Inscribed for
Paul V. Faragher
with the compliments
of
David C Mearns

23-1-48

ABRAHAM LINCOLN
as he appeared shortly before his inauguration
Engraving reproduced from the *Illustrated Times*, 1861

THE STORY OF THE COLLECTION

WITH SELECTIONS TO JULY 4, 1861

THE
LINCOLN
PAPERS

DAVID C. MEARNS

INTRODUCTION BY CARL SANDBURG

VOLUME I

DOUBLEDAY & COMPANY, INC.

GARDEN CITY, NEW YORK, 1948

TO

Anne and the shade of Matthew Vassar

Preface

IN COMMON WITH MOST OF MANKIND, THE LINCOLN PAPERS WERE
not available to me until a few minutes past midnight on Saturday, July 26, 1947. During those early hours it was my privilege, in
collaboration with a group of associates, to prepare the first formal
and public announcement of the composition and content of a collection previously withheld from the world, which for more than
three quarters of a century had stirred the imagination of succeeding
generations of Americans, evoked sentimental speculation, and lent
itself to wild and reckless conjecture. That was a memorable but
frenzied experience, for circumstance permitted only a cursory examination. Thereafter I did not consult the papers again for several
weeks.

But despite the fact that I did not see the collection until after it
had been officially opened, I had for sometime studied its history,
and on the basis of materials, printed and manuscript, had compiled
extensive notes from which it was possible to forecast the probable
nature of the hidden writings. These have since been amplified, or-
ganized, and set forth in the first part of this book. It is not claimed
that all of the mysteries which once clustered about the collection
have now been dispelled, but many have been exorcised, and those
that remain have been so sharpened and so isolated that their even-

tual solution may be simplified. On one point I am convinced: understanding of this vast resource is dependent on a knowledge of its provenience.

As to the significance of the collection, it is necessary always to keep in mind the fact that it is the fundamental record of Mr. Lincoln's presidency. Until now only two biographers working jointly have ever had access to it. Moreover, their use was made at a time and under a condition when objective exploitation was hampered rather than furthered by contemporaneity. It detracts nothing from the monumental and enduring quality of their accomplishment to point out that they labored under the direction of a zealous proprietor, and that they were themselves retarded, inhibited, and, to some degree, shackled by intimate personal relations to the personages and episodes which the papers describe. Frankly partisan, possessed of inescapable prejudices and predelictions, they were the authorized and commissioned exponents of a point of view. To these constricting influences must be added the factor of size. So large a body of materials and so comprehensive a design required of them the most sparing consideration of some matters, and led one of them to warn against the futility of taking "two bites on an atom." And yet it is from the evidence, as presented by them, that Lincoln research has principally developed. For the first time it is now possible to collate these archives with the results of recent scholarly investigation and to apply to them the procedures of modern techniques.

Those who have even casually perused the papers have been impressed with the realization that the Lincoln story will ramify far beyond the limits which formerly had been supposed to exist. They lead inevitably to many subjects hitherto unexplored and unsuspected. The clues are there; the hunt will be exciting and relentless. But the papers are distinguished not only for what they reveal of the personality of Mr. Lincoln himself, but also for the information they contain of other figures, large and small, who shaped the nineteenth century. The papers are, in short, the cabinet of an epoch.

The selections included in this work are not offered under the contention or delusion that they constitute the most "important" specimens discoverable in the first fifty volumes, nor are they offered as being representative of the entire collection. Full coverage will undoubtedly reach the public in due time. "Importance," after all, is meaningless, because it must be relative and particular. I can claim for these examples only that they are typical, and that they seem to me more lively, more moving, more generally interesting than the rest. So far as possible I have avoided abstractions, policies have given way to politics, and politics have yielded place to people, whatever their condition or position, for the reason that only through them can Mr. Lincoln be made intelligible. Pains have been taken to transcribe each document exactly, without editorial impediment or gloss, save only in those infrequent instances where an explanation is suggested by ambiguous allusion, or where the reader conceivably may be advantaged by, or grateful for, interpolated comment. The original spelling, punctuation, abbreviations, etc., have been preserved. Cancels are bracketed and printed in italics. By and large, the letters are self-interpreting and in combination tell an uninterrupted story. Somewhere in each of them it is possible to discern the lean and epic figure that called them into being.

My sense of obligation to the many men and women who have unselfishly and variously had some part in the preparation of this book is as deep and abiding as its expression is absurdly inarticulate. On steaming August evenings a very great American shared with me his rich and vivid knowledge. To Carl Sandburg I am profoundly grateful for generating a sense of confidence, for tempering impulsive estimates, and for allowing me to draw upon his magnificent mastery of material. Dr. James G. Randall, with characteristic consideration, guided me to the location of missing (and therefore essential) information. Dr. Paul M. Angle, the distinguished director of the Chicago Historical Society (of which Mr. Lincoln was an honorary member), has been kind enough to search among the Isaac N. Arnold papers in quest of references to Robert Lincoln. Mr. Oliver R. Barrett has given me invaluable counsel and suggestion. Dr. Louis A. Warren, of the Lincoln Historical Research Foundation, has supplied many of the ingredients which have gone into the history. Dr. J. Monaghan, of the Illinois State Historical Library, has furnished the letter which reflects Robert Lincoln's attitude toward his mother's correspondence. Mr. William H. Townsend, of Lexington, has, at my behest, ransacked his extensive collection of letters

PREFACE

written by Robert Lincoln to his Kentucky relatives. Dr. Jesse Shera, of the library of the University of Chicago, has produced a photostat of Robert Lincoln's letter to Josiah G. Holland. Miss Helen Nicolay has most graciously and precisely responded to my inquiries and has made possible an accurate chronology of events surrounding the early history of the papers.

I am indebted to Dr. Luther H. Evans, Librarian of Congress, who granted me a leave of absence for this undertaking. At the risk of stating the obvious, I feel compelled to acknowledge him as the giver of opportunity and forthwith to relieve him of any responsibility, official or semi-official, for what I have done with it. If there are virtues I am delighted and eager to distribute them, but such faults as persist are solely and strictly and privately my own. My special thanks go to Mary H. Richardson for excellent and adopted suggestions. Robert C. Gooch, Willard Webb, C. Percy Powell, and Ethel M. Walter have sustained and even surpassed the tradition of their helpfulness. The transcribers were Olive M. Seltzer, Dorothy H. Brooks, Edith G. H. Lenel, and Anne E. Herring.

D. C. M.

Washington, D. C.
November 6, 1947

Contents

CONTENTS

Illustrations

VOLUME I

ABRAHAM LINCOLN
AS HE APPEARED SHORTLY BEFORE HIS INAUGURATION
frontispiece

PRESIDENT LINCOLN REVIEWING A PARADE
ON PENNSYLVANIA AVENUE, WASHINGTON, IN 1861
facing page 12

A TEXTBOOK WHICH LINCOLN STUDIED—
ANN RUTLEDGE'S COPY OF SAMUEL KIRKHAM'S *English Grammar*
facing page 154

VOLUME II

ABRAHAM LINCOLN ON HORSEBACK
frontispiece

TROOPS ON THE SOUTH GROUNDS OF THE WHITE HOUSE
facing page 390

xiii

ILLUSTRATIONS

Introduction

THE STRANGE AND COMPLICATED STORY OF THE BIOGRAPHERS OF Abraham Lincoln and their source materials is getting told in a series of books and will probably not come to an end so long as there are generations of men who continue to write biographies of Lincoln.

This book by David C. Mearns concerns the largest single privately owned collection of Lincoln papers, the owner of that collection, the custodians of it who used it in the writing of a ten-volume work they titled *Abraham Lincoln: a History*, others who wanted to use it and were refused access to it, and a variety of myths that arose around the collection.

In the year of 1947, when this collection was declared open for the use of any and all, there appeared a volume *A Shelf of Lincoln Books* by Paul M. Angle which gave a summary narrative of the changing streams and methods of Lincoln biographers. This was followed by *Portrait for Posterity*, by Benjamin P. Thomas, who executes a mosaic panel of Lincoln biographers. These and the present work of Mr. Mearns are basic books, indispensable for guidance through the bibliographical wilderness of more than 4,000 books written about Abraham Lincoln.

A unique task awaited Mr. Mearns. Besides sifting and choosing amid some 18,000 inanimate handwritten letters, telegrams, documents, memoranda—scripts and scrawls often difficult to decipher—he must cover considerable ground not hitherto come to light. As he wrestled and wrangled with the materials he found that the aggregate of papers that came to the Executive Mansion when Lincoln was president began to take on a sort of breathing and independent existence of their own. An involved tale of cold and queer facts moved at times into a fierce drama of passionate moments. The body of documents became a corpus having a living character, moved hither and yon, guarded and tended, valued with affectionate and even greedy eyes, for years slumbering unused, becoming finally a national topic for talk, query, surmise, guess, idle tittle-tattle, and myth.

We have herein the most complete study thus far made of the actions of Robert T. Lincoln and his personality, with relation to the collection of papers left at his father's death. In this extended sketch we often get momentary self-portraits of Robert T. Lincoln and close-ups of the dilemmas and problems of a distinguished, troubled, peculiar, and sometimes smug individual. His father's private papers became his private property to dispose of and administer as he chose. His series of decisions across six decades, as to who could use the collection, saying "Yes" to the request of two young friends, saying "No" to all others, his final decision not long before his death that no one should have access to the papers till twenty-one years after his demise—is one of the oddest tales in American history, whimsical, grotesque at times, and again stark and tragic, as here pieced together from many sources.

As though under admonitions "Be not rash with thy mouth" or "Let us be quite sober" Mr. Mearns takes up the headlined question, "Where are the Lincoln papers?" and collateral inquiries, "What are the Lincoln papers? Who has them? How many of them are there? How do they group and classify? How do specimen texts of them run? Where have they been last year, the year before, and still earlier? Have these papers traveled, and if so what was their itinerary and who held possession of them, and when they changed in possession or custody, who were the parties thereto? Of such papers as are missing, what might be the character of them and can we know how many of them have disappeared and what are the explanations and what might be the various theories as to why they vanished?"

The Lincoln myth in process of fabrication, revision, and reconstruction is set forth in varied bearings on the incessant queries in colloquial, "What's the lowdown on his ancestry, on murder conspiracy in his Cabinet?" Mr. Mearns covers this ground in a way to throw light on how myths arise, though he seems to assume that, no matter what the plain historical facts are, there will be rumor mongers and journals to keep exploded myths traveling.

The vitality of the Lincoln tradition, for the present generation, was attested with a glint of wonder in the year preceding July 26, 1947, when at midnight the stored and locked papers were at last to be opened for public use in all time thereafter. Into the office of the Librarian of Congress poured a constantly increasing number of letters and inquiries. From every part of the country, from editors, ministers, scholars, plain and humble citizens, came the questions about this or that phase of what came to be termed "The Unveiling." Some inquirers were sharp with a whetted curiosity. Some had a nameless anxiety. The Lincoln scholars in general held to a unanimous expectation of no new and startling discovery though believing of a certainty that the newly available materials would deepen and further confirm the known lines of the Lincoln figure and personality.

Mr. Mearns out of twenty-eight years of service in the Library of Congress, and as head of the Department of Reference, understands the use of source materials, primary and secondary. His selections from documents and papers sometimes connect with pivotal historic events or again they give a quick portrait of a fine person worth knowing—or the sudden voice of a pleasant fool who knoweth not his folly. Those who enjoy the study of interesting and varied people in real life can step back into a generation of vanished Americans and see them in speaking likenesses.

Carl Sandburg

PART ONE

The Story of the Papers

CHAPTER ONE

The End of the Prince of Rails

SORROW, IT SEEMED, HAD PARTED FOR A WHILE. THE NEWS WAS good, there was a general lifting of hearts and a sense of exaltation. Relaxed in gossip, the son and the secretary had spent a quiet evening upstairs. Suddenly, at about a quarter of eleven, a panic-stricken mob converged upon the house, shouting cries of murder. The doorkeeper went to the place above the entrance and made an uncertain announcement. The son put down the vial and teaspoon which he had been holding as though to administer a drug. The secretary turned pale. Together they ran down the steps and out upon the portico, climbed into a waiting carriage, and drove through the heavy night to the merchant tailor's house on Tenth Street. Along the way the sidewalks and the road were thronged with people, their first excitement dulled by anxiety or drained by anguish. In the vestibule Dr. Stone tenderly whispered helplessness.

Through the long hours, while inexorable duties absorbed the secretary, the son did what he could, standing by his stricken father whose great frame was too long for the mean bed on which he lay; or comforting his hysterical mother; supporting her in her hourly visits to the fetid, overcrowded room where she would remain until the weight of grief became unbearable; or conferring with frightened authorities and gravely acknowledging expressions of solici-

3

tude. It was a little before seven when his mother entered the room for the last time. She took one look at the distorted features and fell fainting to the floor. Restoratives were applied; she revived quickly; and, as the son helped her to her feet, she appealed in unreasoned urgency to the dying man: "Love, live for but one moment to speak to me—to speak to our children!" But the only answer was that heavy breathing. In less than half an hour it ceased forever. One who was there throughout the long watch remarked that the son "bore himself well, but on two occasions gave way to overpowering grief and sobbed aloud, turning his head and leaning on the shoulder of Senator Sumner." When the end came, the son was standing at the head of the bed, while through the partly opened door came the moaning sounds of a distracted woman. Tomorrow would be Easter. . . .

When Abraham Lincoln and Mary Todd were married they went to live in the Globe Tavern, on Springfield's East Adams Street. There, in three days less than nine months, on August 1, 1843, their first child, a son, was born. The baby was named for his maternal grandfather, Robert Smith Todd, a distinguished citizen and lawyer of Lexington, Kentucky. Not long after the Lincolns moved to the house at the northeast corner of Eighth and Jackson streets which was to be their home until they exchanged it for the "Executive Mansion" in "Washington City."

Shortly after Robert's third birthday his father, in a letter to an intimate friend, insisted that

Bob is "short and low," and I expect always will be. He talks very plainly—almost as plainly as anybody. He is quite smart enough. I sometimes fear that he is one of the little rare-ripe sort that are smarter at about five than ever after. He has a great deal of that sort of mischief that is the offspring of such animal spirits.

According to Robert himself, "I followed the usual pursuits of infancy and childhood . . . until I was four years old, when I was taken by my parents to Washington, D.C., my father being at that time a Member of the House of Representatives. Of my life in Washington my recollections are very faint." But one episode of early domicile he did remember—an expedition with his father to the model room of the Patent Office where, looking at the marvels of modern invention, they reached the rueful conclusion that finality had come to man's mastery of nature; nothing remained to be discovered.

Of the relations of Robert and his father, particularly during Robert's boyhood, the records are scant and usually unsatisfactory. Actually, it is unlikely that Robert Lincoln saw very much of his father. The boy spent the winter of 1848–49 with his grandfather in Lexington, and after his return to Springfield (Mr. Lincoln's one congressional term having expired), Mr. Lincoln immersed himself in professional pursuits and renewed his passionate interest in local politics. A direct result of these preoccupations was frequent absence from home. It is reasonable to suppose, therefore, that Robert grew up largely under his mother's influence.

Of the essays at his education Robert left this account:

I have a dim recollection of being under the slipper guardianship of a School-mistress until 1850, when I became a pupil at the Academy of a Mr. Estabrook, & under his instruction I remained for three years. At this time there had been founded at Springfield an Institution of Learning called the "Illinois State University," at which I was placed and remained until the summer of 1859. This "University" had, I believe, four instructors, Dr. W. U. Reynolds being the President. The government was very easy and we did just what pleased us, study consuming only a very small portion of our time. The Classes were divided as at College, and when I left I was about to enter the Senior Class. I became aware that I could never get an education in that way and resolved to enter Harvard College, imagining that there would be no trouble in doing so, in which idea, it is unnecessary to say, I was very much mistaken.

There is evidence that Robert was at this time endowed with those qualities of bumptiousness, emotional extravagance, and adolescent self-esteem which are penalties paid by parents for the privilege of permitting their children to grow up. But he was also extremely sensitive and socially impeded by an incurable shyness, which, in later years, was to be mistaken for the encrustation of a snob. His schoolmates had given him the unenviable and physically undeserved nickname of "Cockeye"; this had only increased, rather than diminished, his uncomfortable reserve. And yet he was obviously a manly boy, deeply aware of his responsibilities to those about him, and trained in reliance on his own counsel.

He took his college entrance examinations and, instead of passing with flying colors, he went down to ignominious defeat by flunking fifteen out of sixteen subjects. He might justifiably have been dismayed, but despite the "fabulous number of conditions," he "resolved not to retire beaten," and acting on the advice of President Walker, he entered Phillips Academy at Exeter, New Hampshire. He had hoped, by this method, to become a member of the class which, in the following July, would be admitted to Harvard as sophomores, but "the worthy principal, Dr. Soule, soon convinced" him of the vanity of his aspirations. Life at Exeter was pleasant; his father occasionally sent him drafts for $25 or $50; his mother bought him heavy drawers, half a dozen French towels, and a pair of gloves at the store of John Williams & Company in Springfield as well as a pocketknife from C. M. & S. Smith's emporium; and he attained a pleasant status among his fellows. Marshall S. Snow, a classmate, reported that

Bob Lincoln was a very popular young fellow, a gentleman in every sense of the word; quiet in manner, with a certain dignity of his own. He was a very good fellow, however, and always ready for any good time and clean fun. He was very popular with the girls of the town as well as with the boys. He was what would be called nowadays a "good dresser," and always looked as well as acted the part of a gentleman.

Yes and no. Another witness has with unbecoming indulgence testified that Robert Lincoln, "with divers other students, played some innocent but mischievous pranks on the citizens of Exeter, such as making amusing changes of gates and signs in the nighttime." The townspeople were neither amused nor impressed with innocence. They sought relief from the preserver of the peace, "and the students with the exception of Lincoln were called to the justice's office the next morning." When they appeared, Robert Lincoln stepped forth and in words that would have pleased Parson Weems or Horatio Alger made a noble, if tentative, confession:

I see by the reading of the warrant that many of my school comrades are charged with committing offenses last evening against good order and the peace and dignity of this pleasant village. I was in company with many of the parties mentioned in that warrant, and if they are guilty of the charges therein set forth, I am equally amenable before the law. I therefore ask, before proceedings commence, that this warrant shall be amended by having my name inserted with the rest of my comrades, for I do not desire any person to shoulder any responsibility rightfully belonging to myself.

The chronicler of this heroic tale concludes with the statement: "No objection being made, the warrant was amended, also the certificate of summons, and all the students, including the President's, son were fined."

But the one genuinely historic episode of that academic year was Abraham Lincoln's visit. Robert would later say that had he not failed in his first attempt at college, and had not that failure aroused in his father an anxiety for his development, Abraham Lincoln would not have come East, would not have delivered the Cooper Institute address and eleven others en route to New Hampshire, would not have acquired a national reputation, and consequently would not have been nominated for the presidency. On March 3, 1860, the Honorable Abraham Lincoln, of Illinois, treated the audience in Exeter's Town Hall to "practically the same address he had given a few days before in New York." The orator, "tall, lank, awkward, dressed in a loose, ill-fitting black frock coat, with black trousers . . . somewhat baggy at the knees . . . his hair . . . rumpled, his neckwear . . . all awry," made the boys whisper, "Isn't it too bad Bob's father is so homely? Don't you feel sorry for him?" But when he had "untangled those long legs from their contact with the rounds of the chair," had drawn himself up to his full height of six feet four inches, and launched into his speech, "his uncouth appearance was absolutely forgotten," and "there was no more pity for . . . Bob."

After commencement in 1860 Robert Lincoln was able to inform his father that he had succeeded in entering college without a condition, and had become a member of Harvard's sub-freshman class. He brought with him a letter of recommendation from the Honorable Stephen A. Douglas, introducing him as the son of Abraham Lincoln, "with whom I have lately been canvassing the State of Illinois." Mr. Lincoln was pleased with the boy's progress. "He promises very well," he declared, "considering we never controlled him much." As for Robert, he began at once to enjoy the freedoms of Cambridge life, studied enough to satisfy himself, and relaxed in his rooms at "Pasco's, corner of Main & Linden Sts."

For the head of the Lincoln family the summer and fall of 1860 were exciting and momentous months: he was nominated for, and elected to, the presidency of the United States. A Springfield neighbor in October wrote to her son: "I rejoice that this excitement will soon be over. Bob Lincoln, you have doubtless seen, has been styled *Prince of Rails!* I saw Mrs. Lincoln a day or two since, she enquired very particularly after you, and feels quite confident of her husband's election."

Robert's new sobriquet had been inevitable. The Prince of Wales, touring the United States incognito as Baron Renfrew, had been accorded columns of publicity and everywhere had received a tremendous ovation. Moreover, he had been a recent visitor to Springfield. Mr. Lincoln's honors were shared by his first-born. In November the Boston *Traveller* announced in a paragraph:

Young Lincoln, son of the President-elect, now in Harvard College, was, on Wednesday night, called upon by a large body of the students of that institution, and congratulated on the success of his father. He had been previously waited upon by many, but this call was more formal, though not more cordial. The young man is said to be a worthy scion of the old stock and is quite popular among his fellow students.

Early in January 1861 Mrs. Lincoln went to New York to select a wardrobe befitting the mistress of the Executive Mansion. During her absence, Mr. Lincoln had to shift for himself, and he was a most reluctant and unskilled housekeeper. When she returned on the twenty-fifth, bringing Robert with her, the perplexed spouse experienced a tremendous sense of relief. Indeed, Henry Villard, the brilliant young reporter, stationed in Springfield by the New York *Herald* and the Associated Press, noted in his wire that "dutiful husband and father that he is, he had proceeded to the railroad depot for three successive nights in his anxiety to receive them, and that in spite of snow and cold." He added that on the following day Robert, "the heir apparent to the President-elect," had been "the observed of all the observing Springfield girls." He continued: "The effect of a residence within the improving influence of genteel, well-dressed, and well-behaved Boston is plainly noticeable in his outward appearance, the comparative elegance of which certainly presents a striking contrast to the loose, careless, awkward rigging of his president father."

On February 6 Mr. and Mrs. Lincoln gave a farewell party at their home. The crowd was immense; one guest complained that "it took twenty minutes to get in the hall door, and then it required no little management to make your way out. Bob figured quite largely. While I was standing near Mr. L. he came up and in his humorous style gave his hand to his father, saying: 'Good evening *Mr. Lincoln!*' In reply his father gave him a gentle slap in the face."

Five days later the presidential party left early in the morning for Washington and that evening the royal progress reached Indianapolis where it was quartered in the Bates House. At an impromptu reception, held that evening in the principal parlor, beginning at seven o'clock, "Bob was almost as much annoyed as his father by the persistency with which the curious pointed him out and loudly gave vent to their expressions respecting the 'Prince of Rails!'"

The following morning Mr. Lincoln, responding to the importunities of an enthusiastic crowd, appeared upon the hotel balcony, and when he had "bowed himself into his room, the Prince of Rails was called for and reluctantly induced to appear for the first time in his life before the public." There were noisy exhortations for a speech, but he "confined himself to a graceful waving of his hand." It would have been unnatural if these generous attentions did not expand whatever ego Robert Lincoln allowed himself, and there can be no doubt that as the Prince of Rails he gave a magnificent performance. In Cincinnati he was plied liberally with sparkling Catawba by admiring young Republicans, but the following day seemed not "to feel any the worse and contributed much to the general good feeling by his gay, colloquial ways." In Cleveland he led a mounted escort through the mud and rain and snow from the Euclid Street Station to the Weddell House where he was provided with his own suite of rooms on the Bank Street side, corresponding in elegance to the apartments set aside for his father.

Only one episode marred the journey: somewhere along the line

Robert Lincoln lost the long, old-fashioned black bag containing his father's inaugural address, which had been confided to his keeping. The disappearance was only momentary; the precious piece of luggage was soon recovered, but the impression left upon Robert Lincoln cut deep into his spirit, for his father, learning that it had vanished, is said to have been genuinely alarmed, to have explained the embarrassment which its premature release would bring to the new administration, and generally to have scolded his astonished and confused offspring for his carelessness in not observing the security requirements of presidential papers. Never would Robert Lincoln again be accused of such a lapse.

When he had seen his father officially installed in office, the Prince of Rails returned to college, while the mounting American crisis burst into unfathomable war. The next four years would be years of heartbreak, fixed purpose, and the discovery of a new national spirit, and the man in the White House would confess: "If to be the Head of Hell is as hard as what I have to undergo here, I could find it in my heart to pity Satan himself." But for the Cambridge student they were not altogether insufferable. He became a member of the Institute of 1770, and served as its editor for one term; he joined a secret society; and was made vice-president of the Hasty Pudding Club.

From time to time he would hear from his father via the telegraph office. Thus:

Executive Mansion—July 3, 1863

Robert T. Lincoln, Esq., Cambridge, Mass.
Don't be uneasy. Your mother very slightly hurt by her fall.

A. L.

Executive Mansion, July 11, 1863

R. T. Lincoln, New York, Fifth Avenue Hotel
Come to Washington.

A. Lincoln.

Executive Mansion, January 11, 1864

R. T. Lincoln, Cambridge, Mass.
I send you draft to-day. How are you now? Answer by telegraph at once.

A. Lincoln.

THE END OF THE PRINCE OF RAILS

Executive Mansion.
Washington, D.C. January 19, 1864

R. T. Lincoln, Cambridge, Mass.

There is a good deal of small-pox here. Your friends must judge for themselves whether they ought to come or not.

A. *Lincoln.*

Washington, D.C., October 11, 1864

Robert T. Lincoln, Cambridge, Mass.

Your letter makes us a little uneasy about your health. Telegraph us how you are. If you think it would help you, make us a visit.

A *Lincoln.*

But the harried President could find little time for correspondence with his son. Robert would inform the inquisitive Mr. Herndon, October 1, 1866: "I have not any letters which could be of any interest whatever to you or to anyone—you may remember that I did not leave home until my father was so busy in public affairs that it was next to impossible for him to write to me—accordingly the few letters I have, ranging over a period of five years, are with one or two exceptions letters enclosing money—I was much too young for him to write me on general matters—at least he never did so."

Of course Robert Lincoln spent the greater part of his vacations in Washington, renewing his intimacy with the President's gifted private secretaries, escorting his mother to church, talking to his younger brothers, driving the White House horses, dancing with his "Iowa friend," winning the favor of his elders and the cordial admiration of his own generation, and eagerly seeking the company of his presidential progenitor. "I was not unaccustomed to have conversations with him," he told a Board of Inquiry in 1879, "when I would find him alone in his office, on subjects that were then current. Sometimes the conversation would arise from a remark of his own, and sometimes by a question of mine." They discussed, for example, the cashiering of Fitz-John Porter and the rumors of Secretary Chase's willingness to succeed Mr. Lincoln at the end of his first term.

Following his graduation in 1864, Robert came home to the White House. One day he saw his father for a few minutes. Mr. Lincoln

11

asked: "Son, what are you going to do now?" The boy replied: "As long as you object to my joining the Army, I am going back to Harvard, to study law." "If you do," his father remarked, "you should learn more than I ever did, but you will never have so good a time." This comment, partly prophetic, constituted the only advice Mr. Lincoln ever gave his son on the choice of a career.

The Prince of Rails entered the Harvard Law School that fall. And then, on the nineteenth of January 1865, Abraham Lincoln addressed a private note to Lieutenant-General Grant:

Please read and answer this letter as though I was not President, but only a friend. My son, now in his twenty-second year, having graduated at Harvard, wishes to see something of the war before it ends. I do not wish to put him in the ranks, nor yet to give him a commission, to which those who have already served long are better entitled and better qualified to hold. Could he, without embarrassment to you or detriment to the service, go into your military family with some nominal rank, I and not the public furnishing his necessary means? If no, say so without the least hesitation, because I am as anxious and as deeply interested that you shall not be encumbered as you can be yourself.

Two days later General Grant replied:

Your favor of this date in relation to your son serving in some military capacity is received. I will be most happy to have him in my military family in the manner you propose. The nominal rank given him is immaterial but I would suggest that of Capt. as I have three Staff officers now, of considerable service, in no higher grade. Indeed I have one officer with only the rank of Lieut. who has been in the service from the beginning of the war. This however will make no difference and I would still say give the rank of Capt.—Please excuse my writing on a half sheet. I have no reserve but to take the blank half of your letter.

Robert Lincoln's commission as "Assistant Adjutant General of Volunteers with the rank of Captain" was signed by his father and Secretary Stanton February 17. Captain Lincoln's military career was short-lived. He participated in the operations which led to the evacuation of Petersburg by the Confederates, accompanied the President of the United States on his visit to the scene of hostilities, and was present at Appomattox on April 8 when General Lee sur-

PRESIDENT LINCOLN

reviewing a parade on Pennsylvania Avenue, Washington, in 1861. Beside
Mr. Lincoln sits the portly General Scott. The front of the White House is in
the background. Contemporary drawing by Waud reproduced from the
original in the Library of Congress

rendered his army to General Grant. The next day, with General Grant, Captain Lincoln started for Washington, but because of the destruction of the railroads and unforeseen difficulties of travel, they did not arrive at the capital until the early morning of April 14. It was Good Friday, the anniversary of death.

Captain Lincoln found the family at breakfast, recounted the episodes of the closing hours of the campaign, and showed his father a portrait of General Lee. The President examined it carefully. "It is a good face," he said; "it is the face of a noble, brave man." Mr. Lincoln spent a busy day. Those who saw him were impressed by his cheerfulness, but the war years were nearly over and he knew it. In the evening Mr. and Mrs. Lincoln went to the theater. They had urged Captain Lincoln to accompany them, but he had made his excuses. He would talk to John Hay for a while, perhaps study a little Spanish, and then retire. Idleness seemed a strange indulgence. Minutes slipped easily away. Then came those shouts from the darkness of the lawn, and Tom Pendel was standing in the doorway . . .

When the son came out of the Petersen house, where the President had died, the Prince of Rails had preceded him and fled to memory. A giant's shadow stretched across the land. To Captain Lincoln its form was familiar; he knew it was not his; he knew also that always it would follow him. He would honor it and cherish it, sharing it with the world as pride made pleasant and duty made so dear, but first effacing the scratches, burns, and slight disfigurements. Because he found no beauty in its scars, Robert Lincoln, a man who relied upon his own judgment and mistrusted the uses of reality, could not believe that it had power both to sustain and survive understanding, that its strength was stronger than impertinence and malice, starkness and conclusion, time and change.

CHAPTER TWO

Files Upon Parade

I T WAS "A DISMAL DAY." SENATOR BROWNING, OF ILLINOIS, SADLY
recorded in his diary for Saturday, April 15, 1865: "Robert Lincoln told me his mother did not wish to go back to Springfield, and did not want his father's remains taken there but to Chicago, if anywhere in Illinois. I did not see Mrs. Lincoln—she was greatly agitated and in bed."

At noon, less than five hours after the death of Abraham Lincoln, a message was filed in the busy Washington telegraph office—a summons. It was brief. "Please come to Washington at once to take charge of my father's affairs. Answer." It was directed by Robert Lincoln to David Davis, Associate Justice of the Supreme Court of the United States, who was then sitting with Mr. Justice Drummond as a circuit court in Chicago. More than half a century later Robert Lincoln would gratefully recall his helpfulness: "I cannot remember when I did not know Judge Davis . . . of whom I heard as a boy everything good from my father and who was very kind to me. Upon my father's death I went to Judge Davis as a second father, and this he was to me until his death. I am deeply indebted to him for counsel and affectionate help on many occasions and revere his memory."

A native of Maryland, educated at Kenyon College, Gambier,

Ohio, a student of law in Lenox, Massachusetts, and at the law school in New Haven, Davis emigrated to Illinois in the fall of 1835, where he hung out a shingle, first in Tremont, then Pekin, later in Bloomington. He entered politics, was elected to the Assembly, amassed a fortune, and became judge of the Eighth State Circuit. Henry Clay Whitney, who was in a position to observe Judge Davis, has described him as, "on first acquaintance, one of the most genial and companionable men I ever knew."

Judge Davis met Abraham Lincoln in 1836, and their friendship, fast and devoted, was marked in many ways, but to their associates and students they seemed an oddly and completely mismated pair, of contrasting stature and appearance, emanating from conspicuously different backgrounds and characterized by opposing temperaments and conflicting mental habits. The biographer of Davis, Dr. Harry Edward Pratt, has put it this way:

Lincoln was tall, gaunt, and dark with dangling arms, large feet, and hands trained to toil. Davis was light-haired and fair, five inches shorter and massive in build, weighing well over a hundred pounds more than Lincoln, but with small hands and feet. They were the carelessly dressed and the stylishly attired; the college-trained lawyer and the stranger to schools, struggling to gain a legal education. The one with limited means and no faculty of making money; the other acquisitive, with the foresight and financial backing to satisfy his talent. The judge was of a decisive nature; the President bilious, morose, of phlegmatic mind and body; the former holding tenaciously to his views, the latter more yielding and politic. There were certain common traits: both were genial, ambitious, frugal, liking and liked by their fellow men.

At the Chicago convention, where Mr. Lincoln was nominated for the presidency, Judge Davis had been his principal lieutenant, established Lincoln headquarters at the Tremont House and paid the bill, and generally proved himself indefatigable in dealing with the delegations of other states. Mr. Lincoln had notified his managers: "I authorize no bargains, and will be bound by none," but the judge, who, weighing more than three hundred pounds, had once jumped over a horse to prove his freedom of action, and who, convinced that Lincoln in Springfield could not possibly understand the on-the-spot situation, had proceeded to enter into agreements which were later to embarrass the standard-bearer, but in 1862 the judge had been appointed to the Supreme Court.

In Chicago, on the day Lincoln died, the United States Court was the only one in which remarks were made. Said Judge Davis, who disliked speechmaking:

Gentlemen of the bar; this nation is stricken by a great calamity and a great sorrow. My sorrow is a double one. I mourn not only as a citizen of the United States, but as a personal and devoted friend of the President. We cannot, now, talk as we should of this great tragedy, and of the duties growing out of it. A day should be given to reflection. . . . Yesterday the future was all brightness. Today darkness covers the whole land. The President of the United States and his chief constitutional advisor have been murdered. Atrocious crimes, with few parallels in history, have been committed. Let us take a day for reflection, and meet on Monday and give public expression to our feelings and duties. I trust, gentlemen, that you will do whatever is in your power to discourage the holding on this day of public meetings of any kind. They may do harm, and cannot possibly do good. In view of the overwhelming calamity which afflicts this people, this Court will adjourn without transacting any business.

By Monday morning Judge Davis had left Chicago for Washington.

In the capital the judge was extremely busy. On Wednesday, the nineteenth, he attended the funeral; on Thursday, the twentieth, he held a conversation with Robert Lincoln and urged the opinion that his mother should make her home in Springfield; in the afternoon he visited the *Republican* and *Star* offices and "suppressed advertisements calling a public meeting to express indignation against Marshal Lamon, for, as they said, appointing secessionists to act as marshals on occasion of the funeral of the President"; on Friday, the twenty-first, he saw the funeral train; on Saturday, the twenty-second, he called on Secretary Stanton and asked for the promotion of L. B. Parsons from colonel to brigadier general, and later confided to Senator Browning that Mr. Lincoln had "never written him a line, nor asked his opinion upon any subject since he was elected President"; Sunday, the twenty-third, he made some social visits; and on Monday, the twenty-fourth, he wrote to his brother-in-law, Judge Julius Rockwell, of Lenox, Massachusetts, who had signed Robert Lincoln's bond when Robert entered Harvard College:

> The terrible crimes which have saddened the country as country was never saddened before, and the length and breadth of which cannot now be told, brought me here. I should have come, anyhow, but Mr. Lincoln's son telegraphed me to come on and take care of his private affairs.
>
> I could not avoid the responsibility and care.
>
> I went on with the remains to Baltimore, Saturday, and have been busy getting his papers ready to take to Illinois. They will be ready today, I hope, and I will return direct to Chicago tomorrow. I am tired, very tired and worn out with excitement, and want to get with my loved ones for a day. I shall accompany the remains from Chicago to Springfield.

The arrangement and preparation of the papers were carried out under the judge's direction, possibly with some assistance from Robert Lincoln, by the late President's private secretaries, John George Nicolay and John Hay. Major Hay, of course, was at the White House on the night of the assassination, but Mr. Nicolay was returning from an official mission to Cuba, on board a warship, undertaken at the invitation of the Assistant Secretary of the Navy. The first rumor of the tragedy came from a pilot boat, met at the entrance to Chesapeake Bay, but little credit had been given it for the reason that unfounded reports had blown like ragweed throughout the war, and more than once Mr. Nicolay, in the line of duty, had been called upon officially to deny fantastic stories of the President's brutal murder. But when the boat reached Point Lookout the flags along the shore were seen to hang at half mast; the horror, rejected by the ear, became visible in symbols. Mr. Nicolay reached Washington at half-past two on the afternoon of April 17 and hurried through the crepe-lined avenue to the White House. Perhaps, in the days which followed, he thought of this or that task as a last service to a beloved if sometimes exasperating chief, but only his own death would terminate the association; Mr. Nicolay would continue for thirty-five years as Mr. Lincoln's posthumous secretary and archivist.

John G. Nicolay was born in the village of Essingen, Bavaria, February 26, 1832. With his parents he emigrated to the United

States six years later and settled first in Cincinnati, then Indiana, then Missouri, and finally in Pike County, Illinois, where his father and brothers had for a time operated a flour mill. Orphaned at an early age, he clerked for a year in a store, and then found employment in the Pittsfield *Free Press*, rising steadily from printer's devil and typesetter to editor and proprietor. He met Abraham Lincoln in 1856.

Pittsfield, that autumn, was in a ferment of political excitement. It was a time of tension; feelings and oratory had run high. A big meeting had been arranged and Nicolay had been appointed to the committee which had it in charge. Among the more notable speakers in the state were Lincoln and Lyman Trumbull, and as there were scores of counties to be covered, it had been agreed that these two should divide the field rather than appear jointly on any one program. The Pittsfield committee was aware of this arrangement, but because it was "crafty," as such groups sometimes are, and although it would have considered itself fortunate to secure an address from either of these distinguished citizens, it widely advertised the presence and participation of both.

Trumbull arrived on the afternoon of the meeting, and the frankly admiring Nicolay watched him stop in his march along the wooden sidewalks of the town to greet a stranger. The stranger was Mr. Lincoln. Through some accident, both men had come to Pittsfield, and the committee, in spite of itself, had been imposed with honesty. Before the proceedings opened, editor Nicolay had been presented to the honorable gentleman from Springfield; the rugged features, the kindly smile, the earnest, brooding eyes, the hearty handclasp, the conspicuous absence of pretense, all had combined to make an impression of strength and simplicity which had produced an instant response of friendship. Mr. Lincoln's address on that Monday evening in October had done the rest; its logic had found acknowledgment in Nicolay's orderly mind, its fine phrasing had appealed to his sense of beauty, its passionate sincerity had reflected his own beliefs, at its conclusion Mr. Lincoln had won a gifted, loyal, lasting disciple.

Perhaps Mr. Nicolay had gone to Springfield for no better reason than to be near Mr. Lincoln; in any event, shortly after the election

he had sold the *Free Press*, accepted a clerkship there in the office
of the State Secretary of State, and become a correspondent for
several out-of-town papers including one in Chicago and one in
St. Louis. It is said that the office of the Secretary of State, which
adjoined the Supreme Court Library where caucuses were held, was
quite the pleasantest room in the Capitol. It was only natural, therefore, that it should have been a favorite meeting place for politicians.
It was in that room that Lincoln's name had first begun seriously to
be mentioned for the presidency, and frequently in the hearing of
Nicolay, Lincoln felt obliged to deprecate such foolish notions, and
to declare his own unfitness to aspire to that high office. Then in
May 1860 Mr. Lincoln had secured the nomination; his callers had
come in droves; his correspondence had reached diluvian proportions. Mr. Nicolay had been not only gratified by a popular
validation of his own enthusiastic support, but had been eager to
take an active and affirmative part in the contest. Years later he
would tell a reporter how it happened:

The moment I heard of Mr. Lincoln's nomination, it occurred to me
that I might write the campaign biography. This was as much a feature
of the political battles then as tariff tracts are of present-day campaigns.
Full of this purpose and having no idea that anyone would dispute my
right to do the work, I began to prepare for the task at once. A week after
the nomination, however, a newspaper man from Columbus, Ohio, appeared at the Capitol to collect material for writing the life of Lincoln.
I was instantly filled with jealous rage, and hastened to a friendly official,
who was closely attached to Mr. Lincoln, to complain of what I considered to be a usurpation of my just prerogative. I shall never forget that
complaint nor the answer to it. The official heard me out in silence—he
was a quiet, dignified man—and I was very bitter. After I had finished he
looked down at me smilingly.

"Never mind, Nicolay," he said, "you are to be Mr. Lincoln's private
secretary."

In my whole life nothing had ever so taken me aback as this announcement did. He told me that a day or two after the nomination he had said
to Mr. Lincoln that now he had become a presidential candidate, he
would be overwhelmed with letters, and would need a private secretary.
"Yes," responded Mr. Lincoln, "I had thought of that and decided on
young Nicolay." It would have been astonishing for any man but Lincoln
to have thought of it at all so soon.

Early in June Nicolay assumed his new duties in the Governor's Room on the second floor of the State House, which had been made available to Candidate Lincoln. There Nicolay drafted correspondence, received visitors, watched artists at their difficult work of pleasantly portraying the ex-rail splitter, listened to conversations which were sometimes engrossing and sometimes hilarious, made meticulous memoranda, ran occasional errands, and gradually took on the attributes of an indispensable man. From time to time gay John Hay, an old friend from Pittsfield, dropped in and voluntarily pitched in to help with the work.

When Mr. Lincoln left Springfield for Washington, Nicolay had been on board the presidential train. Another occupant of the "cars" was John Hay, Esquire.

John Milton Hay, balladist of Pike County, future diplomatist, historian, journalist, "dear heart" of Henry Adams, discoverer of Lincolnian qualities in Theodore Roosevelt, was born at Salem, Indiana, October 8, 1838, moved to Warsaw, Illinois, was educated at local schools, a private academy in Pittsfield, and the Illinois State University, whence, succeeding where Robert Lincoln had failed, he entered Brown University as a sophomore at the age of seventeen, graduated with academic honors, and in 1859 entered the office of an uncle, Milton Hay, at Springfield, in order to study law. Nearby was the office of Abraham Lincoln, where his friend of Pittsfield days, John Nicolay, was employed. He had had an air of sophistication, a charming manner, a facility of expression, a sense of frustration and expectancy, and a gallant disregard of the conventions of spelling and punctuation. Toward the end of what the newspapers insisted on calling Mr. Lincoln's "stay" in Springfield, Nicolay's work had been seriously in arrears. Nicolay appealed to Mr. Lincoln for a personal assistant and suggested the availability of the brilliant neighbor. Mr. Lincoln agreed, and thus it was that John Hay came to Washington as a member of the President-elect's "cortege."

Following his inauguration, Mr. Lincoln's first official act was to sign Nicolay's commission. Following a time-honored tradition, Hay served as assistant private secretary to the President, but actually derived his compensation from other federal pay rolls. Nicolay wrote in a letter dated March 10, 1861: "As the existing laws do not provide for an assistant for me, I have had him appointed to a clerkship in the Department of the Interior and detailed to special service here at the White House, so that he gives me the benefit of his whole time." On January 12, 1864, he had been commissioned a major and Assistant Adjutant General of Volunteers, assigned to the Executive Mansion.

Throughout the greater part of the Lincoln administration the two Johns shared a White House bedroom, in the northeast corner of the second floor; directly opposite, across the wide hall, was their office, adjoining it the President's office, and beyond that the reception room. Just prior to Mr. Lincoln's death both men were given appointments to Paris, Nicolay as Consul and Hay as Secretary of Legation. They were about to turn over their duties to successors when the tragedy occurred.

These, then, were the men whom David Davis, in the spring of 1865, had selected to arrange the Lincoln papers and prepare them for shipment to Illinois. Intimates of the Lincoln household, familiar with every detail of the executive office, bound by the closest ties of loyalty to the memory of the "Tycoon," they were perfectly competent for the assignment.

There was nothing unusual, clandestine, conspiratorial about it. From the time of Washington a president's papers had been considered private papers, and at the end of each administration the White House files were removed and passed to the possession of the late landlord or his heirs. William Howard Taft, who knew the tradition and had followed the practice, told the students of the University of Virginia in January 1915:

The office of the President is not a recording office. The vast amount of correspondence that goes through it, signed either by the President or his secretaries, does not become the property or a record of the government unless it goes on to official files of the Department to which it may be addressed. The President takes with him all of the correspondence, original and copies, carried on during his administration. Mr. Robert T. Lincoln told me that in his father's day, great as the business must have been during the war, there was practically no correspondence except what was purely personal, carried on in the executive office by two or three clerks. Everything was referred to the different departments for disposition, with sometimes a memorandum by the President.

Precedent, in other words, was not only ample, but thoroughly understood. No one demurred at the transfer of the files; no one disputed the Lincoln family's right of ownership.

CHAPTER THREE

Concerning a Chinese Reverence

IT HAS ALWAYS BEEN POSSIBLE TO KNOW A GREAT DEAL ABOUT THE contents of the Lincoln papers; only in terms of the particularization of documents has there been ground or excuse for conjecture; many have long been published; others have constituted a basis for accepted conclusion; statements have been made which admittedly are fugitive, fragmentary, and usually unrelated but possible of compilation; Robert Lincoln himself was seldom expansive but neither was he altogether mute. Surprisingly, however, through all the tantalizing years of limbo no one bothered to assemble the evidence and substitute reason for rashness. In the first place, it was easy to learn that the private secretaries to the late President had been busied with "the papers of the office." This fact, in and of itself, supplies a focus, marks boundaries, and provides a narrowly definable subject for inquiry. It should, in other words, have been possible to assume *exclusions* and to enumerate, *inter alia*, the following:

1. Wood Shavings. The Cincinnati *Gazette* and the Illinois *State Journal* published a story in 1860, written by "E" from Evansville, Indiana, under the date line of June 12, with the heading *How Mr. Lincoln Learned to Cipher:*

There have been a great many items of interest going the rounds of the press connected with the life of Abraham Lincoln, while working on the Crawford farm, in Spencer County, about twenty-five years ago, but none of them equal the following:

Mr. Crawford, who visited our city a few days ago, speaking of "Abe," said "Abe" was so eager to obtain an education that, after he got through with his day's labor, he would sit down by the light of the fire, take a board which he would make smooth by the use of a drawing-knife, and on that he would write and cipher when all the rest were sleeping; when he would get it written full, he would take his drawing-knife and shave it again, and so on until his board was completely used up.

These sentimentally interesting exercises appear to have been deliberately consumed by their maker.

2. *The Stovepipe Archive*. Marshal Lamon in his *Recollections of Abraham Lincoln,* published in 1911, declared: "His hat for years served the double purpose of an ornamental headgear and a kind of office or receptacle for his private papers." Dr. Louis A. Warren, in the issue of *Lincoln Lore* for May 16, 1932, which discussed surviving examplars of the President's toppers (they vary in size from six and seven eighths to seven and a quarter), goes very much further: "In the high crowns were carried at various times, according to his occupation, surveyor's notes, letters, dispatches, newspaper clippings, lawyer's briefs, and state papers of all sorts." Tyler Dennett, on the other hand, in his *John Hay, from Poetry to Politics,* 1933, denies that the practice extended into the White House period: "Gone was the day when the President could carry his important papers in his hat." There are considerations which compel agreement. A chief executive of the United States is, when abroad, forever acknowledging salutations from his fellow citizens, and when the flag passes or the band blares the national anthem, he uses the ordinarily shocking object to cover, not his scalp, but his patriotic heart. Thus in Mr. Lincoln's case chance of spilling, chasing, and public indignity would have required a change of custom.

3. *Ancestral Muniments*. Recently a self-anointed "Lincoln scholar," in an article published in a widely circulated and usually responsible weekly, under the ridiculous title, *Where Are the Lin-*

coln Papers? has hinted darkly that Robert Lincoln, a man "very sensitive about the humble origin of his father," had, with the complicity of the private secretaries, suppressed ancestral records which would have entitled the President to blazon a bar sinister upon the family arms. Moreover, he has let go with the inescapable inference that Robert Lincoln wilfully destroyed the documents which would have established that prerogative, and has suggested that they had once been incorporated in the Lincoln papers. Come now! Do many men file away the certificates of their parents' births, marriages, and deaths with the business correspondence of their office? Do even churls cherish the seamy memorabilia of a grandmother's peccadilloes, philanderings, and improprieties by wedging them into a pigeonhole where a respectable colleague may come upon them; or by stuffing them in a bureau drawer where children are bound to spy them out; or by passing them down from generation to generation as evidence of a romantic provenience? Would Abraham Lincoln's father, old Tom Lincoln, who, the son said in his starkly candid autobiography, "grew up litterally without education," and "never did more in the way of writing than to bunglingly sign his own name"—would this unexceptional pioneer likely have been interested enough in his first wife's archives, if archives there had been, meticulously to transport them from "cabing" to "cabing" in the prairie, and tenderly to commit them to his grateful issue? The leaf from the Bible, now in the collection of Oliver R. Barrett, of Chicago, begins: "Thos. Lincoln was born Jan. the 6th A.D. 1778 and was married June 12th 1806 to Nancy Hanks who was born Feb. 5th 1784." It is in Abraham Lincoln's holograph. The family record in Mary Todd Lincoln's *Comprehensive Bible*, Philadelphia, 1847, presented by Robert Lincoln's widow to the Library of Congress in 1928, contains entries in Mr. Lincoln's hand of his marriage to Mary Todd, the births of Robert Todd Lincoln, Edward B. Lincoln, William Wallace Lincoln, and Thomas Lincoln, and the death of Edward B. Lincoln; the rest were written by Robert, presumably in his old age. Why, then, impeach Robert Lincoln's credibility when he declares in his Harvard classbook: "I know very little of my father's family"? It sounds reasonable enough.

He used to tell a story about a Todd who came to see his father one day, explaining that now the family had attained national prominence, Mary's relatives should dress up the family name in some way, and asking if it would be a good idea to add a final "e." Mr. Lincoln pondered for a second then shook his head. "I don't think it's necessary," he said. "God seems to get along all right."

The Honorable Abraham Lincoln, of Illinois, was by no means indifferent to his forebears. On the contrary, his correspondence with Solomon Lincoln, of Hingham, Massachusetts, and other enthusiasts exhibited a natural curiosity and a healthy interest. As for Robert Lincoln, it is true that, through the society of people called "nice," he acquired attitudes, reticences, rules of conduct, and traits of character strangely alien to the environment of his sire, but so great was his reverence for his father, so pervasive his pride in him, that to be an aristocrat, as only democracies can create aristocrats, it was enough for him to be his son. The idea that Robert Lincoln was frightened by the prospect of delvings into folkways and lineage books is farfetched and quite too facile. He was, as a matter of fact, not only a Pilgrim Tercentenary member of the New England Historic Genealogical Society, but one of its benefactors as well!

4. Lectures and Literary Essays. Prior to his departure for Washington, Mr. Lincoln packed a carpetbag with the manuscripts of those of his writings which would not be required for the conduct of the White House office and turned it over to Elizabeth Todd Grimsley. In substance, he explained to "Cousin Lizzie" his hope that she would consent to care for his "literary bureau," that if he should return he might want to reclaim it; that otherwise she might dispose of the contents in any way she pleased. After his death, Mrs. Grimsley would gratify the wishes of old friends to possess an "association" item by dipping into the bag and handing over whatever came to her hand. This agreeable custom reached an abrupt end one day, when a maid, confusing these assorted leaves with trash, conscientiously burned them. Five of the survivors of Mrs. Grimsley's bounty were subsequently tracked down: the lecture on discoveries and inventions; two fragments on slavery, one on the Constitution, and Mr. Lincoln's closing speech in the senatorial campaign of 1858. The sleuth who recovered them and in whose possession they now repose is the wonderful Oliver R. Barrett.

Mr. Lincoln's verses beginning, "My childhood home I see again," were presented to the Library of Congress by his granddaughter, Mrs. Charles Isham, in 1937. Other samples of his contributions to beautiful letters are conserved in a score of places.

5. *Legal Documents.* Mr. Lincoln left behind in courthouses and in his Springfield law office the accumulation of his legal papers. Thus some passed to his law partner, William H. Herndon, and those which escaped dispersal, numbering 750 documents, came into government ownership when the Library of Congress purchased the Herndon-Weik collection in 1941.

6. *Intimate and Family Letters.* From the number which exist in various collections, it has been apparent that only by accident would intimate and family letters have found their way into the White House papers. Nicolay and Hay had printed but one letter from Abraham Lincoln to his wife and only nineteen telegrams. Such correspondence did not belong in an office collection.

7. *Some Notable Documents.* Quite obviously there were several distinguished state papers which were not among those which were prepared by the secretaries for shipment to Illinois. For example, Mr. Lincoln himself had donated the Emancipation Proclamation to be sold at auction for charity. It brought a good price and was presented to a soldiers' home in Chicago and was destroyed in the fire of 1871. The first draft of the Gettysburg Address, and the reading copy, both in Lincoln's holograph, and the original manuscript of the second inaugural, together with the printed text from which it was delivered, were presented to the Library of Congress by the children of John Hay on April 11, 1916. On the same day Colonel Nicolay's daughter, Miss Helen Nicolay, gave the Library the memorandum of August 23, 1864, in which Mr. Lincoln expressed the opinion that in all likelihood he would be defeated in the forthcoming election, in which event he would give the President-elect

his full co-operation in order to save the Union. He had sealed the memorandum, the Cabinet had endorsed the envelope and, when the successful issue of the campaign was assured, he had read aloud its contents to his ministers. The famous Hooker letter, once in the Kolb collection, now adorned the magnificent library of Mr. Alfred W. Stern. The note of sympathy to the widow Bixby had been an object of considerable interest and curiosity to Robert Lincoln. If he knew of a rough draft, or possessed related documents, he would probably have shared the information. A long list of celebrated Lincoln manuscripts in other collections might readily be compiled; it is certainly not difficult to learn their whereabouts.

8. *Terminal Date.* That the materials in the Abraham Lincoln papers concluded with the President's sudden death was presumable from the fact that letters of condolence written by eminent personages to his widow were presented to the Library by Mrs. Robert Lincoln eight years after the deposit of the collection and one year after she, too, had been widowed. The unfinished business of the Lincoln administration was, of course, transferred to Andrew Johnson.

9. *Final Negation.* It can never be said that Robert Lincoln scattered his father's correspondence, but from time to time he did delight in making "little gratifications." Thus in 1908 he wrote to the widow of John Hay:

I am very sorry that I have been unable to find any more letters from Colonel Hay to me.

In my father's papers there is as yet found only one letter, which I enclose. It is, I think, very characteristic.

The following year he responded to a request for information from Professor Frank Irving Herriott, of Drake University:

Your note of January 26th was received on Saturday, and a search was begun for the letter to which it refers from Hon. John A. Kasson, to my father, dated September 13th, 1859. It was located this morning, and as it has ceased to be of permanent importance among the papers I have, I take great pleasure in sending it to you, together with the envelope in which it was originally mailed. The pencil notation is in my father's handwriting.

No indication of any response to this letter has been found.

In 1916 he made a handsome acknowledgment to the Honorable John W. Dwight:

You know my gratitude to you for your effective work in the House in the legislation providing for the erection of the Lincoln Memorial here, which is now approaching completion, but I wish you to have something tangible as a testimonial of my feeling and which may be associated by you in your memory of that part of your public work.

In the book by Noah Brooks entitled *Washington in Lincoln's Time*, you will find an account of a public demonstration at the White House immediately after the presidential election of 1864, at which my father made a speech which he had written out beforehand. I am sending to you the original manuscript used by him on that occasion and I beg your acceptance of it, with the renewed assurance of my kindest regard.

Of course there were other instances of such largesse. It would be interesting to know the criteria applied in determining "permanent importance," because if it was clear that, at rare intervals, Robert Lincoln had removed documents from the collection, for one purpose or another, it was equally obvious that others had been withheld from those deposited in the Library of Congress in 1919, and that some remained in the possession of his heirs following his death. For example, the Honorable George Anthony Dondero, of Royal Oak, Michigan, in an article published in the *Journal of the Illinois State Historical Society* for May 1931, in referring to Grace Bedell's letter urging Abraham Lincoln to grow a beard, had made no secret of the fact that

Upon the death of President Lincoln . . . Robert Todd Lincoln, his son, obtained possession of the letter and upon his death, July 26, 1926, it became the property of his widow, Mary Harlan Lincoln, from whom the writer received it.

Certainly there were some papers which the family had decided to retain, and, of course, they had a perfect right to do so. Only the malicious could construe their reluctance to part with the totality of the Lincoln record as suspicious or furtive, and only the malevolent would deny their responsibility to prevent an indiscriminate invasion of privacy.

This, then, was the aspect negatively considered, these were the kinds of material, and these the exceptions which the public should have known better than to expect to find bared and perpetuated in a national collection, but there were positive indications as well, and they were reliable. They were discernible, even discoverable, in many ways: in the existing knowledge of Mr. Lincoln's person, in the problems which confronted and compelled him in his relations to the whole American community, in the manner of men who surrounded him, in the darkness of the days and the darker nights in which he labored, in his contemptuous disregard of office regulation, and most vividly and most assuredly in the one-sided correspondence published in the several editions of his collected or selected works.

A truth, generally acknowledged but abjured in utterance, is the truth that Mr. Lincoln was first and most of all a consummate politician. No stigma, save convention, attaches either to the admission or to him, for his eminence derives entirely from his capture of the people's confidence. Without it, he might have been as undivided a servant of the Union as he was; he might have been as shrewd and wise and kind; he might have possessed as uncanny and mildly supernatural powers of understanding as he did; and still have been among the most inglorious failures in history. His genius for human relations was, moreover, sensitive to other forces. He was not oblivious to the importance of influence; he was familiar with the uses of patronage; he valued favorable publicity; he approved not only the abstract concept of American government but also the sometimes conflicting system by which it worked. To be sure some ineffable extension of character took place between the election of the small-town lawyer and the inauguration of this major prophet of democracy; there was some revelation on some Damascus road; but the vision did not displace but rather was imposed upon his older genius.

If this were so, and both reason and example confirmed it, those whom Mr. Lincoln numbered among his correspondents must have included every specimen of the race. Whether literate or not, the American people have always found an inexplicable release in writing letters, particularly in writing letters to persons in authority. They cajole, scold, beg, command. Sometimes, but with less frequency, they commend. But whatever their tone, nothing can stay the impulse toward articulation. To Mr. Lincoln, who infinitely preferred men to missives, the efficiency of the postal arrangements must more than once have seemed a grave misfortune.

On November 14, 1860, shortly after his election, the Illinois *State Journal* announced:

Today, and till further notice, Mr. Lincoln will see visitors at the Executive Chamber in the State House from 10 to 12 A.M., and from 3½ to 5½ P.M. each day.

The purpose of limiting his reception hours was to allow the President-elect opportunity for private conference with the exacting Republican leaders who hurried to Springfield to present claims and proffer gratuitous suggestions, but it had as its object also time to consult with Mr. Nicolay who was becoming increasingly dismayed by the volume of paper clamorings, and to draft or dictate the tenor of replies. A correspondent who used the pseudonym of "Albany," writing to the New York *Evening Post* on the day this schedule went into effect, reported that

He [i.e., Mr. Lincoln] does not hesitate in his private letters to the South (he has already a large correspondence in that section) and in conversation with his visitors, in answer to proper inquiries, to give any assurances which are consistent with his views heretofore expressed and the party platform on which he stands. . . .
I mentioned that Mr. Lincoln had already quite a large correspondence with the South. There are many of his letters from that quarter which the country ought to see. Missives which no decent man could write are abundant; their postmarks reveal the fact that the vocabulary of Billingsgate is not confined to the Five Points and Marshall Rynder's office. Unfortunately the earmarks of some of them show that their writers are not devoid of education, if destitute of decency. Letters threatening death, in all its forms, as the penalty of his high position, are more

abundant still. They are, of course, mainly anonymous, though a few bear real names. Some are signed in hieroglyphics, said to be known only to the "Sacred Order" or "Southern Brotherhood," which threatens Mr. Lincoln with a sudden and untimely taking-off. A few are ornamented with sketches of executions by the gibbet, assassination by the stiletto, or death by a lightning stroke; and in nearly all the theology of the writers is indicated by rude caricatures of the Devil, ready with his three-pronged fork to receive and pitch into everlasting fire the body of the unfortunate Lincoln, whose offense consists in the belief that human slavery is wrong. He is not, I am glad to say, annoyed by these. Assured that no man who will write anonymous and threatening letters is worthy of being feared, he tosses all such aside, as he says, to illustrate, at some future day, the comical side of his administration. . . .

Aside but not away! And if Mr. Lincoln refrained from writing the appeasing, conciliatory letters he was being urged to write, it was not "merely on punctilio and pluck," but, as he said, because "I have bad men to deal with, both North and South; men who are eager for something new upon which to base new misrepresentations; men who would like to frighten me, or at least to fix upon me the character of timidity and cowardice. They would seize upon almost any letter I could write as being an awful coming down." He intended to keep his "eye upon these gentlemen, and to not unnecessarily put any weapon in their hands." This was temperance but not abstinence. There were many other letters of other kinds. The Lincoln papers were swelling.

Exactly two weeks later the observant Henry Villard, of the New York *Herald*, wired that immediately upon his return from Chicago the President-elect had repaired to his reception room "to open and digest his accumulated correspondence." Mr. Villard continued:

A pile of letters greeted him before which a less determined soul might well have quailed. Until late last night and all day yesterday did it absorb all his attention. With a creditable patience he waded through the contents of several hundred letters, the perusal of which made him no wiser. Even his keen sense of the ludicrous begins to be blunted by the frequency of its imitation. Bad grammar and worse penmanship, stylistic originality, frankness of thought and pertinence of expression, vainglorious assurance and impudent attempts at exaction may do well enough for the temporary excitement of humor. Mr. Lincoln's correspondence would offer a most abundant source of knowledge to the student of human nature. It emanates from representatives of all grades of society. The grave effusions of statesmen; the disinterested advice of patriots reach him simultaneously with the well-calculated, wheedling praises of the expectant politician and the meaningless commonplaces of scribblers from mere curiosity. Female forwardness and inquisitiveness are frequently brought to his notice. Exuberant "wide-awake" enthusiasm, with difficulty pressed into the narrow forms of a letter, is lavished upon him. Poets hasten to tax their muse in his glorification. A perfect shower of "able editorials" is clipped out and enclosed. Artists express their happiness in supplying him with wretched wood-cut representations of his surroundings. Authors and speculative booksellers freely send their congratulations, accompanied by complimentary volumes. Inventors are exceedingly liberal with circulars and samples. More impulsive than well-mannered, Southerners indulge in occasional missives containing senseless fulminations and, in a few instances, disgraceful threats and indecent drawings. A goodly number of seditious pamphlets and manifestoes has also arrived —in fine all the "light and shadow" of Anglo-American political humanity is reflected by the hundreds of letters daily received by the President-elect.

Mr. Villard was privy to the paper in the Governor's Room, and press releases issued eighty-seven years later would not present a more accurate picture.

By December 1860 a new category had intruded into Mr. Lincoln's correspondence:

That popular mania—the collection of autographs of distinguished men —has proved of late a source of considerable annoyance to Mr. Lincoln also, and hardly a mail reaches here without bringing him numerous requests for specimens of his handwriting. Of course all of them wander unnoticed into his waste-paper basket.

The last statement was not strictly accurate, but it probably had the considerate purpose of controlling the callous fashion.

Most troublesome, because they were most important, were appeals or demands for places on the public pay rolls. A cabinet had to be selected, and every Northerner with a favorite candidate would urge his selection with long and irrelevant supporting documents. Sometimes whisperings of choice were overheard, resulting in reams of censure or empty assurances of consent. By the twelfth of January 1861 the New York *Herald* published this item of intelligence:

It has been rumored about town for some days that the President-elect is making the first draft of his Inauguration Address. This report is, however, without any foundation in fact. The change the posture of public affairs is now daily undergoing renders it necessary for him to put off the discharge of this important task to the latest possible moment.

The few visitors he now receives seek him at his private dwelling. To his correspondence he attends, however, with his secretary, in an office rented by him a few days ago in the business part of the city.

Within a few days the paper noted that it had "increased so wonderfully" that he had found it "utterly impossible to read, not to speak of answering it all." In the evenings his servant was sometimes seen standing "in the vestibule of the Post Office carrying a good-sized market basket full of letters." These, it was said, were opened by the private secretary, who, from their signatures, could "determine their relative importance." This was followed by the first hint in history of the burning of the Lincoln papers: "Those emanating from obscure sources are invariably consigned to the stove without the least mercy. Petitions for office especially share this fate."

The situation worsened, deteriorated, scampered from bad to worse. Explained the vivid Villard on January 26:

Written applications for office are now flooded upon the President-elect with unusual vigor and frequency. Mr. Lincoln turns them all over to the tender mercies of his private secretary, who remorselessly consigns nine out of ten to the stove.

As Mr. Lincoln worked on the manuscript of his inaugural address, "the influx of written supplications for executive favors" kept to its distracting course. "Baskets full of petitions and recommendations" arrived with every mail, much to the chagrin of Mr. Nicolay, "upon whose shoulders the main burden of this overwhelming presidential correspondence" rested. "Documents covering from twenty to thirty and more pages, setting forth the claims of the several expectants," were by no means unusual. The indignant Mr.

Villard exploded: "Some fools even went so far as to enclose essays on the duty and destiny of the Republican party and the Republican administration." "To all such indiscreet individuals," he wished to say again that neither Mr. Nicolay nor Mr. Lincoln was "equal to the task of opening, reading, and answering a hundred or so letters every day," and that hence their epistles ran "the ignominious risk of being transferred to the paper basket unnoticed." He urged them, if they were determined to gain a hearing, to "get their papers ready and station themselves at some convenient point selected by Mr. Lincoln for his journey to Washington." He thought it possible that a box for the deposit of such communications would be attached to the presidential train.

A fortnight later the cars rumbled from the Springfield depot, and their joltings made queer splashes of the pencil as Mr. Lincoln struggled to set down the remarks he had made in bidding farewell to the friends who came to see him off. The Lincoln papers went with him, the correspondence of the last few months and the records which reflected his political career. They would be needed at the Executive Office.

Mr. Lincoln was incorrigible. Steadfastly he refused surrender of himself to the heedless disciplines of routine; rebelled with impious stubbornness against submission to an ordered existence; repudiated the easy insistences of time; despised schedules whatever their disguise and blandishments; declined in disgust the ivory towers intended for his isolation; and frequently drove his staff to the corners of despair. As an administrator he left behind no cleverly conceived devices which the future expositors of scientific management might admiringly exhibit as models for the young. Indeed, in his capacity as Chief Clerk of the United States, Abraham Lincoln was completely unsatisfactory.

Long before he left Springfield these marked shortcomings had been sufficiently pronounced to produce palsied heads above the bodies politic. Those about him were filled with dour misgivings, and the public press spouted apprehensions. At moments when conscience and duty required withdrawal to plan the salvation of the Union, or take decisive action, or compose national doctrine, he would be down at the State House, his feet atop a table, talking and joking and exchanging views with the rabble whose franchise had propelled him into public display.

The trip to Washington afforded no opportunities for reform; people would board the train at nearly every stop, ride a few miles, and then give way to others; in the cities where he spent the night he was besieged throughout his stay; and even at Willard's, where he registered upon his arrival at the capital, he was instantly mobbed by the impatient and the captious and the peremptory who for days had laid in wait for him. No wonder that his secretaries shuddered at sight of the accumulated mail. They would have to deal with all of it themselves, or put some aside, which, in the nature of things and Mr. Lincoln, would never receive attention.

Worst of all, this habit of filling life with people persisted in the White House. In those first days the hordes which cluttered the stately rooms were the usurers of power come to exact payment in the currency of patronage. As weeks passed and the paper image of Union was rudely crumpled, there intermingled with those vulgarians noisy men eager for contracts, untutored but cocky little military geniuses, youths bumptiously eager for commissions, frightened mothers and pretty brides seeking releases or promotions for their men; advocates of abdication; impulsive espousers of weird causes; the inflated dispensers of intelligence; the frightened mendicants of peace; in short, the unlovely conglomerate of selfishness bent upon executive acquiescence. Few were turned away; fewer still were dismissed without the suggestion of other recourse.

In such a situation it is not surprising that John Hay looked back upon it with a touch of bitterness. Writing to Herndon in September 1866, he recalled that Mr. Lincoln "was extremely unmethodical." As a matter of fact:

It was a four years' struggle on Nicolay's part and mine to get him to adopt some systematic rules. He would break through every regulation as fast as it was made. Anything that kept the people themselves away from him he disapproved—although they nearly annoyed the life out of him by unreasonable complaints & requests.

He wrote very few letters. He did not read one in fifty that he received. At first we tried to bring them to his notice, but at last he gave the whole thing over to me, and signed without reading them the letters I wrote in his name. He wrote perhaps half a dozen a week himself—not more. . . .

CONCERNING A CHINESE REVERENCE

I opened and read the letters, answered them, looked over the newspapers, supervised the clerks who kept the records, and in Nicolay's absence did his work also.

When the President had any rather delicate matter to handle at a distance from Washington, he very rarely wrote, but sent Nicolay or me.

Miss Helen Nicolay, who inherited from her father an envelope marked "Personal Traits," and who expanded the notes into a book with that title, published in 1912, made this statement:

His correspondence also took much time though he read only one in a hundred of the letters addressed to him. He rarely dictated. He either made a verbal or written summary for his secretary, or carefully wrote out the whole himself—and frequently copied it. All his important state papers and political letters were signed with his full name. His signature on less formal documents was "A. Lincoln." The range of his daily correspondence ran the whole gamut from naming a baby to the most important national and international affairs, and in addition he made many endorsements, some of them lengthy, on communications he did not answer.

By piecing together such fragments as these, written by participants and familiars, it is possible, despite minor disagreements, to reconstruct the operations of the executive office and sense the nature of the White House files.

Nicolay and Hay were assisted by a young man named William Osborn Stoddard. A native of Homer, Court County, New York, the son of a bookseller and publisher, he had graduated from the University of Rochester in 1858, and shortly thereafter had moved to the Middle West where he had become editor of the Central Illinois *Gazette* at Champaign. It was said afterward that his editorial written for the May 4, 1859, issue of his paper had done "more than any other single writing to call to the attention of the people Lincoln's availability as a candidate." He already had a very large current exchange list, but in order to secure the widest publicity for this special edition he had added two hundred more for its distribution. To his immense satisfaction it had been widely copied.

Following the election Stoddard journeyed to Springfield personally to present his congratulations to Mr. Lincoln, who had offered him a clerkship in the government. Stoddard agreed provided he might be connected with the presidential establishment, and was appointed as secretary to sign land patents with an office in the Executive Mansion. It was not very long before he had other duties thrust upon him, and in 1890 he set them down in a book entitled *Inside the White House in War Times:*

This large south-fronting room has been the business office of all the Presidents who have lived in this house. In one sense it is the nerve center of the Republic. It is a wonderful historic cavern to move about in. The hearts and brains of a great people are somehow in connection with it, and they send to this Chamber their blind impulses, their thrills of hope, their faintnesses of disappointment, their shivers of fear, and even their sinking of despair.

Mr. Lincoln will be here in a few minutes. . . .

There is hardly an ornamental or a superfluous article of furniture in the room. This second-hand mahogany upright desk, from some old-furniture auction—or that is what it looks like—here by the middle window, is Mr. Lincoln's working-desk. This is the place where he is expected to perform his political and military miracles. Matters of all kinds are put into shape here for after-consideration by the Cabinet, when they assemble around the long table to be informed why they were sent for. It is not often, however, that a paper or plan prepared by Mr. Lincoln is much changed in its appearance at the end of a meeting. . . .

There is nothing on the desk but a few bundles of papers and an outspread map. It is a map of part of the regions which are beginning to be overrun with armies. . . .

Here is our special work coming in. The big sack that Louis, the President's messenger, is perspiring under, contains the morning's mail. What a pile it makes, as he pours it out upon the table! Why, no, it is no larger than usual . . .

Put aside the journals now, and take up the kind of written papers which come through the post in bundles and bales, mostly sealed a great deal. Do you see what they are? That pile is of applications for appointments to offices of every name and grade, all over the land. They must be examined with care, and some of them must be briefed before they are referred to the departments and bureaus with which the offices asked for are connected. We will not show any of them to Mr. Lincoln at present.

That other pile contains matter that belongs here. They are "pardon papers," and this desk has the custody of them, but their proper place, one would think, is in the War Office. That is where they all must go, after a while; but the President wishes them where he can lay his hands upon them, and every batch of papers and petitions must be in order for him when he calls for it. He is downright sure to pardon any case that he can find a fair excuse for pardoning, and some people think he carries his mercy too far. . . .

There is no sameness in the sizes of the White House mails. Some days there will be less than 200 separate lots, large and small. Some days there will be over 300. Anyhow, every envelope must be opened and its contents duly examined.

Are they all read? Not exactly, with a big wicker wastebasket on either side of this chair. A good half of each mail belongs in them, as fast as you can find it out. The other half calls for more or less respectful treatment, but generally for judicious distribution among the departments, with or without favorable remarks indorsed upon it.

It is lightning work . . .

Written acknowledgments of the receipt and disposal of papers are frequently necessary, and it is well that you have the right to frank letters through the mails, for you never could get the President to spend time in franking.

Noah Brooks, who would have become private secretary in the second term had Mr. Lincoln lived, and who always enjoyed a position of confidence at the White House, wrote his impressions in a book entitled *Washington in Lincoln's Time:*

Naturally, Mr. Lincoln was methodical in his habits; he was scrupulously exact in all the details of his office, and his care for written documents was sometimes carried to an extreme; he appeared to have the Chinese reverence for a written paper. . . .

Lincoln always composed slowly, and he often wrote and rewrote his more elaborate productions several times. I happened to be with him often while he was composing his message to Congress, which was sent in while Sherman was on his march through Georgia. . . . The President's message was first written with pencil on stiff sheets of white pasteboard, or boxboard, a good supply of which he kept by him. These sheets, five or six inches wide, could be laid on the writer's knee, as he sat comfortably in his armchair, in his favorite position, with his legs crossed. . . .

As a rule, Lincoln wrote his most important letters with his own hand. Some of these—perhaps most of them—were read over to confidential friends and were corrected, or modified, before being sent. He kept copies of all letters of moment, and even some of these copies he made himself with painstaking care. In his office in the public wing of the White House was a little cabinet, the interior divided into pigeonholes. The pigeonholes were lettered in alphabetical order, but a few were devoted to individuals. Horace Greeley, I remember, had one to himself; so did each of several generals who wrote often to him.

THE LINCOLN PAPERS

Ben Perley Poore, a gentleman who got about, sent this chronology to the Boston *Journal* in December 1863:

Mr. Lincoln is an early riser, and he thus is able to devote two or three hours each morning to his voluminous private correspondence besides glancing at a city paper. At nine he breakfasts—then walks over to the War Office to read such war telegrams as they give him (occasionally some are withheld), and to have a chat with General Halleck on the military situation in which he takes a great interest. Returning to the White House, he goes through with his morning's mail, in company with a private secretary. Some letters are endorsed and sent to the Departments —others are entrusted to the secretary, who makes a minute of the reply he is to make—and others the President retains, that he may answer them himself. Every letter receives attention, and all which are entitled to a reply receive one, no matter how they are worded, or how inelegant the chirography may be.

Another witness, J. M. Winchell, writing on *Three Interviews with President Lincoln,* published in the *Galaxy* for 1873, recounted an experience when he went to see the President in quest of some favor:

"But let us see what we can do; I will write something to put our ideas into shape"; and with a pleasant laugh he began at once to search for paper and pen. He was aided in this effort by little "Tad," who was present—and, I must say, somewhat troublesome—and toward whom his father manifested the most anxious and considerate affection. He found a piece of paper with some difficulty on the table (littered with documents lying in complete disorder), and a very poor pen with which he at once set to work. . . .

The document thus prepared was in fact a military order, and I wondered if he made any record of its existence. He had not called in the aid of any of his secretaries, and I afterward inquired of Mr. Nicolay if any record of it had been made. He said not, and was even ignorant of its existence; and added a feeling remark on the President's official habits, which were reckless of all order, and gave his secretaries no end of trouble.

Somewhere in these conflicting statements is the truth. If, according to John Hay, he read only one in fifty of his letters, and, according to John Nicolay, the overlooked were twice as many, it makes very little difference after all. There was agreement in substance. It would be more difficult to reconcile Hay's declaration that he "was extremely unmethodical," with Brooks's avowal, "naturally Mr. Lincoln was methodical in his habits," but from the context of the Brooks account it is clear that his reference was limited to Mr. Lincoln's own writing and did not extend either to the documents he received or to his regard for the integrity of the files. Nicolay was meticulously Teutonic in his thoroughness, perhaps Brooks was more lenient, more charitable in his attitude toward such things; more than that, he lacked the same diurnal knowledge which was Nicolay's to acquire and to impart. He and Hay had had the job to do. They had had to grapple with it. Their appraisal had the soundness of intimate experience.

There were times when the secretaries were accused of withholding and sequestering the President's mail. The charge was once leveled by Judge Davis, and provoked an outraged denial which was never allowed to be sent. But there were other times when the President was the secretaries' ghost writer, even going so far as to sign their names to the record copy. Sometimes he, sometimes they, would scrawl on an envelope "needs no answer." Certainly among those which were shipped from the White House in the spring of 1865 were hundreds which he had never got around to. Now he never would. He had been a methodically unmethodical manager, but then he had been Everyman.

CHAPTER FOUR

The Living

DAVID DAVIS COULD "NOT BE RECONCILED TO MR. LINCOLN'S DEATH and the manner of it," but it did not take him long to wind up the Washington business, and by April 27, 1865, he was home in rainy Bloomington. On that day Robert Lincoln wrote to Professor Francis James Child, of Harvard College:

Your letter was received this morning.

I can truly say that I know of no one to whom I would entrust the task you speak of more willingly than to Mr. Norton. Although I am but slightly acquainted with him personally, he is well known to me as a cultivated scholar and gentleman.

It will be impossible, however, for the complete work which Mr. Norton contemplates to be written for a number of years, exactly how long it is impossible to say because there are no doubt many documents (I myself know of several) which are necessary to the history but which would be damaging to men now living.

The papers have been carefully collected by the Priv. Secretaries and sealed and deposited in a safe place. At some time within the next three or four years, I propose, in conjunction with the secretaries and one or two friends of my Father on whose judgment I rely, to open the boxes and glean out what is useless and to classify the remainder in some sort.

No one will have access to them before that time.

Please assure Mr. Norton of my appreciation of his very generous proposition and say to him that I feel indisposed to bind myself at present

45

for so long a time, although as I said at first Mr. N. has my entire confidence, and that I shall most certainly get myself in communication with him at a future time.

Please accept my thanks, Mr. Child, for your kind expression of sympathy. Our loss is indeed terrible. In all my plans for the future, the chief object I had in view was the approbation of my Father, and now that he is gone and in such a way, I feel utterly without spirit or courage. I know that such a feeling is wrong and that it is my duty to overcome it. I trust that for the sake of my Mother and little brother that I will be able to do so.

Charles Eliot Norton, a young man with a brilliant literary reputation who, during the war, had loyally supported the President's policies in the pages of the *North American Review,* had, through the intermediation of Professor Child, expressed a wish to write a definitive biography of Mr. Lincoln. This would require access to the primary source materials.

Robert Lincoln's refusal, polite as it was and firm as it was, took the position that the request was premature. He had become the inheritor of his father's record. Stated differently, this implied that the Lincoln story and its transmission were in his keeping. It was a heavy responsibility which he accepted with more than filial emotion. There were obligations not only to his father's memory, but to the society which had survived him. He, Robert Lincoln, was the final arbiter, and he did not propose to make any disposition of the record without first securing the counsel of his father's intimates. Together they would go through the papers and separate the important from the unimportant. He might have said where they were, but that was irrelevant; enough that they had been "deposited in a safe place." He might have explained the fact that examination must be postponed because the private secretaries were about to take up their posts in Paris, but that would prolong the letter without adding to or subtracting from his decision. He might have named the counselors (David Davis was certainly one) who would assist him to determination, but such disclosure might embarrass them or him; a personal matter of selection, it was nobody else's business.

Thomas Jefferson once said that "the earth belongs always to the living generation." Perhaps Robert Lincoln had come across the quotation. In any event he understood it, subscribed to it, incorporated it in his creed. He would live by it. Neither consciously nor carelessly would he circulate or allow to be circulated lying documents which might damage "men now living." There were such documents among his father's papers. During the war he had himself been charged with making half a million dollars in questionable speculation. It had been absolutely untrue, but it had hurt. Now, in the moment of his bereavement, he was unwilling by any act of his to add to sorrow the shame of dispensing misery. It was such an impulse as his father would approve.

But to read into this resolve, as years later would be read into it, an anxiety to protect his father's murderers, is a fantastic distortion, contrary to everything in Robert Lincoln's nature. It is likewise fantastic to suppose that the Lincoln papers then or ever contained materials which might betray the perpetrators of the crime. Other treacheries perhaps, but not endlessness.

One week later E. D. Townsend, Assistant Adjutant General, from Springfield, telegraphed the Secretary of War:

> The officers of the guard of honor having seen the remains of President Lincoln safely deposited in the vault, and having delivered the key to Capt. Robert Lincoln, will start at ten this evening by the express train via Pittsburgh, Harrisburg, and Baltimore, for Washington.

The Lincoln period was pronounced closed by the military, but those old friends who watched Robert thought him "fine-looking," despite the fact that "he seemed to feel so sadly." On June 10 he resigned his army commission, and on July 5 he wrote to Charles Sumner, on whose arm he had leaned in the Petersen house: "I desire to assure you that I have been deeply gratified by your oration. I have seen no eulogy out of all that have been delivered that has so well expressed what all who knew my father feel but cannot say." Mary Lincoln gave Senator Sumner Mr. Lincoln's cane and the photograph of John Bright which had stood on the office mantel.

The Lincoln family went to Chicago to live. Mrs. Abraham Lincoln, widow, and her younger son, stayed at the Tremont House, while Robert had a room in the building of Crosby's Opera House, and read law in the offices of Scammon, McCagg & Fuller, on Lake Street. The senior member of the firm, Jonathan Young Scammon, had been a friend and correspondent of Robert's father. Robert was admitted to the Illinois bar on February 25, 1867, went into partnership with Mr. Scammon's son, Charles T. Scammon, and, in that year he, with his mother and brother, shared a home at 375 West Washington Street.

Meanwhile memorial sermons, eulogies, and adulatory biographies of Abraham Lincoln poured from the press. Extravagant, unrestrained, wholly uncritical, they presented a divine being who, born mysteriously in the Kentucky wilderness and first revealed to the world athwart a Sangamon milldam, had performed his messianic mission and sacrificed himself for the sins of his fellows. Of course they were bloodless and unreal, the products of the tinsmiths of mythology, but Robert Lincoln liked them very much. A directory publisher in Troy, New York, formed a collection of them.

Opposing them with greater zeal and more remarkable energy was Mr. Lincoln's late law partner, William Henry Herndon, who sought a human explanation of his old friend's greatness. He gathered letters and documents and memorabilia of all sorts, visited the places where Mr. Lincoln once lived, interviewed hundreds of persons whose lives had touched his, took depositions, lectured, and wrote for the newspapers, impugned the legends of domestic felicity, scorned reports of orthodoxy, and generally made himself a painful and probing nuisance. And forever he was talking, criticizing, denying, ridiculing with a Whitman-like torrent of words. Frequently his opinions, based upon deduction, were worthless, but to him more than to any one man must go the credit for the rescue and preservation of the Lincoln story. His materials were and are magnificent. But to this day Mr. Herndon remains a controversial figure, who divides students into hostile schools. It is unfair and it is foolish, for his major achievement was superb.

On the other hand it was only natural that to the traditionalists he should appear as an officious interloper, an unprincipled debunker, a vicious ferret, bent upon reducing Mr. Lincoln to his own mediocrity and re-creating him in his own earthy image. It wasn't long before their contempt for him and his for them became fixed and unrelenting, but it began with cautions. Judge Davis, for example, wrote him on January 14, 1866:

I have always understood that Mr. Lincoln's Emancipation Proclamation was his own conception: that he announced to his cabinet that he intended to issue it, and that he wd. hear suggestions about verbal criticisms &c.—It is mean to try to deprive him of the glory of that.

Robert Lincoln tried to assume a dignified aloofness. With a touch of stern detachment he informed the prober on June 8 of that year:

Even when I differ with anyone in his views of my father's character &c. unless it were something flagrantly wrong, I would not discuss the subject.

Mrs. Lincoln was more openly distressed. In a letter dated August 28, 1866, marked "private—please burn," in which she enclosed a clipping, she appealed to his vaunted sense of justice and sentiment:

Owing to Robert's absence, from Chicago, your last letter to him, was only shown me last evening. The recollection of my beloved husband's truly affectionate regard for *you* & the knowledge of your great love & reverence for the best man that ever lived, would of *itself*, cause you to be cherished with the sincerest regard by my sons & myself. In my overwhelming bereavement those who loved and idolized my husband—aside from *disinterested* motives—are very precious to me & mine. My grief has been so uncontrollable that in consequence I have been obliged to bury myself in solitude—knowing, that many whom I would see, could not fully enter into the state of my feelings—I have been thinking for some time past, that I would like to see you & have a long conversation. I write to know if you will be in Springfield *next* Wednesday week—Sept. 4th—if so—at 10 o'clock in the morning, you will find me at the St. Nicholas Hotel —please mention *this visit to S. to no one*—It is a most sacred one as you may suppose to visit the tomb which contains my All in life—my husband. You will excuse me, enclosing you this sentence of yours & asking its meaning. With the remembrance of years of *very very* great domestic happiness with my darling husband & children—my sons & myself fail to understand your meaning—will you be pleased to explain. If it will not be convenient to you—or if business *at the time* specified should require yr. absence—should you visit Chicago any day this week, I will be pleased to see you.

Further correspondence indicates that the meeting took place. On October 1, 1866, Robert Lincoln told Herndon: "I spoke to my mother . . . and she says she had a talk with you on the subject when at Springfield and that her letters are of too private a nature to go out of her hands."

Between the two men explanation continued to be required and given, along with conciliatory reassurances and promises of corrected impressions. On December 13, 1866, Robert wrote to Herndon again:

Your letter of Dec. 10 is received and it contains just what I understood to be the result of our conversation at Springfield.

As I said then, I have never had any doubt of your good intentions but inasmuch as the construction put upon your language by everyone who has mentioned the subject to me was so entirely different from your own, I felt justified in asking you to change your expression. Beyond this, I do not wish, nor have I any right, to go. Your opinion may not agree with mine but that is not my affair. All I ask is that nothing may be published by you, which after *careful consideration* will seem apt to cause pain to my father's family, which I am sure you do not wish to do.

The following day he wrote again; this time to ask for a certain book on western history, formerly owned by his father, which he wished to present to an old friend, Dr. Smith, who was then Consul at Dundee in Scotland. He remembered having seen it a year before, shelved in a case on the south side of the office. He asked that it should be well wrapped and sent by mail to his mother marked *free;* it would need no postage.

It was not forthcoming. When Robert Lincoln wrote to Herndon on Christmas Eve there were signs that a permanent break would not be longed delayed:

I should have acknowledged your letter sooner but I have been very much engaged. I am sorry about the book but only because our old friend Dr. Smith will be disappointed. In answer to your question I have to say that I do not know of Dr. Smith's having "converted" my father from "Unitarian" to "Trinitarian" belief, nor do I know that he held any decided views on the subject as I never heard him speak of it.

I *infer* from your letter, but I hope it is not so, that it is your purpose to make some considerable mention of my mother in your work—I say I hope it is not so, because in the first place it would not be pleasant for her or for any woman to be made public property of in that way—With a man it is very different, for he lives out in the world and is used to being talked of—One of the unpleasantest consequences of political success is that however little it may have to do with that success, his whole private life is exposed to the public gaze—that is part of the price he pays. But I see no reason why his wife and children should be included—especially while they are alive—I think no sensible man would live in a glass house, and I think he ought not to be compelled to do so against his will. I feel very keenly on this subject, for the annoyance I am subjected to sometimes is nearly intolerable. I hope you will consider this matter carefully, my dear Mr. Herndon, for once done there is no undoing.

This unequivocal position and the insistence upon the inviolability of the living spurred Herndon to an instant response, and on the twenty-seventh Robert wrote to him again:

Your letter of yesterday is at hand and I am very glad to find that I misunderstood your language, and that you do understand my feelings on that subject. There is no need of saying anything more about it.

Dr. Smith did not say the book was *his*—merely that my father had once loaned it to him and that he desired very much to possess it. You did all right about it of course. I can doubtless hunt up something that will please the Dr. quite as well.

The final rupture of relations (so far as the contents of the Herndon Papers disclose) was not marked by any blinding flash of correspondence, but the Lincolns became convinced of Herndon's evil genius for what they could only interpret as denigration and outright perfidy, and wrote him off their books with a loathing as munificent as the loathing he, in turn, lavished upon them. It was complete and irreparable.

At about this time Colonel Nicolay and Colonel Hay were beginning to think about the writing of their biography of Abraham Lincoln. They had planned it in their White House days. John Hay had kept a most engaging diary, and John Nicolay had carefully compiled extensive memoranda of historic transactions. The President himself had promised his help, and they had probably made their intentions known to Robert Lincoln. Now others, such as Henry Villard, their old friend from the New York *Herald*, and the picturesque James R. Gilmore, who, as "Edmund Kirke," so frequently interested himself in the promotion of new and elaborate magazines, were urging them to set about it.

John Hay returned from Europe, announced his "farewell to diplomacy," and on March 5, seated in New York's Astor House, mentioned in the course of a brief note to Consul Nicolay:

Nobody talks turkey as distinctly as we could wish in relation to the Lincoln book. They say the market is glutted, etc. That will be after all, I fear, a labor of love that we will do when we get rich and idle.

Arnold is to publish the works of Lincoln—at least so Colfax tells me—at the request of the family. That dishes our chances at the papers. I will see Bob at Chicago.

He followed this up two weeks later from his home in Warsaw, Illinois:

Nobody is keen for our book. We will have to write it and publish it on our own hook some day when we can afford. You had better not come home till you are kicked out, and our crazy friends in the Senate have legislated all the dead-beats now in office, into an eternity of bread and butter. . . .

Arnold is making a collection of Lincoln's letters & speeches &c., but on his own hook. Bob encourages it but will not give him the key to the boxes. He will keep them for the present & still hopes for our assistance in classifying them. He has commenced practice in partnership with Scammon's son—with brilliant prospects. Mrs. Lincoln was well—was extremely kind—insisted on my moving my traps to her house. I could not as I only remained one day.

In mid-September an ardent Lincolnian and English clergyman, the Rev. Mr. Newman Hall, toured the United States, and later set down his impressions in *The Broadway, A London Magazine*. In Chicago he went to see Robert Lincoln. Part of his interview is reproduced:

. . . Speaking of the memorials sent from England on the death of his father, he said the family preserved them all; and that there were more from Great Britain than from his own country. I asked him if it was true that the Queen had written to his mother. He replied, "Yes, a long letter of four pages. We have often been urged to publish it, but we have decided not to do so, as it was evidently written with no idea of publicity, though it would be greatly to the honor of the Queen if it were made known; but it was so evidently the unrestrained outpouring of sympathy from a full heart, that we felt it would be a violation of propriety to publish it, at least during the life of the writer."

Here again is that same respect for the privacy of the living, and here also is a presumption that the letter was spontaneously and personally inspired. What Robert Lincoln did not know was this: It had been intended for publicity. Mr. Goldwin Smith, of Oxford, whom the Queen considered "a great democrat," had said in a letter to Dean A. P. Stanley, April 27, 1865:

The murder of the President who was the ministry not only of clemency at home, but of moderation abroad, so greatly increases the danger to the peace of the world from that quarter, that I feel it almost a duty to let you know how much good might be done, and how much evil might be averted, by a personal expression of sympathy from the Queen.

At the same moment the Foreign Office got busy. Witness this:

Lord Russell presents his humble duty to your Majesty: it has been suggested by Lord Granville and Lord Clarendon, that a very good effect would be produced in conciliating the feelings of the United States, if your Majesty would deign to write to Mrs. Lincoln privately, condoling with her on her bereavement by so cruel a crime. Lord Russell concurs in this suggestion.

Two days later the Queen, at Osborne, had recorded in her journal:

Wrote to Mrs. Lincoln (widow of President Lincoln), which was much wished, and was quite touched by a letter from Mr. Goldwin Smith . . . who was so anxious that I should write, saying it would do more good than anything else, as I was so much respected in the United States. Told General Grey [private secretary to Her Majesty] what to write in answer, how I felt unworthy of this high opinion of me, but that it was worth struggling on in this wretched life, if I could be of use, could preserve peace and pour balm into wounded hearts. That these many sad and striking events had convinced me more and more of the utter nothingness of this world, of the terrible uncertainty of all earthly happiness, and of the utter vanity of all earthly greatness. That virtue, honesty, fearlessness, truth, unselfishness, and love were the only things truly great and eternal, whether in high or low. That we were alike before God, and that, while difference of position and rank was necessary and must be supported, one could not be sufficiently loving, kind, and considerate to those beneath one. I felt this strongly, and that sorrow levelled all distinctions. I would as soon clasp the poorest widow in the land to my heart, if she had truly loved her husband and felt for me, as I would a Queen or any other in high position. I would as soon grasp the hand of the humblest peasant who felt for or with me, as that of the highest of Princes. General Grey seemed pleased with what I said, but it really comes from my heart! Such a feeling of humility comes over me, such a wish to forgive any wrong, and a try to make all good.

She was recalling her screed to Professor Smith, but the Widow of Windsor had addressed to Mary Lincoln a very moving letter, filled with underscorings and written on her best mourning stationery. It was expected that it would have a healing influence on the American heart, but the people never had a chance to submit to the cure until 1927, when Mrs. Robert Lincoln presented it to the Library of Congress. The Queen had done her best and the President's son had proved his gallantry.

In the months which followed the Rev. Mr. Hall's invitation to breakfast, Robert Lincoln, with that constancy which distinguished him, pursued his career at the bar. From his father he had inherited thirty-six thousand dollars, he had a growing practice, and on Thursday, September 24, 1868, he was married to Mary Harlan with whom he had danced at the Second Inaugural Ball. Bishop Simpson of the Methodist Episcopal Church performed the ceremony, and the bewhiskered Gideon Welles, at whose Washington home Robert had stayed while conducting his courtship, was favorably impressed with his "deportment and character."

CHAPTER FIVE

My Particular Friend

ABRAHAM LINCOLN WHO, LIKE MOST OF HIS INTIMATES, CALLED HIM by his middle name, referred to Ward Hill Lamon as "my particular friend." Born near Winchester, Virginia, January 6, 1828, Lamon began the study of medicine at seventeen, soon abandoned it, and two years later went West. After attending lectures at the Louisville Law School he was admitted to the Kentucky bar in March 1850, to the bar of Illinois in January 1851, and quickly began practice in Danville where his office, above a saloon, fronted a building principally devoted to the simple pleasures of bawdry.

A gusty, boisterous, roystering, impulsive but by no means unlearned man, almost as tall as Mr. Lincoln himself, with an Irishman's love of a brawl, and a fine, full, confident voice, he possessed a gift which he cultivated into a habit for getting into good graces, frenzied situations, and hot water. He once had a trick monkey and from that experience may have come upon the surest means of stirring up the species. From 1852 until 1857, when Lamon became prosecuting attorney, he and Lincoln were in partnership, concentrating their attention on Vermilion County and the eastern end of the Circuit.

Lamon had another intimate friend: the judge of the Eighth

Circuit. David Davis thought of him as "one of the dearest friends I have in the world. He may have faults and few of us are without them, but he is as true as steel, honorable, high-minded, and never did a mean thing in his life."

Through the 1860 campaign Lamon labored with effective enthusiasm for the Republican cause, and had been one of the President-elect's suite on the journey to Washington. When, at Philadelphia, it was decided that Mr. Lincoln should leave the party and enter the capital secretly, Colonel Lamon was selected as his bodyguard, and "wore that night two ordinary pistols, two derringers, and two large knives."

President Lincoln had appointed him marshal of the District of Columbia—a capacity in which he acted as Chief of Protocol at White House functions, keeper of the city jail, and principal guardian of the executive person. His facility for scrapes did not desert him; he enraged the populace by his strict enforcement of the fugitive slave laws, brought down the wrath of Congress for ordering two regiments, which he called Lamon's brigade, brought to Washington without authority; on, or on the way to the field of Antietam he sang to Mr. Lincoln "Picayune Butler"; and, following the funeral of Mr. Lincoln, he was roundly criticized for having permitted Southern sympathizers to serve as assistant marshals in the procession. As early as 1862 he had tried to escape the embarrassments and ingratitudes of office by submitting his resignation, but Mr. Lincoln, who delighted in his companionship, had persuaded him to stick it out. Following his great friend's death, Colonel Lamon remained at his post for a few weeks, and then, on June 8, 1865, filed notice of his wish to withdraw from government. Mr. Seward, in behalf of Andrew Johnson, regretfully accepted his final resignation, pointed out that "since his advent here" the new President "has heard from those well qualified to speak of your unwavering loyalty and of your constant personal fidelity to the late President." By way of conclusion he expressed the hope that Colonel Lamon's "reputation of a faithful and fearless public officer" would gain for him in any new occupation which he might undertake the "same reputation and the same success." And that was that.

Lamon became a junior partner in the Washington law firm of

Jeremiah Sullivan Black, "defender of the Constitution and the Ten Commandments," whom David Davis considered "the most magnificent orator at the American bar." Lamon shared the judge's admiration and presented his senior with a silver tobacco box engraved with the words: "An honest man is the noblest work of God."

For Lamon, the alliance must have been altogether advantageous, for "Jere" Black was a man of great eminence and must have had a lucrative practice. But what gave singularity to the combination was the fact that Lamon, the friend of Lincoln, had associated himself congenially with "Old Buck's" wig-wearing, arch-apologist, Attorney General and Secretary of State. What should have been a collision turned out to be a happy union. Just what it betokened on Black's part is difficult to explain. He was already by instinct and acclaim the exegete extraordinary of what he considered fraudulently maligned and grossly misunderstood Buchananism. It followed that his distaste for the late and inelegant master of the White House was profound and severe.

But this lion-and-lamb tableau did not exhaust Colonel Lamon's exhibits of the bizarre. Perhaps the abuses he had suffered had dulled his fervor and his wits; perhaps there was a momentary diminution of his loyalties; perhaps government employment had rendered him obtuse; perhaps for judgment and perspective he had leaned too heavily on Mr. Lincoln. Certainly he was not a vicious man. Perhaps he sought guarantees of detachment and objectivity. The causes are confounded, but there was integrity in his intention. He proposed to produce a biography of Mr. Lincoln, relaxing the rigid figure of the sentimentalists into the reality which it required. Contrary to popular belief Mr. Lincoln had been human, and it had been his mankindliness which made him great. It would be a sympathetic and strictly honest rendering. Motive and purpose thus were excellent, but the means of accomplishment were startling.

Now Colonel Lamon knew how to write. In the eighteenth century he might have distinguished himself as a pamphleteer; his style was forceful, pungent, clear, but instead of doing the work himself he diverted that responsibility to Black's son, Chauncey Forward Black, an energetic young man of some abilities, saturated with his father's prejudices and psychologically but perhaps unconsciously disqualified for the assignment. On December 10, 1869, they signed a memorandum of agreement. These were the provisions:

It is proposed by the parties to prepare and publish a just, full, and impartial biography of Abraham Lincoln, out of the best authentic materials that can be obtained.

Lamon agrees to furnish papers purchased by him from W. H. Herndon and to get at his own expense all the other documents and papers which may be found within his possible reach, and have them properly verified.

C. F. Black agrees to write the text of the book and arrange the materials for publication, and generally to perform the duties of an editor, as well as to furnish such material as may be possessed or obtainable by him.

In consideration of the premises the parties herein named will be joint proprietors of the book, equally entitled to the copyright, and to an even share of any profits which may be made by publication.

The work is to be done without delay and the publication to be made as rapidly as may be consistent with the joint interests herein provided for. Copyright shall be secured in the names of both parties or of such third party as may be designated by them. Lamon's name is to appear on the title page as the sole author of the book, unless otherwise agreed upon hereafter.

Lamon shall have a right to suppress names or facts found in the documents furnished by him whenever he is bound to do so by any promise he has heretofore made expressly or impliedly. As to other facts and the names by which they are verified it is agreed that a free but judicious use shall be made of them to the end that the interest and value of the book shall be increased. In cases where the judgment of the parties differ concerning the omission or insertion of anything the question shall be submitted to J. S. Black and David Davis whose advice on the subject shall be followed.

Here were all the ingredients of a bibliographical monstrosity. A book was to be produced, based upon the materials of one man whose own personality in the view of the public (which included many of the well-informed) was inseparably and inextricably entangled with them; they would be warmed into an ordered story by a second man to whom the subject was personally repugnant; and a third man, known as an intimate and confidant, would, over his own name, with a natural expectation of devotion, issue the vicarious result.

MY PARTICULAR FRIEND

The Herndon papers were principally concerned with Mr. Lincoln's background and his pre-presidential history. If the biography were to be complete, Colonel Lamon would be obliged to satisfy his undertaking to procure at his own expense all the other documents and papers which might be available. Some, perhaps, he already possessed, but these were probably limited to his own exchanges of correspondence with Mr. Lincoln and his coadjutors. How did he propose to get the other necessary sources? Did he appeal to Robert Lincoln, and, if he did, was he rebuffed? The answers to these questions are important but they are not presently forthcoming. Because of them, however, the following letter written by Judge Black, from York, Pennsylvania, to David Davis July 9, 1870, is particularly interesting:

You are aware that Lamon is engaged in a life of Lincoln—I believe he does conscientiously desire to give the exact truth and that he will not allow himself to be swerved from a perfectly candid statement by any consideration except it be his personal affection for the man. That may induce him to color his narrative more than he himself thinks. The materials are very copious, for which he paid a high price and I think they are perfectly veracious—making allowance for the enthusiastic admiration of the witnesses. I believe he knows nothing and cares nothing for the estimate which L's enemies put on his character. But his best and warmest friends do not conceal the grossness of some incidents in his life. It can hardly be denied that the *tone* of his mind—the thoughts and habits of his daily walk and conversation were lower than those of a *beau ideal* President. He certainly does not compare well with the refined and highly cultivated gentlemen (fifteen in number) who preceded him in the executive chair. He also lacked that lofty scorn of fraud and knavery which is inseparable from true greatness. He was not bad himself but he tolerated the evil committed by others when it did not suit him to resist it. I have told Lamon that he ought not to be an advocate nor even a judge upon any question which is open to dispute. He must content himself in performing the humbler function of a mere assessor for the great tribunal of public opinion and like an Auditor or Master in Chancery report the facts to the court where they can be discussed and decided upon as justice shall require. I think if he adopts this view of his duty he will make a book which the world will give him some credit for—and it will do good—But in order to make a just and full report he should have some evidence which you can furnish him. What he considers more valuable as well as more creditable to Mr. Lincoln than anything else are his own written statements of facts, opinions, &c. Much of this kind of material he has and you also have much under your control. Will you give it to him? Mr. Lincoln kept memoranda of events as they occurred and a record probably of his thoughts and feelings and intentions concerning the most important acts of his administration and you can get these and many other things that will be of great value to Lamon's enterprise. I am quite well aware that those papers may contain much that is not proper for public information. Of course you can dictate what shall be used and what suppressed. But let Lamon see and examine them that at least his views of the subjects he writes about shall be corrected where they are erroneous. In other words I will guarantee that no use shall be made of them which you don't approve. Perhaps I take more interest in this business than you would expect; for I have seen enough of the work to raise the writing and the subject very much in my estimation. I hope you will answer this and say candidly what you think you ought to do.

In all the vast literature of effrontery this letter is without parallel. It pulls no punches. Mr. Lincoln was a vulgarian and complacent boor; the lowest specimen ever to outrage the presidential office. Black's conception of the purpose of the biography was not delineation but destruction. So long as he had anything to do with its preparation no break would be given Father Abraham. The best light would be the worst possible light. And yet it is an appeal. It asks for favors. Making every allowance for Judge Black's candor and eccentricity, one wonders how he dared to write it. Or had David Davis, in the course of their acquaintance, betrayed his own poor opinion of Mr. Lincoln? How would Davis respond? Would he courageously defend the memory of the man to whose mantle he so urgently aspired? His answer was written from Bloomington on August 19:

Your letter of the 10th inst. [*sic*], only received a day or two ago caused me both pleasure and pain. I was exceedingly gratified to learn that Mr. Lamon's work met your approval, for I have every confidence in your judgment. You are well aware, both on acct. of my attachment to the dead & the living, that no one can rejoice more than I at the success of the work, and whatever I can or ought to do towards making it a *success*, I will do most cheerfully.—But I am powerless in the matter whereof you speak, and it pains me that you misunderstand my relation to Mr. Lincoln's private papers, which you think I control and have declined to give Col. Lamon. It is true the papers are in the vault of the National Bank in this place, & would not be delivered up without my order, but if Robert Lincoln and his mother demand them, how could I refuse to surrender them?

If Mr. Lincoln had made a will & confided his private papers to my care, of course I could retain them—But this was not the case—I administered on his personal effects—at the request of his wife who had the right of administration—& this is the only legal connection I have had with this estate—When, at the time of his death, I gathered up his notes and securities, I suggested to Robert that his father's private papers, which concerned his public career should be securely boxed & sealed & sent to me at this place.—This suggestion met his approbation & the other friends of Mr. L., & Mr. Stanton undertook to have them transported here—Robert and the Secretaries attending to the boxing of them, and it was the understanding at the time, that at a future day, when the secretaries could be present, and some of Mr. Lincoln's particular friends, the papers should be examined and arranged with a view to preserve those of any value & destroy the remainder—This has never been done though I brought the matter to Mrs. Lincoln's notice before she left the country, & to Robert since—My object in having the papers removed here was principally to get them fr [om] Washington—& to give advice when they were examined as to what should be done with them—I never dreamed that I had any right to control them, without the full assent of the wife & son—I did not want some persons to get hold of them and considered a great point gained when I got them here—All this I thought Col. Lamon fully understood—The Journal he speaks of is doubtless in the boxes, but I have no knowledge on the subject, for I did not superintend the packing of the boxes, & am literally in ignorance of their contents—

You will readily see, my Dear Sir, that I have no authority to break the seal without the permission of Mr. Lincoln's heirs—If Col. L. wishes me to see Robert Lincoln again on the subject, I will do so, or I will send him your letter, or what would probably be better, send it to Mr. Swett with a request that he communicate with him.

I know nothing personally of his reasons for withholding the desired paper, but I can readily imagine what they are—Mr. Herndon has troubled the family greatly, by his indiscreet letters & publications, and they judge the character of the papers gathered by Mr. Herndon which are not published & in Mr. Lamon's hands, by the pieces which have been communicated to the newspapers—They have never seen these materials, and cannot be blamed for judging of them harshly, for all the intimate friends of Mr. Lincoln in Illinois have been pained by Mr. Herndon's Lectures & letters to the press, on the life & character of Mr. Lincoln—

This motive which I ascribe to Robert, for his reluctance to yield to Mr. Lamon's request, is mere conjecture, but it has struck me as being the true one—

I suppose Col. Lamon's work is in two volumes—if the 1st vol. satisfies the family, it wd. seem to me that there wd. be no difficulty in procuring the "Journal" for the second, and I suppose it will not be needed to complete the first—

I have written hastily, & in the midst of interruptions but I trust I have made my position clear to you & I need not say that this letter is confidential, though of course I have no objection to the communication of its contents to Col. Lamon.

Your friend
DAVID DAVIS

This is a curious document. There is in it no natural scorn for the proposal to expose "the grossness of some incidents" in Mr. Lincoln's life; it is devoid of anger and resentment and repudiation. Instead, Davis promises collaboration to the limit of his abilities. But it is most informative. He makes known the fact that the papers remain unopened in the vault of the National Bank of Bloomington; and repeats the substance of the plans for their examination as outlined by Robert Lincoln to Professor Child five years before. He suggests that Leonard Swett, one of Mr. Lincoln's most intimate friends, has been selected to share with him the duty of advising Robert Lincoln on the disposition of the papers. He chides Herndon for his public utterances, but only obliquely extends that criticism to Colonel Lamon. He counsels patience. He infers that Colonel Lamon has previously sought access to the collection both through him and through Robert Lincoln and that he has been denied. But ostensibly frank and disingenuous as he is, he adds to the growing column of still-unanswered questions by such statements as these:

My object in having the papers removed here was principally to get them fr [om] Washington.

I did not want some persons to get hold of them and considered a great point gained when I got them here.

Why had he been so anxious for their speedy evacuation from the capital? Who were the persons who might have got hold of them and what would have been the dangers if they had? If he was "literally in ignorance" of the contents of the papers, and if he had "no knowledge," what were the reasons and why the satisfaction for their deposit in Bloomington? It would be helpful to know.

Without the Lincoln papers, Chauncey Black worked steadily on the manuscript of what Paul M. Angle has called the "first . . . challenge to the filio-pietistic school" of Lincoln biography, and Judge Davis became a candidate for the presidential nomination. Lamon, meanwhile, was boasting of the explosive character of "his" book. The judge's managers became alarmed lest the public should assume his agreement with anything Lamon might say. Lawrence Weldon, in a letter to Lamon marked "Personal-Private and Confidential," dated May 7, 1871, urged him to delay publication "until in the progress of events" it should be determined how the judge stood in relation to the presidential contest.

In June Samuel C. Parks wrote:

I am really very anxious that you should not publish your life of Mr. Lincoln or if you do publish it that you should delay it for a few months or years. I am sure that it will injure you & some of your friends if published now. It is too soon after Mr. Lincoln's death if for no other reason. But unless I am greatly misinformed there are things in the book that will make it very offensive to very many people of this Country. And they will believe that some of your nearest and dearest friends are partly responsible for its publication—that you would not have published it without showing it to them & that they acquiesced in its publication if they did not advise it. You can never make the world believe that our mutual friend, Judge Davis, did not know the contents of your history & that you would not have published it if he had advised you not to do so. . . . They will be very likely to consider you the maker and him the endorser of the book—& *everything in it.*

Colonel Lamon's position was unenviable; the judge was exceedingly uneasy; Chauncey Black was obstinate in his determination to disseminate his shocking revelations to the world. On September 20 James R. Osgood and Company, of Boston, signed a contract for its publication, the manuscript, with the exception of the last chapter, was delivered and set in type, and as proofs were pulled, John Spencer Clark, a member of the Osgood firm, who from the beginning had objected "to a life of Mr. Lincoln being prepared under such apparently hostile influences," became gravely concerned. "They showed," he recalled in 1910, "a lack of appreciation of the finer qualities of Mr. Lincoln's nature, and a disposition to keep the rougher, coarser aspects of his pioneer life prominent," and when he reached Chapter XV, "purporting to give a brief history of the Kansas struggle," he "saw well-known historic facts perverted to shield the pro-slavery democratic party." He protested, and "after considerable discussion and the exhibition of much feeling on the part of Black, Colonel Lamon fully sustained" the publisher, and the text was altered. This experience made Clark "suspicious of Black's good faith, and when the proofs of the chapter pretending to give a historic record of the very memorable period between Mr. Lincoln's election and his inauguration came, it was only too evident that justice to Mr. Lincoln during this critical period was sacrificed to an effort to extenuate if not excuse the shambling policy of the Buchanan administration." Accordingly Clark, "put the matter squarely before Colonel Lamon and he saw the unwisdom, if not the absurdity, of compromising Mr. Lincoln in the slightest degree at this great period when in the swirl of political complications his was the sanest mind of all."

Chauncey Black was furious at the tamperings with his tract. He quarreled with Lamon, with the publishers, and with any and everyone who advocated revision. But the chief objection was not political, but personal. Much was made of Mr. Lincoln's alleged infidelity, his early romances, his predilection for obscenity. More than that he was coolly represented as a bastard. Neither Herndon nor Lamon had managed to locate the marriage bond of Thomas Lincoln and Nancy Hanks, and, as a matter of fact, it was not found until 1878. But Black had not even given the parents the benefit of the doubt, but had tried, on the basis of Herndon's evidence, to identify another man as Mr. Lincoln's father. John Hay, who heard that the book would contain this aspersion, circulated Mr. Lincoln's friends with appeals to bring their influence for omission to bear. David Davis could no longer appear personally indifferent, while permitting his lieutenants to seek expurgation in his interest. What he did about it was told in a letter which Horace White wrote to Jesse W. Weik, of Greencastle, Indiana, February 24, 1913:

I will give you my recollection of the conversation I had with Leonard Swett in the year 1872. He came into the office of the Chicago *Tribune* of which I was then the editor & said that he & David Davis had had a severe struggle with Ward Lamon in reference to a chapter in the Life of

Lincoln which he (Lamon) had been writing for a Boston publisher. The book was nearly ready for publication & Lamon had submitted the page proofs to Swett & Davis for their criticism. They found in it a chapter showing or arguing that Lincoln was not the son of Thomas Lincoln, his reputed father, but of some other man. In short that although born in wedlock, he was really illegitimate. They (S. and D.) were horrified. The [y] got Lamon into a room, locked the door & kept him there nearly a whole afternoon, trying to force him to take that chapter out of the book, & they succeeded after great difficulty. Swett did not tell me what proofs L. advanced to support his statement but he said they were *prima facie* strong.

For six weeks, beginning April 4, 1872, the biography was advertised in the *Publishers' Weekly* under the title "The True Life of Abraham Lincoln from His Birth to His Inauguration as President of the United States," but when it was deposited for copyright on May 15, *True* had been omitted. At first it received some favorable notices, and then the loyalists went to work with reviews so savage and so outraged as to fill columns with expletives and disdain. Only 1,900 copies were sold.

Robert Lincoln did not read it himself, but he could not close his ears to the unpleasant echoes. Perhaps it hardened his grim distaste for autopsy. Out of this episode there comes the suspicion, faint and inconclusive to be sure, but persuasive nevertheless, that he had been infected with distrust and abhorrence and mysteriously morbid fears by the political "heir to the Lincoln tradition," the Honorable David Davis.

Perhaps it was because the judge had never quite understood Mr. Lincoln, who, the judge felt, had "had neither strong friendships nor enmities." He would think of him as "a very kind-hearted man," who "disliked to do a harsh thing, and never acted from passion." And yet Mr. Lincoln had never written him a line "nor asked his opinion on any subject since he was elected President." This was the more puzzling because pending the election the judge had often addressed the candidate. He had, however, been discouraged into discontinuance by silence. During the war years the judge had "often talked to the President," and had given him "his opinions very freely," but Mr. Lincoln "would sit with his head down and make no reply." It was too late now for an explanation.

CHAPTER SIX

Two Everlasting Angels

Following the appearance of colonel lamon's book in the
spring of 1872, Robert Todd Lincoln, counselor and attorney
at law, spent six months in Europe, and, upon his return to Chicago,
formed a new partnership, this time with Edward S. Isham. His
practice was good and his affairs prosperous. His brother Tad had
died the year before, and he was now the "sole surviving child of
Abraham Lincoln." He had a three-year-old daughter. His mother,
"widow of the chief magistrate of a great nation," was manifesting
symptoms of mental abnormality. There was always some situation
to prevent his attainment of serenity.

In Washington John George Nicolay became marshal of the
Supreme Court of the United States, an office which, if not quite
a sinecure, was certainly less exacting than it has since become. It
was supposed that he might now pursue his long-postponed research. In November came a letter from John Hay, dated the twenty-
second, in which the young diplomat declared:

I am convinced that we ought to be at work on our *Lincoln*, you might
as well be putting in your time collecting material as not. I don't think
the time for publication has come, but the time for preparation is slipping
away.

It is probable that Nicolay had already begun some desultory spadework; once he had adjusted and accustomed himself to his new position he might take it up in earnest. What made it important to start was the fact that gentlemen of Mr. Lincoln's generation either were dying off, taking their recollections with them, or they were themselves breaking into print and contributing to the surfeit of the market. Moreover, there was always the chance that something might happen to those papers which were still shut away in Bloomington.

But Nicolay and Colonel Hay betrayed no sign of hurry. On the contrary, they prided themselves on the circumstance that "after the war was over, and the triumph of the national arms had received its pathetic and tragical consecration in the martyrdom of the President, they did not take advantage of the excitement of the hour to throw upon the world a hasty and ill-digested compilation." They were no more restive, no more impulsive, no more impetuous now. Theirs would be the definitive, final statement which once and for all would relate the Lincoln story. It would not have to be told again.

As Nicolay and Colonel Hay, with their sense of mission, contemplated their special qualifications, they enumerated the following:

. . . Both grew up in the same region with Mr. Lincoln; they were intimate from boyhood with his friends and companions. Mr. Nicolay took charge of his correspondence before his election to the Presidency . . . He held this position [Private Secretary] throughout Mr. Lincoln's term of office, and enjoyed his closest intimacy and confidence. Mr. Hay, like Mr. Nicolay, accompanied the President from Springfield to Washington, where he remained several years as Assistant Secretary; he then entered the army as an Assistant Adjutant General of Volunteers, and after a brief period of staff service was ordered back to Washington and assigned to duty as an aide-de-camp to the President where he remained till the war ended. One of them, and generally both, were on duty at Mr. Lincoln's side every day from 1860 to 1865; Mr. Nicolay was his official medium of communication with Congress and the Cabinet; both were continually employed by him in delicate and important missions to every part of the country; both stood beside him at his two inaugurations; one saw him die. . . .

At an age when the faculties of memory and observation are at their best, they made frequent notes and memoranda of important events occurring about them. The President himself was aware of their intention, and encouraged and assisted them in their work. Some of his most precious manuscripts were given them by his own hand.

But in 1873, when Nicolay at last buckled down to the serious business of assembling sources, their most formidable asset was the compliance of Robert Lincoln. In June he promised to see Judge Davis about the possibility of turning over his father's papers to them. Nicolay, who possessed the instincts but not the training of an archivist, appears to have begun his work with materials in his own possession. On March 14, 1874, he showed Ainsworth Rand Spofford, Librarian of Congress, a "Carpetbag bundle of 'Lincoln Papers' somewhat damaged by water, preserved by Nicolay and transcribed by him." It wasn't long before there were rumors of the commencement of the enterprise. In May Herndon reported that he had heard "it hinted that Hay and Nickolay [*sic*] were writing a life of Lincoln." By July 17 the corpus of the Lincoln papers from Bloomington (there may have been a stopover in Chicago) had been delivered at the marshal's office in the Capitol, but were still unopened. Then Mr. Nicolay undertook the gigantic task of putting them in order, sorting them, classifying them, establishing dates, relating them to other documents in his keeping, and, for him most important of all, devising, on the basis of their contents, plans for a comprehensive treatment of the Lincoln period. Necessarily it was a one-man job, and necessarily it was slow, but the tall-browed, meticulous Mr. Nicolay was not deterred by its proportions. Only those who have seen the Lincoln papers can fully appreciate the difficulties which confronted him.

It was said afterward that "all the manuscripts of whatever nature belonging to the estate of Mr. Lincoln were absolutely and unreservedly placed" in the hands of the joint authors. This statement, which presumably was made with their concurrence since it preceded the first installment of "Abraham Lincoln: A History," in the pages of *The Century*, must be considered skeptically. Although it is unlikely that there existed a formal contract, as in the case of the agreement between Lamon and Black, it is nevertheless certain that conditions were imposed and that these conditions were clearly and perfectly understood. In the first place, "the manuscripts . . . belonging to the estate of Mr. Lincoln," might better have been described as the White House files which the prospective authors had packed immediately after the President's funeral in 1865. Robert Lincoln is known to have had in some of his "boxes" other manuscripts of his father's which, for one reason or another, were not regarded as a part of the Executive Mansion collection, and probably never had been. In those days he seldom looked at them and may not have known precisely what he had. They may have been gathered up with other family belongings in the living quarters, when the Lincolns left Washington.

In the second place, it is evident that Robert Lincoln either required or was granted the right to edit, amend, or cancel any use of the papers which he disapproved. His decision in such instances would be final.

In the third place, it seems likely that Robert Lincoln had been induced to surrender the papers because Associate Justice David Davis would be on hand to consult with the marshal of the Supreme Court on fragile problems of inclusion or exclusion, and to act as Abraham Lincoln's literary executor and keeper of the privy seal of confidence.

Finally, it is necessary to understand that the "gleaning out," which Robert Lincoln had promised himself, had not yet taken place. Actually, aside from the cursory glimpses he may have had of some of them, in the casual course of assisting in their bundling nearly a decade before, it is improbable that he had more than the faintest glimmerings of what they were. To him they were tragic mementoes, laden with disturbance and distress.

On the other hand, he could depend completely on the discretion, conscience, and earnest purpose of these old friends. The loyalty they had brilliantly demonstrated to his father had now been transferred to him. Both were competent writers, and Colonel Hay was an accomplished stylist. Their good faith was unquestioned; just as they would do nothing to taint his father's fame, so they would deliberately never displease him. In other words, the papers would be safe in their custody. More than that, he could insist that their work satisfy him. It was high time for an authorized version, and this would be it.

But if Robert Lincoln insisted on concessions to himself, he did not grudge some to his associates. Their work would be exhaustive, complicated, sometimes onerous, often dull. They would devote years of their lives to its accomplishment. In return for their sacrifice, he was willing to allow them all of the compensations for their labor. They would be the only licensed transmitters of the Lincoln era. Beyond their rights as authors to their literary property he gave them the freehold of his father's record. It was a monopoly which he felt they eminently deserved.

In April 1875 Robert's mother returned from Florida, pathetically but dangerously insane. It was obvious that she must be committed to an institution. After a conference with her cousin and Major Stuart, of Springfield, and Judge Davis, of the Supreme Court, Robert Lincoln filed charges. The case was heard May 19, with Leonard Swett, who had not so long ago prevailed on Colonel Lamon to alter the text of "his" biography, and Isaac N. Arnold, who once had sought access to the Lincoln papers, among the counsel. Robert Lincoln told the court:

I do not regard it safe to allow her to remain longer unrestrained. . . . She has no home, and does not visit my house because of a misunderstanding with my wife. She has always been kind to me. She has been of unsound mind since the death of her husband, and has been irresponsible for the last ten years. I regard her as eccentric and unmanageable.

The jury's verdict delared her insane and "a fit person to be sent to the State Hospital," adding that her disease was of unknown duration and unknown cause, that it was not hereditary, that she was not subject to epilepsy, that there was no evidence of homicidal or suicidal tendencies, and that she was not a pauper. Robert Lincoln was appointed conservator to manage and control her estate. For him it was a harrowing experience, not only because of his natural emotions and sorrow, but also because of the publicity which unavoidably attended the proceedings. More than ever he longed to opaque the walls of his house. Then, on the following day, while awaiting removal to a private asylum, Mrs. Lincoln managed to elude her attendants and attempted to poison herself. Fortunately the druggist who sold her a concoction labeled "laudanum and camphor" had been warned of her condition and possible purpose, and handed her a harmless mixture. She was seen to drink it, and returned a few minutes later for more. Again she swallowed the innocuous fluid. Robert, who had been summoned, arrived on the scene almost immediately afterward and took her in charge. She was placed in a private car, under the care of her physicians, and sent to the Bellevue Place Sanatorium, in Batavia, Illinois. But the story got into the newspapers and Robert Lincoln, with the instincts of a recluse and the destiny of an exhibitionist, felt incurably afflicted by the prying press. He probably concurred with the doctors, who held that part of his mother's trouble was attributable to Herndon's lectures.

The two young men went ahead with their plans. In June Nicolay was in Springfield, interviewing and taking notes. On the seventeenth he spent two hours talking to Senator Browning and writing memoranda of the information he obtained. By autumn enough material had been assembled to justify the first attempts at writing. Nicolay on November 16 wrote to Colonel Hay who had married and settled in Cleveland: "I send you today by express the first installment of material." On December 4 Colonel Hay acknowledged its receipt, promising to "go seriously to work upon it." He hoped "to make considerable progress by next spring." One of Colonel Hay's biographers, William Roscoe Thayer, has described their method of work:

Being marshal of the United States Supreme Court from 1872 to 1887, Nicolay resided in Washington where he was near the official archives. His library was the central storehouse of material; but Hay collected also, and, as the work went on, he bought many manuscripts and documents and rare books for their joint use. Nicolay blocked out the schedule of chapters, which they then discussed together, and, after coming to a decision, each chose the topics he preferred. As fast as these were written, they passed to the other partner, for criticism, trimming, verification, and additions.

The library of Civil War literature which Nicolay formed in his B Street home, facing the Capitol, was notably comprehensive; for ancillary material he had access to the Library of Congress, a block across the plaza. Moreover, in addition to the Lincoln papers he sought and obtained "the private . . . correspondence of most of Mr. Lincoln's Cabinet," while "leading statesmen and generals of the time . . . afforded . . . every possible assistance in the elucidation of difficult points." The practice of exchanging drafts, of rewriting each other's chapters, of amending, correcting, and canceling succeeded in the object of uniformity but sterilized the individuality of the contributors; so much so, in fact, that when the work was completed the publisher would ask Colonel Hay: "Have we your permission if it be thought best to let the newspapermen know what parts are from your pen and what are Mr. Nicolay's?"

Progress was discouragingly slow. Colonel Hay "went industriously to work" in the winter of 1875–76, "got a fine start" on his material, and "commenced putting it in shape." He had "even written a few pages," when he was "struck with partial blindness." He had a long and tedious convalescence. The duties of marshal intruded upon Nicolay's productivity. In August 1877 Colonel Hay reported to his colleague: "If nothing happens adversely, we can have Lincoln inaugurated by the fourth of March 1878. I have been very hard at work for a month or so, and sat down some weeks ago to writing. I have written from nine to ten thousand words (that is the only way of stating it) and have brought up to 1830." On St. Valentine's Day in 1878 Colonel Hay notified Robert Lincoln:

. . . I have been spending a fortnight in Washington with Nicolay and am very much gratified at the work he has done in arranging your papers and in preparing for our history. Besides putting the MS. in admirable order, he has made a first-rate beginning at the chapters allotted to him. I also have had pretty good luck during the last season and we now consider the big job well begun. It will take a long time yet, but we are in no hurry and I presume you are not. We have made such arrangements that in case either of Nicolay's death or mine your property is safe and the work as far as done is available for the survivor.

In January 1879 he told Nicolay that he had "made considerable progress," had almost "got to the Shields duel time," and asked for "any original matter not included in the Lamon book." By March he had "written . . . in all, over 50,000 words." In that year his literary work was retarded by his appointment as Assistant Secretary of

State. He discharged the duties of that office until the end of the Hayes administration, and represented the United States at the International Sanitary Conference, of which he was elected president. Then, despite the urgent solicitations of Garfield and Blaine to remain in public life, he retired to devote himself to the life of Lincoln.

But the silent partner came to Washington in 1881, when James A. Garfield, President of the United States, "reposing special trust and confidence in the Patriotism, Integrity, and Abilities of Robert T. Lincoln, of Illinois," nominated and appointed him Secretary of War. It was a popular move.

There was, of course, much to commend him, but, on the other hand, he could not be said to be widely versed in public affairs. In April 1876, as part of a movement to oust a corrupt gang of petty office holders, he had been elected supervisor of the town of South Chicago, and had held the post for the year he had agreed to serve it. He had been a member from Cook County to the State Convention at Springfield, which had nominated delegates to the National Convention held in Chicago June 2, 1880, and had been one of the electors on the Republican ticket for the state of Illinois. Early in 1880 he had been appointed by the governor of Illinois as one of the trustees of the Illinois Central Railroad. He was conservative, taciturn, adept at administration. But what particular significance he brought to the War Department was the fact that he was not just *a* Lincoln, but the *only* Lincoln of that time. There was majesty in that. By way of family, he had a charming wife and three small children: Mary, born October 15, 1869; Abraham, born August 14, 1873; and Jessie Harlan, born November 6, 1875. Although he made an excellent civil servant, he was not distinguished for fostering public relations.

When General Garfield died, President Arthur asked Robert Lincoln to continue in the Cabinet, and he complied. In Washington he may from time to time have looked in on Nicolay and followed the gradual emergence of the history. The Lincoln story did not languish. Soon after he became Secretary of War, the Honorable Isaac N. Arnold sent him a copy of a paper which he had written and read before the Royal Historical Society, in London, on Abraham Lincoln. In acknowledging Mister Arnold's gift, Robert Lincoln assured him: "I tell you sincerely that I have never seen anything of the character so gratifying to myself and so complete."

From Cleveland, on January 27, 1884, Colonel Hay wrote to "Dear Bob":

Nicolay tells me he has laid before you or is about to do so, the first volumes of our history containing the chapters in which I have described the first forty years of your father's life.

I need not tell you that every line has been written in a spirit of reverence and regard. Still you may find here and there words or sentences which do not suit you. I write now to request that you will read with a pencil in your hand and strike out everything to which you object. I will adopt your view in all cases whether I agree with it or not, but I cannot help hoping that you will find nothing objectionable.

When the manuscript was returned every one of the passages had been marked, and Hay wrote to Robert Lincoln on April 20, 1885: "I will do what you suggest in final revision. It is better, even as a matter of taste and without regard to your wishes which would, of course, be conclusive." But Lincoln was upset, and on January 6, 1886, Colonel Hay felt impelled to write to him again:

I was very sorry to see by a letter you wrote to Nicolay the other day that you were still not satisfied with my assurance that I would make those first chapters right. Even before you read them I had struck out of my own copy here nearly everything you objected to and had written Nicolay to make the changes in his which he had not time to do. Since then I have gone over the whole thing twice again, reading every line so far as possible from your point of view, and I don't think there is a word left in it that would displease you. But of course before final publication I shall give you another hack at it, with plenary blue-pencil powers. . . .

We have been making great progress for the last year or two—the book is nearly two-thirds finished. We have finished the fifth volume and are well on in the sixth. If we live two years more we shall get through. I am more anxious than I can tell you to live that long. There has been so much irresponsible and untrue writing of late years, that I feel a solemn sort of pressure in me to do my part—to putting the truth before the country. Year after year of study has shown me more clearly than ever how infinitely greater your father was than anybody about him, greater than ever we imagined while he lived. There is nothing to explain or apologize for from beginning to end. He is the one unapproachably great figure of a great epoch.

Now the original manuscript of the first four chapters of volume one has survived, and it contains the alterations in the text. Most of them relate to the shiftlessness of Abraham Lincoln's father or to the less glamorous aspects of the prairie civilization in which he lived. Modern scholarship agrees that with one exception the changes were made by John Hay in accordance with his concept of Robert Lincoln's taste. The exception was Robert Lincoln's insistence on the deletion of "the ludicrous incident of sewing up the hogs' eyes," which Abraham Lincoln had included in his autobiography, and which John Nicolay had carefully omitted in copying that document for distribution to the press. But the point is that in writing the account of Mr. Lincoln's early youth, Colonel Hay had been under the necessity of relying on "secondary sources" and old wives' tales. He had even resorted to the objectionable work of Colonel Lamon, who had got hold of the pig story and printed it in his outrageous volume. In other words, it could hardly be said, on the basis of a single instance, that Robert Lincoln had purged his father's papers. There was at that juncture nothing in them to worry about. Nevertheless, future critics would abuse him without knowing what the papers contained for that period. This would be unfair; he was more proficient as an editor than as an addicted censor. Hay and Nicolay, on the other hand, had from those markings received a lesson in decorum and acceptability. Robert Lincoln's "plenary blue-pencil powers" would unconsciously impose circumspection. Herndon would put it differently: "Nicolay and Hay handle things with silken gloves and a camel-hair pencil," he declared. "They do not write with an iron pen. . . . They are writing the Life of Lincoln under the surveillance of Bob Lincoln. Nicolay and Hay, in my opinion, are afraid of Bob. He gives them materials and they play hush." If there were any justice in this supposition, the authors themselves were unaware of it. They went on record with the statement that

We can only claim for this work that we have devoted to it sixteen years of almost unremitting assiduity; that we have neglected no means in our power to ascertain the truth; that we have rejected no authentic facts essential to a candid story; that we have had no theory to establish, no personal grudge to gratify; no avowed objects to subserve. We have aimed to write a sufficiently full and absolutely honest history of a great man and a great time; and although we take it for granted that we have made mistakes, that we have fallen into such errors and inaccuracies as are unavoidable in so large a work, we promise that there shall not be found a line in all these chapters dictated by malice or unfairness.

This was perfectly honest, perfectly sincere, and in conflict neither with their obligations to Robert Lincoln nor with their own personal inhibitions.

When Grover Cleveland moved into the White House, for the first time Robert Lincoln returned to Chicago and his practice. Looking back on his four years in the War Department, he would think there was nothing in his administration "worth recording." He was "satisfied to have got out of it without more grief."

Meanwhile the work of Nicolay and Colonel Hay on a more enduring monument had reached a point where its sturdy outlines had become visible and alluring. In the years of its construction it had passed from the stage when publishers would not talk turkey to the time when all of the larger houses gobbled loudly for the privilege of sponsorship and the authors had the pleasant sensation of discouraging them. Most persistent because they were most eager (and, perhaps, most opulent) were representatives of *The Century* magazine. First Robert Underwood Johnson tried his hand, and then he turned the transaction over to the redoubtable editor, Richard Watson Gilder. On June 11 Mr. Gilder wrote to Mr. Nicolay:

I have been thinking a great deal about your book lately. I have a scheme in mind which is not yet definite enough for me to ask Mr. Roswell Smith [president of The Century Co.] to put it in the form of a proposition, but I will nevertheless mention it to you.

You said if we printed any of the book in the magazine we would want the cream of it and this you would not like. But I have another idea—not to take the cream, but to take the whole!—and to make you (the authors) such a proposition therefor that any possible slip up on the book sale would be more than discounted. For the book might be reserved only those long and dull documents, if any there be, which add dignity and value to a library volume, but which the ordinary reader skips.

Before any such definite proposition were made it would be necessary for me to get a clear idea of the book, with your permission. I should indeed prefer to read the whole thing rapidly. I think that the book could be published in the magazine inside of twenty-four months beginning one year from next November—by that time it would doubtless be completed by the authors. We could illustrate with a few *real* pictures, I mean pictures of persons and places, which could be used in the book or not as you preferred, or as might be determined upon.

If your object is that Lincoln's story should reach this generation, how could it better be accomplished? As for remuneration for your long and faithful labors, that would be assured from the beginning; then would come the further profit and the full-blown historical and literary dignity of library volumes. A further consideration would be the opportunity of correcting possible errors and enriching the volumes with material elicited by serial publication.

John Hay, to whom Nicolay sent this letter, considered "the offer of *The Century* very tempting." He admitted to his colleague: "Of course we could cut down a good deal and present what would be a continuous narrative in about half the space we have taken for our book." On August 10 he wrote to Nicolay again:

. . . There will be no difficulty whatever in beginning the series—if ever—next fall (1886). The only contingency in which we should not be able to keep up would be death. If we live we can do it. . . . I have toiled and labored through the chapter over him (McClellan). I think I have left the impression of his mutinous imbecility, and I have done it in a perfectly courteous manner. . . . Gilder was evidently horrified at your saying that Lee ought to be shot—a simple truth of law and equity. . . . The war has gone by. It is twenty years ago. Our book is to be read by people who cannot remember anything about it. We must not show to the public in the attitude of two old dotards fighting over again the politics of our youth. . . . We must not write a stump speech, eight vols., 8vo. We will not fall in with the present tone of blubbering sentiment, of course. But we ought to write the history of those times like two everlasting angels who know everything, judge everything, tell the truth about everything, and don't care a twang of our harps about one side or the other. There will be one exception. We are Lincoln men all through. But in other little matters, let us look at men as insects and not blame the black beetle because he is not a grasshopper. S.P.C. [Salmon P. Chase] is going to be a nut to crack, so is Seward.

Whether they liked it or not, the "two everlasting angels" were unreconstructed unionists and their insects (or most of them) spoke with a Southern accent. While negotiations with *The Century* were going forward, they pressed on with their writing. There were times when Colonel Hay was ashamed of his "feverish anxiety to boil down and condense—but," he observed, "when your job is to get the universe into eight volumes, you must not take two bites of an atom." He told his fellow angel on August 29: "There is enough in Chase's letters abusing Lincoln behind his back for a quiet scorcher —but think of Mrs. Hoyt, if you please." Mrs. William Hoyt was Chief Justice Chase's surviving daughter. The authors, naturally, found no pleasure in the prospect of provoking people they knew. In November they sold the serial rights for fifty thousand dollars to The Century Company. It was said to be the largest sum an American magazine had ever paid. Gilder was delighted; he wrote to Edmund Gosse: "It is not only what you might call the secret history of the secession conspiracy, and the inside history of the war, but it also contains a complete, authentic, and logical account of the great political struggle in connection with the subject of slavery. But what gives it its greatest value, at least in this country, is that it is the authorized—the only authorized life of the greatest man this country has ever produced—at least since Washington—and not only the greatest, but by far the most interesting; in interest Lincoln even surpasses Washington."

It was agreed that most of the military chapters would be omitted from the magazine publication and reserved for the book, for the reason that The Century had already covered much of the ground in its war series from which it was reputed to have made a million dollars. This reduced the manuscript by approximately half its actual size. As for the larger work: "We shall never get through in a million words," moaned Colonel Hay, "and so must seize every opportunity to condense." With the signing of the contract, the authors discovered that, in addition to Robert Lincoln, they had another editor in the person of Mr. Gilder, who never hesitated to insist on the elimination of personally uncomplimentary adjectives, the tempering of obvious exhibitions of partisanship, the revision of awkward sentences and phrases, and even the deletion of whole chapters when they contradicted the opinion of Mr. Buel, The Century's expert on warfare.

Just the same, it could not be denied that The Century provided an elaborate production. Its art staff performed magnificently in rounding up portraits and photographs; Joseph Pennell and Augustus Saint-Gaudens were retained to furnish additional illustrations; and the serialization was announced with almost ecstatic pleasure. *Abraham Lincoln: A History*, in its abridged form, ran for forty months—from November 1886 to February 1890.

Gilder was terribly pleased. He wrote to Colonel Hay: "I enclose a small batch of criticisms and notices, good, bad, and indifferent. The great fact remains, no matter what is said, that the Work is a phenomenal success as published in *The Century*. We know what we are about, and it is all right. It is so right that any help which comes from even adverse criticism ought to be welcomed by all of us."

William Dean Howells, formerly of Columbus, Ohio, now of Beacon Street, Boston, who, for the campaign of 1860, had written one of the first biographies of the late President, was extremely generous. "I get a chance at about one chapter in each installment of the Lincoln," he wrote. "It seems to me admirable—easy, dignified with solemnity, and extremely interesting; the frankness of it is just what should be."

James Ford Rhodes in Paris was equally kind: "From this side of the water a word of congratulation may perhaps not be amiss on the clever and entertaining way in which you begin your history. I expect that your book will demolish the modern theory that an author cannot write modern history impartially."

Even Robert Lincoln was unstinted. He told Colonel Hay: "Now that you have as one may say dropped the curtain at the end of the first act—I want to tell you how much pleased I am with the result of your long work. It is what I hoped it would be." That was enough for him.

All the comment wasn't praise. General Fitz-John Porter was aggrieved and asked for public retraction. Armchair strategists found fault with minutiae of battle accounts. A few of the characters felt slighted. Herndon noted that "some of the finest episodes in Lincoln's young life are omitted or evaded or swallowed up in words." But generally speaking the reception was heartening and the authors had every reason for gratification.

The most pointed criticism came from *Life,* then an intentionally humorous magazine. On March 10, 1887, it asked, "Is it a joke?"

Readers of *The Century* have been much confused by a History of the United States published serially in that magazine under the somewhat personal title of "Abraham Lincoln." There certainly existed a president of that name, and we believe he is alluded to once or twice in this history; but such a reputation should not be used for advertising purposes. If we remember rightly, the editors of this magazine once announced with some ceremony that a life of Mr. Lincoln was soon to appear in their pages. Where is it?

Several more criticisms of a similar nature appeared in *Life.* Some of their carping was not without foundation. Nicolay and Hay's *Abraham Lincoln,* as the monumental record of an era, was a remarkable achievement, but it was a source book for history and was never intended as "popular" biography. That treatment they planned to undertake at a later date, when the great work had been accomplished and put away in type. On the other hand, they realized, better than people who had not examined the Lincoln papers could possibly realize, that Mr. Lincoln's life was a part of many lives, a part of the lives of the individuals who together composed the people of the United States. Sometimes they, sometimes he, were in the brighter focus, but he was always there. It was his identification, fusion, partiality with them which made their task so difficult and the result so compellingly commendable.

But while the history was appearing in *The Century,* things were happening to the little group which controlled the Lincoln papers. David Davis had died in June 1886. Without him, Robert Lincoln had to assume the problems of the papers alone. But he had made a place for himself in the world and could stand on his own feet.

James Grant Wilson, editor of Appleton's Cyclopaedia of American Biography, wrote to Colonel Hay on February 14, 1877:

I think you may properly devote about 500 words to Robert T. Lincoln, but if you desire a little more space for his story pray take it. Will you kindly add to your sketch of the President a brief notice of Mrs. Lincoln, as the plan of the Cyclopaedia includes portraits of the ladies of the White House.

Colonel Hay, having completed his draft, submitted it to Robert Lincoln, who returned it on Washington's Birthday, with a covering note:

Many thanks for your kindness in sending me your MSS. I beg you will cut it down at least to the extent I have indicated, for you have let your enthusiastic kindness overcome the stark realities. As I have changed it, I think no one can take serious exception to it.

My mother died of paralysis July 16, 1882. . . .

The altered draft survives in the shirt-box miscellany of Hay papers in the Library of Congress. Robert Lincoln's changes are interesting as reflecting his economical phrasing, truthfulness, and editorial capacity. From them it is possible to imagine the nature of his revisions in the later chapters of the history. For example, Colonel Hay, in connection with Robert Lincoln's participation in the Civil War, had written:

He served throughout the final campaign before Richmond and Petersburg, distinguishing himself by his zeal, courage, intelligence, and modesty.

This Robert Lincoln had corrected to read:

He served throughout the final campaign which ended at Appomattox.

Again Colonel Hay had written:

On the accession of Vice-President Arthur to the presidency, Mr. Lincoln was the only member of the former Cabinet who was requested to retain his portfolio and this request of the new President was supplemented by so universal a demand from the country that Mr. Lincoln felt compelled to accede to it.

This was toned down:

On the accession of Vice-President Arthur to the presidency, Mr. Lincoln was the only member of the former Cabinet who was requested to retain his portfolio and he did so to the end of the administration.

His comments on the account of his mother, contained in a letter of March 3, 1887, are also illuminating:

I return you the sketch of my mother, with the date of her birth—I suggest in pencil the omission of certain prefixes merely to please my own taste in an article of this kind. I like the sketch very much. Please consider the propriety of striking out the clause "a brother-in-law . . . Chickamauga." I suggest this because it seems to me that it would be better not to name one person & omit others exemplifying the "division," e.g., my mother's half brothers were in the rebel army—Samuel was killed at Shiloh. Her brother George was a Surgeon in the rebel army while as you know Dr. Wallace & Mr. Edwards held commissions in the Union Army & it seems to me better to leave the matter with the general phrase as to the division.

Confederates were always only rebels to Robert Lincoln.

There were now too many demands upon Nicolay. On November 29, 1887, he wrote to Morrison Remick Waite, Chief Justice of the United States:

As the literary and historical labors upon which I am engaged as a co-worker will, during the next few years, require the whole of my time, I herewith tender you my resignation as Marshal of the Supreme Court of the United States, to take effect on the [blank] day of December next.

In severing my official relations with the Court I desire to convey my warm appreciation of their personal friendship and kindness during the whole of my fifteen years' service.

At this time of the year there was a minor episode which stirred up no little excitement in the land. A box of Confederate flags was discovered in the War Department, and it was said that a former secretary had planned to restore them to the Southern states. "Well, what of it?" snapped Robert Lincoln. "What if the old rags were boxed up? I don't see that there is any reason for such an insinuation. . . . I don't know anything about the matter. I don't recollect ever having heard a word spoken on the subject of rebel flags. I don't recollect having once seen them. I don't even know in whose charge they were. I have some reason for thinking that they were in charge of the Adjutant General, and I have some grounds for believing they were in charge of the Chief of Ordnance. I have a dim recollection of the Chief of Ordnance speaking to me once about some old rags of rebel flags which he had in his museum, and which, from rottenness and general decay, had become unfit to be seen, and suggesting that they be boxed up, but cannot say that was so, mind you. If the flags were boxed and anybody wants to insinuate that they were so boxed for the purpose of returning them to the Southern states, it is all poppycock. The thing was never once spoken of, nor even thought of while I was in the Department. We had more important things to think about when I was there than the disposition that should be made of a few rotten old rebel flags."

It was as easy to misunderstand as to annoy him. It may have been in that knowledge that Colonel Hay wrote to him on April 12, 1888:

I own a few of your father's MS. which he gave me from time to time. As long as you and I live I take it for granted that you will not suspect me of boning them. But to guard against casualties hereafter, I have asked Nicolay to write you a line saying that I have never had in my possession or custody any of the papers which you entrusted to him.

I have handed over to Nicolay to be placed among your papers some of those which your father gave me. The rest, which are few in number, are very precious to me. I shall try to make an heirloom in my family as long as one of my blood exists with money enough to buy a breakfast.

We are nearly at the end of our lifelong task and I hope you will think your father's fame has not suffered any wrong at our hands.

The following March President Benjamin Harrison nominated and the Senate confirmed the appointment of Robert Lincoln as "Minister Plenipotentiary of the United States of America to Great Britain." Mr. Lincoln was taken completely by surprise, but he put his affairs in order, and sailed for his post on May 15, 1889. He was a popular and conscientious diplomat, dined with Mr. Gladstone at Henry Labouchère's, and impressed Her Majesty as a very pleasant and sensible sort of man. But tragedy which had struck first with his father's murder, and next with his mother's madness, followed him abroad. On March 5, 1890, a little after eleven o'clock in the morning, Master Abraham Lincoln II, who had been suffering for a long time from blood poisoning arising from a malignant carbuncle, died. It was said that he suffered no pain and passed away quietly. The old Queen promptly sent another message of sympathy to the bereft Lincolns. But the loss of "Jack"—Abraham had been too ponderous a name for the boy among family and friends—was very hard to bear. There had been no limits to the hopes which his parents had set for him.

Robert Lincoln came home to take part in the campaign of 1892, and in 1893 was succeeded by Bayard as Ambassador to England. In that year Harvard College conferred on him the degree of LL.D. He did not resume the practice of his profession, but "found himself sufficiently occupied in the business affairs of various companies in which he had an interest." During his absence Herndon, in collaboration with Jesse W. Weik, had published *Herndon's Lincoln: The True Story of a Great Life*, and it was generally supposed that some of the attacks which that work received had been inspired by Robert. He was convinced that Herndon "was actuated by an intense malice, and was possessed of a most ingenious imagination." He was inclined to believe that it was caused by the fact that his father "could not see his way, in view of Herndon's personal character, to give him some lucrative employment during the War of the Rebellion." Herndon retaliated by calling "Bob" a "damned fool" and a "wretch of a man." There would never be peace between them.

John G. Nicolay and John Hay's *Abraham Lincoln: A History*, had been published in book form in the summer and fall of 1890, and The Century Company had sold 5,000 sets by subscription. It was made up in ten volumes, containing 4,700 pages and about one and a half million words. It was the longest biography ever produced, and as history it bulked twice as large as Green's *English People*, contained 300,000 more words than Gibbon had required to trace the twelve centuries of the *Decline and Fall of the Roman Empire*, and was equaled only by Bancroft's *History of the United States*. It was dedicated "To the Honorable Robert Todd Lincoln . . . in token of a lifelong friendship and esteem."

He was pleased by this distinction and on May 30, 1893, wrote to Nicolay:

As you and Colonel Hay have now brought your great work to a most successful conclusion by the publication of your life of my father, I hope and request that you and he will supplement it by collecting, editing, and publishing the speeches, letters, state papers, and miscellaneous writings of my father. You and Colonel Hay have my consent and authority to obtain for yourselves such protection by copyright, or other-

wise, in respect to the whole or any part of such a collection, as I might
for any reason be entitled to have.

This was a post-facto document, a ratification, for on the ninth of
February preceding "a formal contract, duly signed by Hay and
Nicolay, for the publication of the *Complete Works of Abraham
Lincoln,* had been entered into by The Century Company." The
Complete Works, in two volumes, appeared in April 1894. Naturally
Nicolay had had to retain the papers for this purpose. When they
first came into his custody he had kept them at his home at 121 B
Street, S.E., but about 1880 he was forced to move because the block
on which he lived had been acquired by the Government in order to
erect a structure to accommodate a great collection. For the rest of
his life he resided on the square immediately east of his previous
dwelling, at 212 B Street. It was there that Edward Marshall, an
editor of the New York *Press,* on a morning in the winter of 1894
found him and recorded his impressions, part of which follows:

. . . It is now twenty years since Nicolay and John Hay began the
actual writing of their great biography of Abraham Lincoln, which was
completed and issued two years ago. During all that time and since no
other interest has been allowed to come between Nicolay and his work
of telling the future of the great man who had passed. His workroom,
with its great desk and many bookcases, is a place in which the present
is not known. There are gathered practically all the Lincoln manuscripts
in existence. Some of them are owned by Mr. Nicolay, most of them
are the property of the Lincoln family.

The morning of my visit he showed me many of them—there are
thousands in all—and the contents and history of each was ready to his
tongue, almost without a glance of identification. They are filed away in
great manila envelopes, and are all so well preserved that one wonders
when he realizes how many years have passed since they were penned.
Two of them particularly interested me. One was a letter written before
the nomination and expressing in modest simplicity Lincoln's own sense
of his unfitness for the great place of President. The other was the
original manuscript of a message to Congress, which contrasts strongly
with another message to Congress within a few weeks by another President in circumstances somewhat similar.

There appears to have been no secrecy, no cloture then. When
Marshall's article was published in the *Press* for Sunday morning,

February 11, it was illustrated with portraits of Lincoln and "photographic facsimiles of parts of the famous peace conference message [February 10, 1865], reproduced for the *Press* from the original manuscript, by courtesy of John G. Nicolay, Lincoln's Private Secretary." There was also a facsimile of Abraham Lincoln's letter of January 30, 1865, to Thomas T. Eckert.

Nicolay thereafter busied himself with magazine articles and the preparation of a one-volume biography of Lincoln. One day in the mid-nineties he was visited by Ida M. Tarbell, an attractive young woman whose acquaintance he had formed at the meetings of the Washington Literary Society. She told him that she had been commissioned by Samuel Sidney McClure to write a "popular" life of Lincoln, and had come to ask for his help. However, he was most discouraging. There was nothing of importance to be had. The collection of letters and speeches which he and Colonel Hay had compiled was complete, the subject had been exhausted, he would advise her not to touch so helpless an assignment. Miss Tarbell felt that he never forgave her for going ahead, and after her story began to appear in *McClure's* he came to her one evening and exclaimed: "You are invading my field. You write a popular Life of Lincoln and you do just so much to decrease the value of my property." However unchivalrous, it is easy to understand his attitude. He had devoted his years to Lincoln and had come to regard himself and Colonel Hay as the only legitimate dispensers of the story.

Miss Tarbell persisted. She went to Chicago, and through the intercession of a friend met Robert Lincoln. It was sometime after November 1897; he had become president of the Pullman Company, and his daughter Jessie, under most romantic conditions, had eloped with Warren W. Beckwith, a splendid athlete, of Mount Pleasant, Iowa. Miss Tarbell later recorded her recollections of that interview:

To be drinking tea with the son of Abraham Lincoln was so unbelievable . . . I searched his face and manners for resemblances. There was nothing. He was all Todd, a big plump man perhaps fifty years old, perfectly groomed with that freshness which makes men of his type look as if they were just out of the barber's chair, the admirable social poise of the man who has seen the world's greatest and has come to be sure of himself; and this in spite of such buffeting as few men have had. . . .

I devoured him with my eyes. He was very friendly. . . . But he went on to say he was afraid he had little that would help me. Herndon had taken all his father's papers from the law office. I think he used the word "stolen," but I am not sure; at least I knew he *felt* they were stolen.

Robert Lincoln did, however, allow her the use of a daguerreotype, the first picture of Abraham Lincoln ever taken. When she inquired for his father's letters he explained that those belonging to the presidential period were stored in Washington, having been completely exploited by Nicolay and Colonel Hay.

On Thursday, September 26, 1901, John G. Nicolay, who "had been in feeble health for several years," died at his home in Washington, leaving an estate, consisting of real property, bonds, household furniture, books, personal articles, and money in the bank, amounting to about forty-eight thousand seven hundred dollars. His daughter Helen was the sole heir at law and next of kin. She would also inherit his copyrights.

But the Lincoln papers which John Nicolay had made the substance and the motive of his living would not return to the President's son. They were symbols of change.

CHAPTER SEVEN

Intangible Memorial

W HEN JOHN NICOLAY DIED, THE LINCOLN PAPERS WERE DIVIDED into two lots: one, consisting of manuscripts in Abraham Lincoln's holograph, was boxed and stored in the vault of the National Capital Bank; the other and larger section, made up of communications addressed to the President, was still in Mr. Nicolay's home on B Street. Miss Nicolay promptly wrote to Robert Lincoln requesting instructions as to their disposition. Mr. Lincoln at the moment was preoccupied with pressing business matters and found it impossible to come at once to Washington to take them off her hands. Instead he wrote to Colonel John Hay, who had become Secretary of State in President McKinley's Cabinet and continued to hold that office under Theodore Roosevelt, asking for his suggestions. Secretary Hay wrote to Miss Nicolay on December 4, 1901: "I . . . have a letter from Mr. Lincoln accepting my proposition to place the papers now in the Safe Deposit Company in the State Department temporarily. Will you kindly send me an order on the bank so that I can have them transferred and relieve you of that responsibility?"

A few doors away from Miss Nicolay, in the Library of Congress, the work of assembling the record of a people made steady progress. At the head of the imposing institution was a young man whose red hair contrasted strangely with his outward calm, inflexible purpose, and irreproachable dignity. Knowing precisely what he intended to attain, he could present an appearance of infinite patience which belied his genius as opportunist. Herbert Putnam was at the beginning of his incomparable career in public service. On December 31, 1901, he wrote to the Honorable Robert T. Lincoln of Chicago:

I have learned from Miss Tarbell that the collection of your father's papers upon which Mr. Nicolay and Mr. Hay based their work still remains a unit, and that so far as she has information you have not yet determined upon a final place of deposit for it. Is there any chance that it may be placed in the National Library?

There is, of course, no need that I should state, much less that I should explain, the considerations which would make this, not merely the most appropriate, but, as far as concerns the investigator, the most efficient place of deposit. You know that the Library of Congress is the National Library. It has a building safe, commodious, and prominent; it has, and is increasingly to have, manuscript material bearing upon national affairs. It has now the organization, the equipment, and the funds which will insure that any material in its custody will render the amplest service.

The American Historical Association is just concluding a meeting in Washington. Dr. Judson, the dean of the University of Chicago, is among those present. He, with the others, has had opportunity to inspect the Library as it is and to learn of its plans for the aid of historical research in the United States. If you should be interested to have him do so, I am quite sure that he would be very glad to express his opinion as to the ability of the Library to conserve and to make useful any material of this sort.

I should be extremely sorry to advance a suggestion in any way intrusive, and I write this, not to anticipate any other disposition of the collection that may seem to you fitting, but merely to indicate the great interest which the authorities of this Library would feel in the deposit of the collection here, and their confidence that if here it would be in the most eminent degree safe and useful.

From the Pullman Building Mr. Lincoln replied within a week:

. . . I have been so very busy at the beginning of the new year that I have not been able to take up, until now, your letter of December 31st.

The subject you speak of is one which is often on my mind. The papers were taken over by Mr. Nicolay and Mr. Hay, as you know, very many years ago, and amidst my many occupations I was not pressed to take the matter up until after the death of Mr. Nicolay, when, of course, it became necessary to relieve Miss Nicolay of the care of the papers. Mr. Hay was good enough to take them in his personal charge until I am able to go to Washington. This I am hoping to do soon, and to confer with him there.

If my son was still alive, I should probably leave the papers in his hands, but as it is, I think it my duty to select some depository for them, just what it will be I am not yet prepared to say, but in considering it, your suggestions are very valuable, and will have great consideration.

I shall hope to have the pleasure of calling upon you when I am next in Washington.

Perhaps Mr. Lincoln did see Putnam when he came to Washington at the time of Prince Henry's tour, but there was a lull in correspondence for several years. Presumably the Abraham Lincoln papers remained in the crypts of the forbidding State Department. Robert Lincoln, who had stayed in Manchester, Vermont, in the summer of 1863 and had renewed his fondness for the charming place through frequent visits to his partner, Isham, purchased extensive property there in 1902, and built an imposing country house which he called "Hildene." There he was to spend many months of every year, play golf, receive distinguished guests, and entertain at least one President of the United States.

Putnam bided his time; on August 18, 1905, he wrote to Robert Lincoln again, addressing him at his Chicago home, 60 Lake Shore Drive:

The death of Secretary Hay removes unhappily one consideration that had prevented you from determining the final disposition of your father's papers. Since my last word with you concerning them, I have, of course, refrained from further suggestion. Mr. Ford, however, urges that a line reminding you of our great interest in them could not now be deemed intrusive, so I write it.

Our collections include now the papers of no less than nine of the Presidents.

Robert Lincoln had not yet made up his mind, and did not reply for several weeks. Finally he wrote from Manchester on September 14:

I have delayed acknowledging your letter . . . on account of the uncertainty of my plans.

It is now my expectation to visit Washington before the end of this month, in regard to the matter you mention, and I shall hope to have the pleasure of calling on you there.

Putnam was out of town from October 26 to November 4, but at some time during that fall or winter the two men probably met. In any event, Putnam wrote again to Robert Lincoln on June 23, 1906:

Further important accessions to our manuscript collections, including additional material from the Department of State, and a review in prospect of this department of the Library, and its possible service, necessarily remind us anew of your Father's papers. I understood you to say that you were intending to go over them. I have wondered if you have yet had an opportunity to do this. We find that, as a rule, such a task is for a man of affairs not very readily accomplished, the "spare moments" which he anticipates never seeming to be at hand.

In the case of one or two other collections we have made a suggestion which (though we apologize if it seems to presume too much) I now venture to you. It is this: that if you are prepared to assume that the collection in the main will ultimately be deposited here, and the chief reason for your delay is your desire to reserve out from it any material too personal in your judgment to be laid open to the public, or for other reasons inappropriate, and you are unable yourself to give the time to an examination of it piece by piece for the purpose of discriminating this, we would undertake here to sort the collection and set aside for your inspection any pieces that would seem to come within this latter category. Mr. Ford [i.e. Worthington Chauncey Ford, Chief of the Library's Division of Manuscripts] himself would do the sorting.

I do not mean, of course, that his judgment would be precisely yours, but neither would the final decision be his. His work would simply be preliminary, and as far as possible to save you time and labor.

Until your decision, the collection to be in our hands confidentially, and accessible neither to the public nor to members of the Library staff apart from the Chief of the Division, upon whose discretion you could, I think, fairly rely. And, of course, the deposit with us for this purpose would be provisional merely, not carrying the title nor any ensuing obligation which you did not care to express.

I make the suggestion at this time, because the summer recess offers freer opportunity for such work than other seasons of the year; but also because the hazards to such collections through fire and accident have been newly brought home to us by the catastrophes of the past year, including the destruction at San Francisco of the original Spanish archives which were in a building supposed to be reasonably safe.

Charles A. Sweet, Robert Lincoln's secretary, forwarded the Librarian's letter to him at Manchester. Robert Lincoln's answer was written on July 20:

Please excuse my undue delay in acknowledging your letter of June twenty-third, but I have been somewhat out of sorts and neglecting all my correspondence that I could lay aside. I regret to tell you that since I had the pleasure of seeing you in Washington I was so foolish as to permit myself to go down very much in the condition of my nerves, so that instead of devoting some time last Winter, as I had hoped to do, in the examination of my father's papers, I was compelled to lay up for more than three months, and did absolutely nothing whatever, not even replying to private notes. I am, I believe, a good deal better, and hope for a complete recovery in a few months.

In the meantime the papers are in my office in Chicago, and my secretary there, who is a gentleman in whom I have the highest confidence, is occupying his leisure time this Summer in putting them in order, and making some examination of them, so that when I get back in the Autumn I hope to find the task, which I dreaded so much, not really as serious as it might be.

I think, therefore, it will be better to let the matter rest in this way. It is a subject which is constantly present in my mind, and I do not intend to let it drag along much longer. I should, however, prefer to go over the papers in this way before letting them get into any hands whatever.

Lincoln's mail was heavy in those days. He was constantly importuned to release the papers to this or that would-be biographer, but without exception he denied every request. On the other hand, he delighted in being as helpful as he felt he could or ought to be. An example was his helpfulness to the learned James Schouler who was working on a study of Abraham Lincoln's appearance at Tremont Temple, Boston, in 1848. In response to an inquiry from Professor Schouler, Lincoln's secretary, Sweet, "was able at once to lay his hands upon some correspondence," which made it possible to "answer . . . with certainty." On another occasion, Robert Lincoln wrote Professor Schouler: "Mr. Sweet, my assistant in Chicago, who is about as familiar with my personal affairs as I am myself, and in some respects more so, sends me your letter, saying that he had gone through my father's papers but finds nothing in them relating to his visit to Massachusetts in 1848, except a paragraph in his autobiography in which he speaks of his advocacy of General Taylor's election and of his speaking several times in Massachusetts. You probably have access to this document yourself, but for your convenience I send you the copy which Mr. Sweet sent to me." He concluded regretfully: "I am very sorry that I cannot give you any further information on the subject, but I do not know where I could obtain anything additional."

What gives a special force of kindness to his many acts of willing and earnest co-operation is the knowledge that nearly every question submitted to him involved matters personally unfamiliar and required, therefore, recourse to records and research. In this connection it is necessary to keep in mind his rueful admission: "My Father's life was of a kind which gave me but little opportunity to learn the details of his early career. During my childhood & early youth he was almost constantly away from home, attending courts or making political speeches—In 1859 when I was sixteen & when he was beginning to devote himself more to practice in his own neighborhood, & when I would have had both the inclination & the means to gratify my desire to become better acquainted with the history of his early struggles, I went to New Hampshire to school & afterwards to Harvard College, & he became President—Thenceforth any great intimacy between us became impossible—I scarcely ever had ten minutes' quiet talk with him during his Presidency, on account of his constant devotion to business."

"I am not a collector," he once wrote, and not being a familiar either, Robert Lincoln had to become a student and gradually accumulate a creditable store of information, but he was always an amateur, and because his own inquiries were ordinarily prompted by generous impulse rather than intellectual curiosity or compelling quest, it is doubtful if he ever came to comprehend those qualities which made his father's influence unique. Despite a filial fidelity amounting almost to piety, he sometimes begrudged his father's memory his own sense of inferiority. There would always be, no matter how hard he might try to ignore or dispute or overcome the fact, a Lincoln major and a Lincoln minor. Morally a Victorian among Victorians, appearances assumed for him exaggerated importance. His principles were high, his motives unassailable, his purpose completely proper, but inner dissatisfactions imposed on him a distrust of posterity's judgment, and this purely personal restraint produced artificial and misshapen obligations. Those whose counsel he once had taken now were dead. He was painfully but courageously on his own. He was on his own that day when he frightened Miss Tarbell. This is her account of the episode:

If Robert Lincoln was always friendly he threw me once into the greatest panic I suffered in the course of my Lincoln work, though this was long after the Life was published. I had gone to ask him if he would arrange for me to consult the collection of Presidential papers. "Impossible," he said. "They are in the safety vault of my bank. I won't allow anybody to see them. There is nothing of my father's there that is of value—Nicolay and Hay have published everything; but there are many letters *to* him which, if published, now would pain, possibly discredit able and useful men still living. Bitter things are written when men are trying to guide a country through a war, particularly a Civil War. I fear misuse of those papers so much that I am thinking of destroying them. Besides, somebody is always worrying me about them, just as you are, and I must be ungenerous. I think I will burn them."

Nothing altered the status of the Lincoln papers for several years.

By 1910 Robert Lincoln had begun to think about retirement. Perhaps his poor health explains his failure to answer a letter which Putnam wrote to him on March 28, 1910; perhaps he considered it merely a confirmation of recent discussions:

Mr. Gaillard Hunt, who has just returned from Chicago, reports to me his call upon you and that your intention of placing here finally your father's correspondence and papers remains unaltered. I cannot resist the temptation of reiterating our strong hopes in the matter.

The manuscript collections of the National Library are assuming greater importance each year. They are resorted to more and more by scholars in American history, for constructive work and for confirmation of historical facts already published. The Library now has the collected papers of nine of the Presidents, and the acquisition of several others is more than probable. The most extensive of the collections is that of General Washington's papers, and it is felt by all who have considered the subject that only here can Mr. Lincoln's papers find fitting companionship. The interest in his achievements and personality is enduring, and embraces everything written by him or to him; however trivial an item may appear to be by itself, it is important if it relates to him even remotely. No one state can properly lay claim to his papers over any other state; more than any other figure in our history, his surviving correspondence is of national import. Because of the sad experience the Library has had on several occasions through some unforeseeable intention, we are naturally anxious that your present disposition with reference to President Lincoln's papers may take a different form at no distant date.

We had, of course, understood that your chief reason for deferring action was a desire to make some final examination of them and segregation of those which might be inappropriate for permanent deposit in a public institution. Is there no possibility that we could aid in such a segregation? The suggestion may seem odd, and yet experience has shown that the experts in our Division of Manuscripts, long familiar with the treatment of such material and the natural attitude toward it, are able to afford such an aid to the considerable saving of labor on the part of the owners.

Beyond the Librarian's mounting impatience, this letter is chiefly remarkable as a reflection of an obvious and natural rivalry among institutions with competing but dissimilar interests to secure the custodianship of the Lincoln papers.

In May 1911 Lincoln's poor health compelled him to resign the presidency of the Pullman Company and become chairman of its board of directors. The following year he moved to Washington, but before breaking up his Chicago home he "destroyed . . . an immense number of old letters and papers." From the context of this statement which was made in 1916 and published in 1921, in the *Journal of the Illinois State Historical Society*, it appears that he was referring specifically to his own files rather than to his father's correspondence. He preserved, however, anything which he "regarded as worth keeping" together with his "letter-press books in perfect order." These were housed "in a special room" of his country house in Manchester.

As for the Abraham Lincoln papers, it is said that, after his retirement, Robert Lincoln guarded them more jealously than ever. When he was in the District of Columbia, they reposed in his fine Georgetown residence, but when he went to Hildene for the summer the papers went with him. Leisure brought new opportunities. He was an expert auditor, and at periodic intervals he would shut himself away in his study and cast up his accounts. With less regularity, but with equal zeal and concentration, he would withdraw from other pastimes or occupations methodically to go over his father's correspondence. It is improbable that any leaves of paper were ever so widely traveled or the objects of such rigorous contemplation.

Presumably the Librarian of Congress did nothing to reopen the subject until 1917, when, on January 6, Miss Tarbell wrote to him:

Here I am again, with my old hobby! Is there any chance of Robert Lincoln giving his letters to the Congressional Library in his lifetime, or leaving them for it? I want to refer to the subject in an introduction I am writing for a new edition of my "Life of Lincoln." I don't want to do anything that you would think unwise, but I should like to say, of course, that these letters should go to the National Library, along with the collections of other Presidents that you already have. (I would be glad if you would have your secretary send a list of these to me.) I should like to suggest, too, that the proper thing for all collectors who have Lincoln letters—and there are of course a great number scattered over the country—would be to arrange to give them to the National Library as soon as Mr. Robert Lincoln makes his gift. I would be very much obliged if you would let me know whether it is possible to state what Mr. Lincoln's intentions are.

Forty-eight hours later Dr. Putnam replied:

I have talked with Mr. Lincoln in the matter, but I have nothing in writing from him which indicates a definite *intention* in the matter. Your purpose offers an opportunity to secure one. Why will you not write to him direct? He certainly could not take such an inquiry amiss.

I presume that you know his address.

The Presidents already represented here by collections of their papers are: Washington, Madison, Jefferson, Monroe, Jackson, Van Buren, Polk, Pierce, Johnson and Cleveland. The last named is a deposit under special proviso that the papers are for the present to be kept confidential. At least one other collection is to come to us upon similar terms.

Miss Tarbell's letter of January 15 brought disappointment:

I followed your suggestion and wrote Mr. Robert Lincoln. He replies: "I would be glad to give you the information you request if I had come to a determination on the subject myself, but I have not done so, and I would prefer not to have the subject mentioned at present, because it would probably result in a good deal of letter writing of which I already have so much that I shudder to think of a new subject being started just now."

I take it that this means that there should be no pressure brought upon him now. I of course shall do nothing more than thank him for his letter. I felt perhaps it would be well for you to know this, as you might lay your lines accordingly; and of course you will regard it as confidential.

But Ida Minerva Tarbell did do something more. When the new edition of her *Life of Abraham Lincoln* appeared a few months later its Preface contained a wish:

The collection of original Lincoln letters and documents owned by Mr. Robert Lincoln, including practically all of the manuscripts, letters and papers published by Nicolay & Hay in the first edition of the "Complete Works," is of supreme importance. It is to be hoped that Mr. Lincoln will one day place this collection in the Congressional Library. . . . Those who own Lincoln manuscripts could not do better than to arrange as speedily as possible to give them whenever Mr. Lincoln shall decide to place those in his possession.

If Mr. Lincoln read this exhortation, and it seems probable that someone called it to his attention, he was not moved to impetuous action.

In the capital was a cultivated and engaging widower named Charles Moore who possessed excellent taste and rare judgment. He was at the head of the Fine Arts Commission, and Mr. Lincoln, like the hostesses who considered him such an excellent dinner guest, found his acquaintance delightful. From him, on March 5, 1919, came a gentle suggestion typed on the Commission's impeccable stationery:

I understand that it is your intention to place in the Library of Congress your father's correspondence and papers. The collection of Washington papers in the Library is believed to be the largest existing collection of the papers of any one man. The Lincoln collection, which will be of equal importance, will increase from year to year; because there is a natural gravitation to the Library of Congress of papers of the highest value.

INTANGIBLE MEMORIAL

The Library has recently received the papers of Presidents Tyler, Roosevelt, and Taft, together with many Buchanan letters.

May I suggest that the time of the dedication of the Lincoln Memorial, next October, would be a happy occasion for the deposit of this correspondence, to be held subject to your order as to examination and use? . . .

Mr. Lincoln's reply contained this paragraph:

In regard to the Lincoln papers, I will reflect seriously upon your suggestion; I have further examination of them yet to make and I am so short of help for such a job that I am not at all sure that I would then be ready to make a disposition of them; I must be careful to avoid a preliminary announcement, for I should be flooded with letters on the subject which it would be burdensome to deal with.

Although he acknowledged these tidings under the Commission's letterhead March 15, Mr. Moore disclosed his new identity:

Your very kind letter has been received, and I am pleased that the suggestion as to the deposit of the Lincoln papers in the Library was received with some favor.

The Library has, either in originals or in letter-press copies, about ninety per cent of all the letters written by George Washington. This is an intangible national memorial, comparable to the tangible one we have in the Washington Monument.

Naturally the Library desires to utilize every opportunity and to put forth every effort to make the Lincoln collection equally or even more complete. I have been led to take up this matter with you, because Mr. Putnam has asked me to act as Chief of the Division of Manuscripts, as a means of promoting a much-needed building for the national archives. The Lincoln papers would come to this Division; and therefore I can promise you the utmost consideration in the treatment of them.

If it would be of assistance to you, we can send to you the Assistant Chief of the Division of Manuscripts [John C. Fitzpatrick], a man of good judgment, quick perceptions, and rare discrimination. He would get your point of view, and would carry out your ideas to the letter. You would find him both expert and conscientious, and in every way agreeable.

We have known so many collections to be lost by fire, and so many papers destroyed as of no value, that we are always apprehensive. Moreover, we would like to give you any assistance in our power in sorting the papers.

As to the dedication of the Lincoln Memorial: the building will be finished about July; the trees will be placed on the encircling mound this spring; and probably an appropriation will be made for the basin this year, so that the work can be done this summer. Mr. Jules Guerin's decorations have been placed, and they give just the right touch of color, without being obtrusive. I saw the head of Mr. French's statue being cut last Monday. The work will be finished and in place by October. The date of the dedication has not been settled. . . .

Moore, as it happened, was much too sanguine; the dedication did not take place until Memorial Day three years later, but he had delivered a *coup de grace*.

Dr. Putnam was in Paris at the moment winding up the affairs of the American Library Association's War Service of which he had been general director; acting for him in Washington was his chief assistant, the dapper and skillful Yankee, Appleton P. C. Griffin. On March 17 Griffin dispatched a characteristically brief note to Mr. Lincoln:

Mr. Moore . . . tells me that he has had some correspondence with you in regard to your Lincoln manuscripts. I am writing this to express the hope that you are favorably inclined to his proposals and to give them official endorsement.

What he proposes seems to take account of the best interests of all concerned.

If the rest of the peaceful citizens of Washington was shattered by the baying of ghostly hounds; if the shade of Mrs. Epimetheus was seen to shake her head in doleful warning; if Freedom atop the lantern of the Capitol was caught waving her arms in exultation and led three cheers; if Father Time on "Mr. Flanagan's Clock" waltzed Elihu Vedder's Minerva through the dusty galleries of the Library; if there were signs and wonders of one sort or another, the press, mindful of a duty to prevent general alarums, ignored them utterly. Indeed, the people at large were deliberately kept in ignorance; darkness obscured excitement, tension, and event; and the only papered whisper was a memorandum from Moore to the chief of the Mail Division on May 6:

Please have the wagon call at Mr. Robert T. Lincoln's house, 3014 N Street, N.W., for seven trunks of papers to be delivered unopened to the Manuscript Division.

The wagon should be there at nine o'clock tomorrow. . . .

This historic document bears a penciled endorsement: "8 trunks received." The following day the Acting Librarian of Congress, Griffin, formally instructed Moore:

The Papers of Abraham Lincoln, belonging to the Hon. Robert T. Lincoln, have been deposited in the Library under the following conditions:

1. The fact that the Papers are in the Library is to be kept from the public.

2. One of the officials of the Library is to examine and arrange them under the direction of Mr. Lincoln.

3. The papers are to be consulted only after permission has been granted by Mr. Lincoln.

Memoranda in the files account for the return of all of the trunks and the transfer of the Lincoln papers to other containers. On May 13 Mr. Fitzpatrick informed Theodore Wesley Koch, chief of the Order Division and the officer responsible for registering all accessions to the collections:

Hon. Robert T. Lincoln, 3014 N Street, N.W., has deposited in the Manuscript Division eight trunks, full of papers of Abraham Lincoln, dating from 1834 to 1865.

This is for your official information but no official record is to be made of this deposit; no mention, official or otherwise, is to be made of it; and no receipt is to be sent. Mr. Griffin has acknowledged the papers in a note to Mr. Lincoln, which states the conditions, which are, generally, that the public is not to be informed that the papers are here; that they are to be examined and arranged by an official of the Library, under the direction of Mr. Lincoln; and that no one is to be permitted to see them without his permission.

Having satisfied himself that the papers had been delivered to the Library without public detection, Lincoln went off to Manchester for the summer, and on October 17 three residents of Chicago witnessed his last will and testament. The second clause of that instrument contained this statement:

THE LINCOLN PAPERS

I have heretofore deposited in the LIBRARY OF CONGRESS in said city of Washington, to be there kept for me temporarily, subject to my order, certain manuscripts and papers of, or relating to, my father, Abraham Lincoln. Such of said manuscripts and papers as I shall not have withdrawn from such custody before my death, I hereby give and bequeath to the GOVERNMENT OF THE UNITED STATES to be kept and preserved in said LIBRARY OF CONGRESS.

Conspicuously absent is any requirement to impound or close the papers. If he were to die without revoking or amending the bequest, the papers of Abraham Lincoln would immediately become available to the American people. In the light of later transactions this indication of purpose is particularly interesting.

A few months later, specifically on March 20, 1920, Moore wrote to Mr. Lincoln:

Can you not now remove "the injunction of secrecy" in regard to the Library having the Lincoln Papers? I do not mean that you shall allow them to be consulted, but simply allow us to announce in the coming Annual Report—which will not be ready until the autumn—that you have given the papers to the Library.

We are getting news of various letters from Lincoln to his many correspondents; and if we should make known the fact that we have the body of the papers here, it would make it easier to get the outlying papers.

Perhaps Lincoln actually demurred, perhaps he signified refusal by ignoring the request; but he was a frequent visitor at the Library in those days and had ample opportunity to make his wishes known. Sometimes he would come to pore over the cards on which one of his secretaries had compiled a partial list of Lincoln "autographs," sometimes to observe Fitzpatrick's progress on a catalogue. As it turned out, Mr. Fitzpatrick's chore did not last very long; he covered less than 10 per cent of the collection before he was permanently diverted from it.

From time to time Moore wrote to Lincoln. For example, on February 21, 1921, he corrected a misapprehension concerning the first two drafts of the Gettysburg Address; and on January 10, 1922, he asked for information concerning the Journal which Jeremiah Black had sought to borrow from David Davis so many years before. If replies were received they do not now constitute a part of the archives of the Library.

In the months after the dedication of the Lincoln Memorial on May 30, 1922, something transpired, which impelled Lincoln to a new decision concerning the security of the documents in the Library, and on January 23, 1923, he signed a "deed of gift of manuscripts and private papers of President Lincoln by his son, Robert Todd Lincoln." Carefully drawn in the office of Messrs. McKenney & Flannery, Washington attorneys, the deed reads as follows:

I, ROBERT TODD LINCOLN, of Washington, in the District of Columbia, sole surviving child of ABRAHAM LINCOLN and the absolute owner of all of the letters, manuscripts, documents and other original private papers left by my father and heretofore temporarily placed by me for safe keeping in the custody of the Librarian of Congress, do hereby give the same in perpetuity to the UNITED STATES OF AMERICA, to be deposited in the LIBRARY OF CONGRESS for the benefit of all of the PEOPLE, upon the condition, however, inseperately connected with this gift, that all of said letters, manuscripts, documents and other papers shall be placed in a sealed vault or compartment and carefully preserved from official or public inspection or private view until after the expiration of twenty-one (21) years from the date of my death. This condition is imposed by me because said papers contain many references of a private nature to the immediate ancestors of persons now living, which, in my judgment, should not be made public, and also much information and matter of a historical character which I have heretofore authorized and permitted JOHN G. NICOLAY and JOHN HAY to use in the preparation of their Life of my father as indicated in their Preface to said Life and in my letter to them of May 30th, 1893, published in volume one of the supplemental volumes of said work.

The gift herein made, upon the conditions expressed, shall be binding upon my heirs, personal representatives and assigns.

Having affixed his signature, and having had it witnessed by Bertha P. Isaacs, a notary public, Lincoln personally presented the document to the Librarian of Congress. If he offered any explanation, he offered it in confidence, and no hint of it has ever been vouchsafed, but later that day Dr. Putnam wrote to him:

I have just received from your own hand the deed of gift executed by you today of the manuscripts and private papers of President Lincoln, constituting the collection heretofore temporarily placed by you for safe keeping in the Library of Congress: the present gift being on the condition that the entire collection be placed in a sealed vault or compartment and carefully preserved from official or public inspection or private view until after the expiration of twenty-one years from the date of your death.

In behalf of the United States of America, to whom the deed runs, I accept the gift with full understanding, appreciation, and acceptance of the condition inseparably connected with it.

With profound satisfaction at the definiteness of this action . . .

The deed, of course, superseded the second article of Mr. Lincoln's will, and in obedience to its provisions, all work on the papers ceased instantly. By February 5 Moore was able to report to the Librarian:

All the Lincoln papers are now in six specially made cases, sealed and deposited in locked compartment No. 19, third floor, Manuscript Division [North Curtain, second floor, Main Building], to remain untouched until the conditions governing them are fulfilled.

A list of the contents of each case will be furnished for the Librarian's file.

In view of the fact that these papers are not to be opened until twenty-one years after the death of Mr. Robert Lincoln, has the Librarian any suggestions to make as to the special marking of the cases? At present they have no mark indicating that the contents are Lincoln papers.

The Librarian directed that the labels should read:

PAPERS OF ABRAHAM LINCOLN
Given by Hon. Robert T. Lincoln
with proviso that they are
not to be opened
until twenty-one years after his death.

List of contents in Manuscript Division

The man who sealed Nicolay's manila envelopes and bored holes in the sides of the cases to admit a circulation of air still remembers the figure of John Fitzpatrick leaning over him and making certain that the work was properly done. The catalogue cards were packed along with the papers.

Now Lincoln's action was entirely consonant with his lifelong purpose to avoid personal injury. Had it been known and perfectly understood, the consternation and wild surmise which followed upon the announcement of cloture might have been reduced. His motive certainly would have been universally respected. But he was so uncommunicative, so reluctant to discuss his personal feelings, so accustomed to reliance upon his own judgment that it is doubtful whether he realized the interpretations which would be placed upon it. The laconic account, published in the Librarian's report for the fiscal year 1923, did little to allay suspicion:

The Abraham Lincoln papers, given by his son, Hon. Robert Todd Lincoln, are the most important accession of the year. These papers have been in the Library as a deposit since 1919, but no announcement was permitted until the gift was completed by Mr. Lincoln. The papers will not be opened to inspection until 21 years after his death. These are the papers used by Mr. Nicolay and Mr. Hay in preparing their Life of Abraham Lincoln. The collection having been examined closely by such competent writers, may contain little unpublished material calculated to change estimates of men or manners. In any case, however, its preservation in the National Library, in association with the papers of 18 of our Presidents, is completely fitting; and Mr. Robert Lincoln's now final action in the matter has been most welcome.

When the "son of Lincoln, 82," returned to his "palatial capital home" in November 1925, the Washington *Sunday Star* marveled that there was "no record of a single utterance, either spoken or penned by him, on the subject of Abraham Lincoln."

He led a regular life in those days, following a fixed routine. His affairs were in admirable order. In 1919 he had "established trust funds in favor of their two daughters, in the amount of approximately $1,000,000 each, partly in order to save the trouble of drawing checks for their monthly allowances." His investments were sound. He was still a director of the Pullman Company. Physically he was in enviable condition also. He had had to abandon golf at eighty, but during the last fifteen years he had not suffered organic trouble of any kind. His old friend, Robert M. Janney, of Philadelphia, had died, but those other companions of the Ekwanok links, Horace G. Young and George H. Thacher, survived in the Lincoln foursome.

On January 16, 1926 he adverted to a habitual interest when he wrote to Dr. Putnam:

Referring to a certain deed executed by me under date of January 23, 1923, wherein I made a gift to the Library of Congress of all the letters, manuscripts, documents, and other original private papers left to me by my father and owned by me at the time of making said deed, upon the condition, however, that all of said letters, manuscripts, documents and other papers should be placed in a sealed compartment and preserved from official or public inspection until twenty-one years from the date of my death:—

It is now my desire to modify the condition of the above deed with regard to inspection of these papers, and I do hereby modify it, so as to give access to said papers to my wife, Mary Lincoln, and to vest in her power and authority at any time during her life or until the expiration of the twenty-one years from my death to grant a permit to examine said papers to any person or persons who, in her judgment and discretion, should have permission to make such an examination.

And I hereby further modify said deed of gift so as to give the Librarian of the Library of Congress power and authority to have made a complete index of said letters, manuscripts, documents, and other private papers to the end that their safety may be preserved against the time when they shall be opened to the public.

Lincoln's note was delivered by his attorney, Norman B. Frost, on January 26, and Putnam responded that he was "happy promptly to accept" the change of terms. The following morning the Librarian informed Moore that when "an arrangement preliminary to an index should have proceeded far enough to make an inspection . . . by him worth-while in search of material on Mrs. [Abraham] Lincoln," Frost "would be glad to be advised and would come here, with an authorization from Mrs. Robert Lincoln, for the purpose." Within a week the Librarian informed Frost that "such progress with the identification of the items" in the collection had been made that it might be profitable for him to make his inspection at any time. Instead of coming himself, Frost's associate, Frederic N. Towers, appeared, accompanied by Miss Katherine Helm, who was then engaged in writing her *Mary, Wife of Lincoln*. They found almost no relevant material, but the visit seems to have been the only authorization ever granted to examine the papers while the cloture was in force. For a time work on the organization of the collection was renewed. On June 13 a strangely garbled story appeared in the New York *Times*, from which some subsequent confusion may be assumed to have stemmed:

Robert T. Lincoln, 90-year-old son and sole surviving descendant of the Civil War President, has let it be known that the mysterious trunkful of Lincolniana which he recently presented to the Congressional Library contains nothing for hunters of unprinted historical matter to get excited about—nothing, in fact, that has not already been published.

Mr. Lincoln, who has steadfastly refused to discuss the trunk's contents, still refuses to talk; but he has whispered enough into the ears of the Congressional Library to quiet the heart palpitations of those Lincoln enthusiasts who have known of the trunk and have spent their good time, their good money and the good influence of wealthy and social friends in an effort to get a peep into the chest while it was in Mr. Lincoln's possession.

The trunk has been a great mystery. There has been a belief that in particular it contained data having to do with Lincoln's ancestry or private family affairs. The son, it has been hinted, was keeping it all quiet for fear of the explosion that might follow its release.

Energetic writers have camped on the Robert T. Lincoln doorstep, confident of their ability to gather in this greatest of all Lincoln scoops. But they have got nowhere. Money, they were told, could not buy the trunk, and the contents were destined to disappear with the last of the Lincolns. There has been nothing much else in the Lincoln line to unearth and this quest has been unabatedly pursued.

Lord Charnwood before he completed his "Abraham Lincoln" heard of the trunk, and, through the British Embassy at Washington, appealed to Mr. Lincoln to tell him of its contents. He was courteously informed that Mr. Lincoln did not wish to go into the matter. William A. Barton [i.e., William E. Barton], another biographer, also urged Mr. Lincoln, it is said, to make the contents public, but met with no favorable response.

This Spring Mr. Lincoln surprised the world by calling the express-man and sending the trunk to the Congressional Library, with the proviso that under no circumstances was the trunk to be opened before twenty-five years had elapsed after his death. But he vouchsafed the suspense-relieving information that the writings have all been published and that there is nothing for anyone to keep awake about. Still there are some who cannot understand the twenty-five-year tie-up, and these will watchfully await the expiration of the period.

For reasons unknown this report went unchallenged. Had Lincoln from his home in Manchester issued a prompt correction, pointing

out that these were the White House papers, and that, in consequence, the skeletons in the family closet were excluded by defini-
tion, much of the legend which came to cling about the collection
might permanently have been uprooted. But there were no vigorous
contradictions. After all, only Robert Lincoln could have made
them, and it is always possible that he never saw the article, for in
his youth he had made no bones about the business. Lincoln was in
"feeble health." On Sunday, July 25, he went for a ride in his auto-
mobile, dined with his family in good spirits, and went upstairs with
his valet and to bed. The next morning, when the butler entered the
room, carrying Mr. Lincoln's breakfast on a tray, he found him dead.
The immediate cause was determined to have been a cerebral
hemorrhage.

The Rutland *Daily Herald* editorialized: "In the national treasury
in Washington is a trunk filled with matter relating to President
Lincoln which his son presented to the nation. Under the terms of
the gift the box cannot be opened until fifty years from now and
there are many who think that Mr. Lincoln may have left his personal memoirs of his father among the collection." From the Library
of Congress was issued a misleading statement in answer to tele-
phone inquiries from the press: "During his lifetime Robert Lincoln
modified his restrictions relating to the time limit during which the
Lincoln papers . . . were to be closed to the public. But the collection is still closed to the public and the papers are held like other
closed collections." This led to some embarrassment and the Librarian's report for that year noted firmly: "The death of Mr. Robert T.
Lincoln has made no change in the condition which he, during his
lifetime, attached to the gift of the papers."

The son of Lincoln was gone, but he had fulfilled his promises; he
had protected his father's fame; he had done what he had supposed
was acceptable, right, considerate. He had built monuments over
the graves of Thomas Lincoln and his wife Nancy Hanks. He had
given his father's home in Springfield to the state of Illinois and it
had become a national shrine. He had contributed a thousand dollars toward the beautification of the park in Hodgenville, Kentucky,
where he had once attended the unveiling of a statue. It was said
that no matter where he rode, the itinerary always included a turn

around the temple on the Mall, and that as the car approached the steps he would call to the chauffeur, "Stop the carriage, stop the carriage!" and looking up at that luminous, brooding figure, he would exclaim, "Isn't it beautiful?" And the Lincoln papers—had not some-one called them an "intangible memorial"?

CHAPTER EIGHT

Doomed for a Certain Term

For TWENTY-ONE YEARS THE AMERICAN PUBLIC WAS A THWARTED Pandora. Private curiosity turned to general speculation, wonder gave way to conjecture, study was almost quite forsaken in favor of prophecy, and, in some quarters, with amazing disregard of contrary evidence, chicanery was not only permitted but approved. The sober division between the Lincoln fundamentalists who repudiated Herndon as an apostate and the assured but usually temperate modernists who could take him or leave him alone widened to a permanent rift, and this unhappy but basic disagreement encouraged the emergence of those forlorn and solitary racketeers who preyed upon credulity and common sense. Documents, long proved spurious, received fresh currency and acceptance. Only the universality of Abraham Lincoln explained the phenomenon, for his compatriots in every generation were conscious of an intuitive kinship to him which transcended learning and surpassed intelligence.

Of course the extent to which the conditions surrounding the Lincoln papers *per se* produced or provoked confusion must await the careful measurements of a social historian, but it is certain that they were principal contributors and that they provided both excitement and charm. Every anniversary elicited references to them, accompanied by hints of questionable motive and dark design. The press, the radio, and the book trade were forever stirring the leaves of secrecy, and forever enjoying the exercise, but without ever risking the loss which discovery would bring to the pleasurable pastime. In all of this they were abetted by the attitude of the officers of the Library of Congress, who, from the very beginning, adopted a policy of belittling the importance of the collection. Perhaps the purpose was avoidance of foreseeable pressures and hopeless correspondence, but two days after Robert Lincoln's death Moore informed a reporter of the *Evening Star* "that there was nothing of historic interest in the papers that had not already been given to the public by John G. Nicolay and John Hay in their biography of Lincoln." He added the further interpretation that "Mr. Lincoln was loath to have the papers put on public view for many years, fearing that they might become the object of commercialization by irresponsible writers." Perhaps he had forgotten (if he had ever known) the fact that some of the "prestige pieces" had been exhibited at the Chicago Historical Society at the time of the Lincoln Centennial Celebration.

What would have been reprehensible, had it not been unwitting, was the failure of the Library ever to announce Mr. Lincoln's expressed reason for withholding the papers: "This condition is imposed by me because said papers contain many references to the immediate ancestors of persons now living"; but, although the Library freely and frequently supplied inquirers with copies of the deed of gift, the complete text, including this explanation, seems not to have been published until Mr. Arthur Krock sent it to the New York *Times* a few months before the collection was released. Unable to understand, people grumbled. Aware of the limitations of the authorized version, realists deplored "the action of Robert T. Lincoln in locking up for a long period the Lincoln manuscripts." Others felt excused for their suspicions.

But the Library was never so careless of its fiduciary responsibilities. On October 15, 1927 Putnam wrote to the American Security and Trust Company, coexecutor with Mary Lincoln of the estate of Robert T. Lincoln:

Referring to paragraph second of the last will and testament of Robert T. Lincoln, wherein he refers to the deposit in the Library of Congress of certain manuscripts and papers of or relating to his father, President

Lincoln, and makes gift to the Library of such of those papers and manuscripts as shall not have been withdrawn before his death.

This is formally to advise you that prior to his death and subsequent to the execution of his will in October, 1919, by deed of gift he presented all of the papers and manuscripts in question to the Library upon certain conditions respecting their being opened to public inspection, etc. Hence, so far as the Library is concerned, the gift referred to having been completed by Mr. Lincoln in his lifetime, nothing now remains to be done by his Executors with reference to said paragraph second of his will.

On Abraham Lincoln's one hundred and nineteenth birthday, February 12, 1928, an article on the papers published in the Washington, D.C., *Sunday Star*, contained these statements:

Certain provisions have been made, however, in accordance with Mr. Lincoln's will, whereby some of the papers can be examined by qualified students seeking for keys to the character of the Emancipator. They can be used only to furnish background. They cannot be quoted, or any inkling given of their contents.

They will make no change, it is understood, in the broad outlines of the accepted figure of Lincoln. The intimate details which they contain, however, will give a sharper picture of his thinking processes and his reactions to the men and events of his time.

After all, it is not the actual Lincoln manuscripts in the collection which are expected to prove of the greatest value to historians, but the letters to him, from persons all over the country and in all walks of life. His replies to some of these letters have been known for years, but will mean much more when the original communications can be placed alongside them.

It was unfortunate that so accurate an appraisal of the characteristics of the collection was marred by the suggestion that the restrictions on its use had been relaxed. Mrs. Lincoln might, of course, grant access, but there were no qualified students taking notes with her approval. Miss Helm was the single exception.

However, on April 16, 1928, she wrote to the Librarian of Congress:

As you know, Mr. Lincoln has given me authority at any time during my life or until the expiration of twenty-one years from his death, to grant a permit to examine certain papers placed in the Library of Congress under Deed of Gift executed by him on January 23rd, 1923, to any person who, in my judgment, should have permission to make such an examination. Accordingly it is my wish that my daughter, Mrs. Mary Lincoln Isham, should have permission to examine said papers at any time during her lifetime.

Dr. Putnam at once recorded this authorization.

On December 18 of that year he received an inquiry from Dr. Nicholas Murray Butler:

Can you conveniently let me know the date, or the approximate date, when the late Robert T. Lincoln sent to the Library of Congress a box or trunk containing a collection of family papers, with the prescription that they should not be opened for a number of years, I think it was fifty.

I am trying to reconstruct the story of a discussion which I had with him over those papers, and a reminder of this particular date will help me.

Dr. Putnam referred the request to John Franklin Jameson, the eminent historian who had succeeded Charles Moore. Dr. Jameson's memorandum sought to be precise:

The Lincoln material was originally received in the Manuscripts Division May 8, 1919, with the stipulation that it was to be examined and arranged under the direction of Mr. Robert Todd Lincoln and to be consulted only by permission of Mr. Lincoln, and not to be opened to public inspection until twenty-one (21) years after the death of Mr. Lincoln, namely 1947. Mr. Lincoln died July 26, 1926.

In accordance with a deed executed January 23, 1923, this Lincoln material (originally deposited) was turned over to the Library as a gift, and on January 16, 1926, a modification of this deed gave access to said papers to Mrs. Robert Todd Lincoln (Mary Lincoln), vesting in her power and authority to grant a permit to examine the papers to "any person or persons who, in her judgment and discretion, should have permission to make such an examination."

Dr. Putnam forwarded Dr. Jameson's report to Dr. Butler on December 20, and on the twenty-second Dr. Butler sent his acknowledgment:

I thank you cordially for your letter . . . transmitting the memorandum of Dr. Jameson regarding the date when the Lincoln material was sent to the Library of Congress. This accords with my own recollection and notes.

It may be of interest to you to know that I had the greatest difficulty in inducing Mr. Lincoln to deposit these manuscripts with the Library of Congress, since he had fully made up his mind to destroy them without further examination by anyone.

This exchange is especially interesting because of its discrepancies. For example, Dr. Butler speaks of *a* box or trunk, whereas there had been eight trunks; he recalls the prescript as covering a period of fifty rather than twenty-one years; he describes the collection as consisting of *family papers*, whereas they might readily have been ascertained to be the papers of Abraham Lincoln's administration. Dr. Jameson, on his part, owing possibly to oversimplification, suggests that the condition of a twenty-one-year cloture was imposed by Robert Lincoln at the time of the original deposit, specifically in May 1919, whereas it was not imposed until he executed the deed of gift in January 1923. Finally, Dr. Butler replies that the statement accords with his own recollection and notes, and for the first time mentions the fact that he had induced Robert Lincoln to place the papers in the Library. Because of future statements concerning the history of the gift, these details are not without significance.

The Library continued its policy of playing down the importance of the papers. On February 13, 1929, the New York *Times*, under a Washington date line of the day before and the heading "Dr. Putnam Doubts if the Lincoln Chests in Congress Library Hold Data of Value," published this interview:

Dr. Herbert Putnam, Librarian of Congress, today gave it as his opinion that the five sealed chests of Lincolniana willed to the Library by the Emancipator's son contain nothing important enough to alter the general historical record of the martyred President.

Except under certain conditions, according to the deed of gift, the chests are not to be opened until 1947, which will mark the twenty-first anniversary of Robert Todd Lincoln's death.

"Although I have never seen the contents of these chests, and may never live to see them," Dr. Putnam said, "I don't believe they contain the kind of material that will cause us to change or condition our attitude toward President Lincoln.

"My reason for saying this is the knowledge that all these documents have been seen by two of Lincoln's biographers, Nicolay and Hay, his personal secretaries. Undoubtedly these men used part of this material in writing their famous ten-volume biography.

"Just a few months before he died Robert Lincoln changed the terms of his original bequest. He understood that there might be historians and biographers who needed access to these papers, and, accordingly, he gave us authority to open the seals under such conditions, providing that each inspection was authorized by Mrs. Robert Todd Lincoln who still lives."

To date no member of the Library staff has seen the contents of these chests, and unless a request comes from Mrs. Lincoln, it is probable that they will remain unopened and unread until 1947.

This provides a striking example of the admixture of fact and fiction which always attended any attempt to discuss the Lincoln papers. The New York *Times,* of course, is a most distinguished newspaper with the highest standards of reportorial accuracy, and yet it is almost inconceivable that Dr. Putnam, one of the most astute and informed men ever to hold public office, could possibly have made the statements here attributed to him. It may be quibbling to complain that the headline is misleading, but there is nothing in the text of the interview to justify it. Admittedly Dr. Putnam was, in his usual modest way, deprecatory, but when he expressed his doubts that the papers contained material likely "to change or condition our attitude toward President Lincoln," he was almost certainly replying to the scandalmongers and sensationalists who were always prepared to suspect the worst of anyone. He realized fully, as he remarked, that "part" of the papers had been appropriate to the uses of Nicolay and Hay and that they had examined the remainder, but he did not question their total significance, or the fact that they were subject to interpretations not previously placed upon them. He knew that the controlling instrument was not a bequest because he knew that the provisions of Robert Lincoln's will had been voided by his deed of gift. Finally, he was perfectly aware that the modifications of the deed had not bestowed any discretion on the Library beyond the direction to make an index. Mrs. Lincoln held the power of access and she held it tight.

On at least one occasion the Library tried to prevail on Mrs. Lincoln to authorize an exception in favor of the scholar who had been selected by the editors of the Dictionary of American Biography to prepare the sketch of Abraham Lincoln. She wrote to Dr. Jameson from Manchester on July 22, 1929:

I regret exceedingly that I cannot comply with the request contained in your letter of the 12th instant; but my opinion as to what I can and should do in the circumstances is so definitely fixed that I find it necessary to refuse to Professor Randall the permission he seeks to examine the papers of President Lincoln lately deposited under conditional Deed of Gift, in the Library of Congress.

In the first place, as you are aware, Mr. Lincoln, for reasons satisfactory to himself, saw fit to surround the gift of his father's papers with the condition that they should not be made public until twenty-one years after his (Mr. Lincoln's) death; and, during his lifetime subsequent to this gift, he never saw fit to change this condition or to give to anyone any special permission or privilege in respect to them. Needless to say, he was often importuned in this regard. His giving to me of authority to appoint an individual who might inspect the documents was for a special purpose only and was the subject of an understanding between us.

Secondly, since his death I have felt it incumbent upon me to carry out his every wish, so far as it is within my power to do so; and, naturally I suppose, I feel that as he saw fit to impose a condition upon the placement in the Library of these papers, it is for me only to see that this condition shall be observed. In short, I have followed what was his practice during his lifetime—that of refusing to each and every one alike the privilege of seeing the documents; and I cannot at this time consistently make an exception in the case of Professor Randall, meritorious though I believe his claim to be and much as I would like to comply with your very courteous request.

It is my sincere hope that you and the Librarian will understand the position I take in this matter.

There was no appeal from this, and Dr. Putnam hastened to reassure Mrs. Lincoln: "We entirely understand the scruples which you have been so considerate as to explain, and now that we have your explicit decision in this case, we can avoid submitting others to you." "The special purpose" which was the subject of an understanding between Mr. and Mrs. Lincoln has never been disclosed. But rumors of a lowering of the bars, emanating perhaps from the *Times* story, were put in circulation. Typical of other inquiries was a letter from the Rev. Dr. William E. Barton, a noted Lincoln student, addressed to Dr. Jameson on November 16, 1929:

THE LINCOLN PAPERS

I have this minute a letter from Lexington, Kentucky, stating that Mrs. Helm, sister of Mrs. Abraham Lincoln, said to my correspondent that Mrs. Robert Lincoln had determined to permit Lincoln students to have access to the Robert Lincoln papers. Is this correct?

Dr. Jameson had to disabuse his hope:

What you have been told about Mrs. Robert T. Lincoln is the reverse of correct. I made an application, in a capital instance, not very long ago, and she replied emphatically, though expressing regret, that she considered herself bound not to give any access to the papers.

There the matter stood for a number of years. It became fashionable in some circles to scoff at the prospect of enlightenment. But those who attempted to reconcile this view with the obvious fact that some purpose other than pure perversity must account for Robert Lincoln's action found themselves confronted with tantalizing fears that there must be something there which would extend the boundaries of their knowledge. Then in January 1936 the *American Historical Review* published a paper read, in part, two years before at a joint session of the American Historical Association and the Mississippi Valley Historical Association. The work of Professor James G. Randall, of the University of Illinois, one of the most learned men ever to apply genius to the Civil War period, it asked the question, "Has the Lincoln Theme Been Exhausted?" and proceeded systematically, cogently, and convincingly to answer with a thundering negative:

The general reader, vaguely aware of the multitude of Lincoln writings, or the historian who had specialized elsewhere, might suppose that the Lincoln theme has been sufficiently developed. If, however, one finds that in the sources there is both spadework and refining work to be done, that the main body of Lincoln manuscripts is closed to research, that no definitive edition of the works is to be had, that genuine Lincoln documents are continually coming to light while false ones receive unmerited credence, and that collateral studies bearing upon Lincoln are being steadily developed, then any conclusion as to the exhaustion of the theme would appear premature. . . .

Foremost among the sources are the Lincoln papers in the Library of Congress with which is closely related the Nicolay-Hay edition of the *Complete Works*. These papers, partly personal and partly official, were for a long time in the possession of Robert Todd Lincoln. They have been physically in the Library of Congress as a deposit since 1919, where they occupy 126 boxes. . . .

Though the papers are sealed, certain facts concerning them are known. It is evident that the only biographers of Lincoln who have used them are Nicolay and Hay, by whom they are edited under the incorrect title *Abraham Lincoln: Complete Works*. It is also possible on the basis of existing evidence to generalize concerning the main contents of the collection. Mr. J. C. Fitzpatrick, who as assistant Chief of the Division of Manuscripts in the Library of Congress attended to the boxing of the papers, states that they contain about ten or twelve thousand pieces dating from 1834 to Lincoln's death, and that about one sixth or one seventh are Lincoln autographs. Over 99 per cent of these autographs, he writes, have been printed by Nicolay and Hay, but he adds that the value of the collection lies in the great mass of letters to Lincoln. These not only clarify the Lincoln side of the correspondence, but are further useful as containing endorsements and jottings in Lincoln's hand. The little checking that he was able to do showed that the texts of Nicolay and Hay "were accurate and [that] they were not guilty of omissions." He further states, however, that they were "too close to the emotional boilings of the Civil War," and that they had the partisan attitude.

As to the manner of Nicolay and Hay as editors a fair criticism can now be given without awaiting the unsealing of the Robert Lincoln collection, since many of the Lincoln originals are in open collections, such as those of McClellan, Welles, Stanton, and Johnson, while most of the Lincoln items owned by collectors, dealers, and libraries elsewhere are also open to historical examination. Comparisons between the originals and the printed versions show that the secretarial biographers did not seek to reproduce the originals as they were, but rather to "edit" them in the broader sense in order to achieve a certain formal correctness of the printed edition. They adhered, in brief, to the older canons of historical editing.

This manifesto, coming from a recognized authority, constituted one of the most brilliant statements and by all means the most thoughtful forecast of the inevitable influence which the opening of the Lincoln papers would exert. To the conservatives, the gay deceivers, and the old pretenders the assertion that earlier studies might have to be revised, discarded, or discredited came as a shock and a surprise. To investigators impatient to publish the result of long, painstaking, and ingenious research it brought disappointment for the reason that it imposed on scholarship the choice of delay or only partial pronouncement. Even the prominent Emanuel Hertz, whose enthusiasm and energy demanded consideration, was baffled and hastened to express concern. He wrote:

In an article by Prof. Randall, Prof. Randall states in discussing the Lincoln papers in the Library of Congress, that the papers turned over by Robert Lincoln occupied 126 boxes and he recites for his authority the report of the Librarian of Congress for 1923, page 43. [Incidentally, Dr. Randall had made no such citation.]

When you were kind enough to show me the closet in which are contained the folders containing the papers, I did not see any boxes at all, but simply folders, nor did I see any large collection of letters to Lincoln of which they all speak of. What justification is there for this statement of Prof. Randall?

In 1927 Mr. Robert Lincoln told me [it must have been very late at night because Robert Lincoln was dead] that all of the papers he turned over were contained in a schedule attached to the deed of gift which we compared with the two-volume edition of Lincoln's *Works* by Nicolay and Hay. I thereafter printed a list in Volume II of my book [*Abraham Lincoln, a New Portrait*] on pages 971 to 977 of those items which had not been printed. When the list was prepared I was told that that was all there was to the gift of Robert Lincoln.

The wonderment of Hertz might easily be cleared away. The boxes were "manuscript boxes," that is to say a kind of Solander case in which unbound papers are stored. These may have been the objects which he had seen ranged behind a locked enclosure. It is certain that he had never seen the papers themselves. As for the "schedule" which had been furnished him by Norman B. Frost, one of Robert Lincoln's attorneys, and which he had printed in 1931, it may have been based on one of the informal and woefully incomplete lot inventories compiled by Messrs. Sweet and Schumacher, of the Pullman Company, at some time prior to 1918, or upon Robert Lincoln's own list of Lincoln "autographs." The index which Mr. Fitzpatrick had undertaken had not progressed beyond the first eleven boxes. But the fact remained that Mr. Hertz, like the host of other supposedly informed Lincoln students, was completely unaware of the extent and general composition of that vast collection of source materials.

Although there was much to be learned and much to be refuted, there were persistent mysteries which would not be dismissed.

DOOMED FOR A CERTAIN TERM

Another was added in April 1937, when *The Collector, A Magazine for Autograph and Historical Collectors,* published a letter from a correspondent, whose name was withheld, to William Romeyn Benjamin, the proprietor of that journal:

Mr. X, who formerly lived in Albany, N.Y., but died a few years ago in Greenwich, Conn., told me the following:

He was an intimate friend of Robert Lincoln, the son of Abraham Lincoln, and he and Mr. Lincoln were accustomed to spend part of each summer together. A few years before Mr. Lincoln's death Mr. X went as usual to visit him at Mr. Lincoln's home in northern N. Y. (or N. H.?). On arriving at the house he found Mr. Lincoln in a room surrounded by a number of large boxes and with many papers scattered about the floor, and with the ashes of many burned papers visible in the fireplace. Mr. X asked Mr. Lincoln what he was doing, and Mr. Lincoln replied that he was destroying the private letters of his father Abraham Lincoln. Mr. X at once remonstrated with Mr. Lincoln and said that no one had any right to destroy such papers, Mr. Lincoln least of all. Mr. Lincoln replied that he did not care and intended to continue his destruction—since the papers he was destroying contained the documentary evidence of the treason of a member of Lincoln's cabinet, and he thought it best for all that such evidence be destroyed.

Mr. X told me this incident just a few years before Robert Lincoln died. I wonder how much history was lost because of this remarkable action.

Mr. X was subsequently identified as Horace Gedney Young, the Albany banker, who was one of the "Lincoln foursome" at Manchester, and who died in 1933. The anonymity of *The Collector's* correspondent likewise disappeared when it became known that he was Mr. Frederick Coykendall, a well-known collector and president of the Columbia University Press. Before very long Mr. Coykendall wrote to Mr. Benjamin again:

The publication of the incident . . . has had an interesting aftermath. . . . While dining at the house of Dr. Nicholas Murray Butler . . . reference was made to the article . . . whereat Dr. Butler said: "I remember the incident very well for I was there at the time. Mr. Young came over to my hotel greatly agitated, and told me of Mr. Lincoln's action. The following morning I went to see Mr. Lincoln and told him he had no right to destroy such papers. There was still one trunk full of papers not destroyed and I persuaded Mr. Lincoln to send that trunk to the Congressional Library."

Dr. Butler's version of the incident was told at firsthand in a letter he wrote to Emanuel Hertz on November 5, 1937:

It was Mr. Horace G. Young, then at Manchester, Vermont, who brought to my attention within a few hours after I arrived from Europe the fact that Robert Lincoln was about to burn a collection of his father's papers, and that he, Mr. Young, had been unable to persuade him not to do so. I went immediately to his house and had a most earnest discussion of the whole subject with Mr. Lincoln in his library. I went so far as to insist that the papers did not belong to him, since his father had belonged to the country for half a century and the papers therefore belonged to the country also. Robert Lincoln finally acceded to my earnest and insistent request for the preservation of the papers and sent them under seal to the Library of Congress, there to remain unopened for fifty years.

Once again Dr. Butler had rescued a single trunk whereas Mr. Young had spoken of a number of large boxes; again he had placed the period of cloture at fifty years, despite the fact that his impression had been corrected by Dr. Jameson years before; but this time he had added the information that the incident occurred "within a few hours" after his return from Europe. Young had told Coykendall that it transpired "a few years before Mr. Lincoln's death." Dr. Butler's reference to the fact that Abraham Lincoln had belonged to the country for half a century was not intended to be understood exactly; had it been, the date presumably would have been fixed at sometime after 1910 or 1915. Dr. Butler's letter was printed in *The Hidden Lincoln: from the Letters and Papers of William H. Herdon,* by Emanuel Hertz, which the Viking Press published February 11, 1938. The book contained, in addition, an account of Young's participation in the episode as recounted by "a friend." The account was presented in quotation marks and, with one or two minor exceptions, was a literal reproduction of Coykendall's letter to *The Collector.* The location of Mr. Lincoln's home was correctly given this time as at Manchester, Vermont, but the strangest divergence from the earlier rendering occurred in the last of these two sentences:

Mr. Young at once remonstrated with Mr. Lincoln and said that no one had the right to destroy such papers, Mr. Lincoln least of all. Mr. Lincoln replied that he did not intend to continue his destruction—since the papers he was destroying contained the documentary evidence of the treason of a member of Lincoln's Cabinet, and that he thought it best for all that such evidence be destroyed.

In the previous version Mr. Lincoln was reported to have said that he intended to continue his destruction, now he was reported to have said that he did not intend to continue, and if this were so, how could Dr. Butler be said to have persuaded him to stop? Presumably Mr. Lincoln had done away with the treasonable documents before he got there.

Contradictions by such eminently credible witnesses are very perplexing. Less distinguished gentlemen might be supposed to have been confused. When Miss Tarbell read an advance copy of *The Hidden Lincoln* she wrote at once to Dr. Putnam:

I hope you have not quite forgotten me and that you will not mind my asking through whose intercession the Lincoln papers came to the Library of Congress.

It was some thirty or more years ago that I asked Robert Lincoln, with whom I had a pleasant acquaintance, to let me examine the Lincoln papers. He refused flatly and told me he was thinking of destroying them, his reason being that there were letters from associates of his father which if made public would give pain to the families of certain men who had been associated with him. He did not want to be a party to pulling down any man's reputation.

I remember going at once to you. You told me you were already in communication with Mr. Lincoln, that you hoped to persuade him to give you the papers. The fact that he did so had led me to believe that you succeeded.

Now there has just appeared a book called "The Hidden Lincoln"—an unexpurgated collection of the Herndon papers. In the Preface Mr. Emanuel Hertz claims that Robert Lincoln was on the point of destroying the papers and that it was Dr. Nicholas Murray Butler who saved them and persuaded Mr. Lincoln to give them to you. He publishes Dr. Butler's account of the episode.

Have you any recollection of how the papers were secured for the Congressional Library? Is Dr. Butler after all responsible?

I will greatly appreciate your recollection of this matter. I have in manuscript form my account of my talk with Robert Lincoln about the papers. My appeal to you, my supposition that it was through your intercession that the papers were saved. I do not want to publish this in the form it stands if I am wrong. I shall greatly appreciate it if you will put me right.

Dr. Putnam's reply was dated February 4:

I have this morning your note of yesterday.

In connection with it I have identified some correspondence with you in January 1917 in which you raised the question as to whether in a preface to a life of Lincoln you could appropriately mention our possession of the Cleveland papers; and, incidentally, whether it would be inappropriate for you to suggest to Mr. Robert Lincoln the desirability of depositing them here. On January 8, 1917, I wrote you that I had talked with Mr. Robert Lincoln in the matter, but had nothing in writing from him indicating a definite intention, and I added that I could see no objection to some suggestion from you to him.

If, however, you are now endeavoring to identify the influences which had induced his final decision, I should note that our records show approaches to him, on behalf of the Library, as far back as 1905, when Mr. Worthington Ford was Chief of our Division of Manuscripts. The correspondence then was succeeded by correspondence at intervals later, down to the date (1919) when he actually made the deposit. As early as 1910 he had pretty definitely expressed his intention of making it, explaining, moreover, that he must delay it until an examination had been made of the papers for the purpose of eliminating any items that he deemed unsuitable for deposit in a public collection.

I should therefore infer that, within his own mind, his intention became definite before 1917.

I find no record of any expressions or communications to him from Dr. Butler.

Dr. Putnam had overlooked the fact that he had first solicited the papers in 1901, at the suggestion of Miss Tarbell herself! On February 7 Miss Tarbell thanked him for his "prompt and satisfying answer," and surmised:

Evidently Dr. Butler found Mr. Lincoln making the examination which he had told you he must make before turning them [i.e., the papers] over to the Library. I am asking Mr. Hertz for the date of Dr. Butler's visit to Mr. Lincoln. If I am able to get it I shall send it to you for your record. It is a small point of course but sufficient to establish the early alertness of the Congressional Library in the matter.

Miss Tarbell was apparently unsuccessful in securing the information from Hertz for there is no record of the further communication which she had promised. Chronology, however, was no longer "a small point" in the history of the Lincoln papers. Dr. Butler himself raised the question in a letter to Dr. Putnam, written November 28, 1938:

Can you refresh my memory as to the date—I think it was in the autumn of 1923—that Robert T. Lincoln deposited a trunk of Lincoln papers and letters with the Library of Congress, not to be opened for a considerable time? What was the date he fixed for setting them free to the public? When he discussed the matter with me, he had in mind to keep these letters from the public for fifty years, but I have a notion that he changed his mind and made the period a shorter one. I have been going over lately my correspondence with Robert Lincoln and I am trying to get these two dates definitely fixed.

Dr. Putnam's answer, dated November 30, stated, "the deposit of the collection by Robert Todd Lincoln was made in 1923. The stipulation was to cover a certain period after his death. It still extends to the year 1947." This, of course, was inaccurate; the deed of gift had been executed in 1923, but the deposit had been made four years earlier. It may be that Dr. Butler's recollection that it had taken place in 1923 accounted for the confusion, but Dr. Butler had placed the season as the autumn, whereas the deposit was made in the spring and the deed was executed in the winter.

The second Butler version, under the title, *Lincoln and Son,* was published in *The Saturday Evening Post* for February 11, 1939, and was surrounded with circumstantial detail. He had returned from Europe in August 1923 and gone to the hotel in Manchester to spend a few weeks. Immediately upon his arrival Young, greatly excited, had come to see him, saying, "You are the only person who has any influence with him. He is going to burn a lot of his father's papers. For God's sake, see him at once!" It was too late to make a visit that evening, but the next morning he went to Hildene to pay his respects, "and to have a chat after a considerable absence abroad, during which time President Harding died and Calvin Coolidge succeeded to the presidency." He found Robert Lincoln seated before a wood fire, reading a newspaper. The morning was chilly.

For a time the two men talked at random, and then Dr. Butler spied "an old-fashioned trunk, which was standing near one of the book-shelves." This prompted him to ask if Mr. Lincoln were planning to go away. Mr. Lincoln gave him a negative answer, and Dr. Butler asked for an explanation of the presence of the trunk. Robert Lincoln replied: "Well, it contains only some family papers which I am going to burn." Dr. Butler, horrified, exclaimed, "Burn your family papers! Why, Robert Lincoln, those papers do not belong to you. Your father has been the property of the nation for fifty years, and those papers belong to the nation. That you should destroy them would be incredible. For heaven's sake do not do anything like that!" An excited and indeed difficult argument had ensued, lasting for more than an hour. At last Mr. Lincoln capitulated: "Very well," he said, "but no one must see them while I live." Thereupon Dr. Butler urged him to send the papers to the Library of Congress, and to "fix a date before which they" should not be opened. Mr. Lincoln followed his advice. Dr. Butler observed: "The letters, whatever they may be, are in the Library of Congress where he had already deposited other family papers, and are not to be opened until twenty-one years after Robert Lincoln's death."

Dr. Butler did not share the opinion of those who supposed that the Lincoln papers "contain evidence of the charge which has since been made, that Secretary Stanton conspired to wreck Lincoln's policies and to bring about his murder." His own belief was that they "contain records and evidence of various happenings in Abraham Lincoln's own life and family which it was just as well not to make public; certainly not while his son was living." Dr. Butler made it clear, however, that this impression was not made on the basis of "any definite statement of this sort" made by Robert Lincoln, but he drew "the conclusion both from some things which he said and from some things which he left unsaid."

It would be easy to dismiss the anomaly of the year on the ground that Dr. Butler had been misled by Dr. Putnam's error were it not for other considerations. In the first place he had always associated the incident with his return from a trip to Europe. Between the years 1917 and 1924, according to the New York *Times Index* Dr. Butler was twice abroad. He spent the summer of 1921 in London,

Paris, and Louvain; in 1923 he was reported as being in London and Cardiff in May, Glasgow and St. Andrews in June, and Paris and Louvain in July. Either of these dates would have been too late for the deposit of the corpus of the Lincoln papers in the Library, but the latter would have accorded with his recollection. In the second place, his memory of his call on Robert Lincoln was vivid, he had been absent for a longer period than usual, President Harding had died in August. In the third place, Dr. Butler discounted the theory that the papers which he saw contained letters from the Cabinet. Finally, Mr. Coykendall wrote to me on June 16, 1947: "I have questioned Dr. Nicholas Murray Butler about the date of 1923 and asked him if there was any possibility of their being a mistake in that date since the Library had received Lincoln's papers in 1919. He replied that as far as he could find out his record was correct." Throughout every one of his accounts of the transaction Dr. Butler was definite about his having seen only one trunk, and it has been impossible to adjust that statement to any influence on, or relation with, the delivery of eight trunks in May 1919. Obviously, Mr. Lincoln's public and impulsive spirit at that time was a response to Charles Moore's beguiling allusion to an "intangible memorial." What, then, is to be made of the encounters of Young and Dr. Butler?

In 1923 Dr. Butler was sixty-one, Mr. Young was sixty-nine, Robert Lincoln was eighty. They were all mentally alert. Still all of them lived long enough to look backward, and reminiscence is an insidious disease, complicated by garrulity and second guessing. Moreover, the story of the rescue of the Lincoln papers was not published for more than a decade after Robert Lincoln's death. It may have been subjected to some of the inseparable changes of time. But it is given plausibility by reason of two considerations: (1) Robert Lincoln's lifelong threats to destroy the papers, and (2) the inviolable integrity of the narrators. It is this circumstance which imposes the requirement of closer scrutiny. There is another factor also which impels further analysis: the evolution of the story to a point where it bears little factual resemblance to the original.

By way of example, Emanuel Hertz, in *The Hidden Lincoln*, wrote: "Before presenting them to the Library of Congress, Lincoln subjected the papers to a purge." He based his statement on the accounts of Young and Dr. Butler, but it is not clear from either that anything so ruthless as legitimately to be termed a *purge* ever took place. Again, Mr. Philip Van Doren Stern in *Afterword,* a pamphlet which accompanied his *The Man Who Killed Lincoln* (1939), wrote of the papers:

The material in question was deposited in the Library of Congress with the reservation that it was not to be consulted until 1947. In that year, when these secret papers will be made public, we shall find out who it was that sat at the cabinet table betraying the President and the people he served. Perhaps we shall even be able to trace some connection to the men who shared with John Wilkes Booth the responsibility for the murder of Abraham Lincoln.

To accept any such theory it is necessary to believe that Robert Lincoln was a man so vicariously patricidal as to cover up and shield the most outrageous perfidies of his father's friends, while at the same time he despised and denied even the virtues of those whom he construed to be the enemies of Abraham Lincoln's memory. Any such assumption violates what is known of Robert Lincoln's character. He was sometimes petty, but disloyal he never was. Moreover, the poisons which were present in the papers were there in 1865, at the moment when the world, including Robert Lincoln, was seeking vengeance, and he knew that they were there and what they were. Would he then or ever have protected conspirators, accomplices, or the most remote of accessories? It is nonsense to suppose that he would; it is nonsense also to suppose the Lincoln archive a possible *locus* for material which would indict them. That would be the last place to look, for if it had ever existed, it would certainly have been turned over to the government for use at the trials.

But *treason* at law, and *treason,* a careless word formed readily on the tongue, are very different. It is conceivable that the Lincoln papers contained records of *political* treason, of confidences betrayed, or ambitions to succession. There were members of Mr. Lincoln's cabinet who were not distinguished for remarkable gifts of silence, or for suppressing their love of place and power, or even for personal loyalties. It is possible that Robert Lincoln deplored and condemned some evidence of their occasional transgressions, but the materials on such episodes as the Pomeroy Secret Circular urging the election of Salmon P. Chase in 1864, and the more than a thousand letters from the Cabinet which Robert Lincoln committed to the Library are emphatic denials that he destroyed very much.

Turning now to Dr. Butler's story, it is important to note that in his *Saturday Evening Post* article (subsequently reprinted in his autobiography, *Across the Busy Years*) he spoke of the imperiled papers as additional to, and distinguishable from, other papers already deposited in the Library of Congress. If that were so, and there is every reason to believe it, then Dr. Butler was duped—perhaps in fun, more probably from anxiety to close a debate and avoid future recrimination—into the supposition that Robert Lincoln had acted upon his counsel, for there were no accessions to the Abraham Lincoln papers after the original deposit in 1919.

It has already been said that family correspondence did not belong with the White House papers, that Robert Lincoln insisted on a firm differentiation between his father's domestic and public life, and that Mrs. Abraham Lincoln flatly refused to permit her letters from her husband ever "to go out of her hands" because they were of "too private a nature." The only letter from President Lincoln to his wife, which was printed in Nicolay and Hay's edition of the *Complete Works*, is still in the collection, and although it is dangerous to assume a rule from an isolated instance, it seems reasonable to suppose that its presence in the collection was entirely accidental. On the other hand, it appears to be a fact that, following his mother's death, some of her letters came into Robert Lincoln's keeping and that he never incorporated them with the documents of the administration. The letter which Robert Lincoln wrote to James Schouler on January 29, 1908, which was published in Volume 42 of *The Proceedings of the Massachusetts Historical Society* substantiates this view:

. . . I have come across a letter written to my mother on March 4th [1860], at Exeter, N.H., in which he wrote to her of what he had already done, and of his engagements up to and including the speech made at Woonsocket, R.I., on Thursday March 8th.

But what became of this message is not known. It may survive among mementos owned by his descendants; it may have been confided to the flames; it seems certain that Robert Lincoln did actually destroy some Lincoln letters, for the family tells how his granddaughter, Mary Lincoln Beckwith, once watched him as he threw some on the grate. Whether they were official or private was not disclosed. Moreover, it is generally understood that he retained for some time the services of Henry E. Barker, proprietor of Barker's art and secondhand bookstore, in Springfield, to collect for him letters from his mother in order that he might erase the pathetic testaments of her madness. There is now in the collections of the Illinois State Historical Library an acknowledgment which he wrote from Manchester to Le Grand Van Valkenburgh, of New York, on May 26, 1913:

I find here your kind letter of a week ago upon my return from a short absence and I greatly appreciate your thoughtfulness. Of course I regret the existence of these relics of the long years of the distressing mental disorder of my mother but it is idle to think of gathering them up. Hundreds of them have been kindly sent to me for destruction and I am quite sure that there exist still other hundreds. All that I have known are of the same tenor; many have been printed in newspapers and catalogues; and I long ago came to the conclusion that one could not imagine a more hopeless work than an effort to collect them or even a large fraction of them.

Beyond the fact that President Lincoln's letters to and from his family have disappeared, and the fact that they constituted a second, small, almost infinitesimal collection, always kept separate, the release of which in Robert Lincoln's view would have violated a proud privacy, or battered the false façades of propriety, or wrenched scabs from shame for infelicities and excesses, it is impossible to go. When a representative of the Security Storage Company of Washington went to Hildene to make an inventory for estate purposes, he found no papers in the house.

Robert Lincoln must have been indifferent to, but perfectly aware of, the consequences of his position; he must have realized that his tenacity would only quicken the initiative of those who were enthralled by his father's memory and resolved to penetrate the invisible cloak in which he had enshrouded him. No mortal man was ever the object of such intense and particular research as was Abraham Lincoln, and because the days before Washington offered a more accessible field, the inquisitors ransacked the records of his forebears for diagnosis of his hormones; sought from gossip and idle mendacity or from veracious reminiscence and public knowledge to retrace his propulsion into national affairs back to unpleasantness at home, amassed a thousand corroborations to clarify a single instance, pried open desks and drawers and neglected closets, dug through ancient files of newspapers and forgotten dockets of county courts, unearthed the manuscripts of contemporaries, disputed with one another the formal tenets of his religion or the lack of them, compiled elaborate catalogues of his misfortunes and embarrassments, resurrected the commonplace and turned it into spectacle, but always moved by reverence for him and resolved to add understanding to honored luster. The result of their selfless searching was the discovery of those very inwardnesses which Robert Lincoln had hoped to hide. And now, when so much is known of his household, his habits, his beliefs, his intimacies, the forlorn fragments of misery which Robert Lincoln extinguished could only confirm, or reinforce matters already revealed, analyzed, and reduced to perspective. Interesting they would be, of course, but they would not, in all likelihood, be substantial enough, or numerous enough, or startling enough to mourn.

On the other hand, the period of the presidency, the period when Abraham Lincoln matured and came to being, has escaped the microscopic examination which has been applied to his earlier unexceptional career. It is because he was so much in and of his world that Abraham Lincoln is the foremost American. He is foremost because he was the central, the focal character in a bruising, bitter, wretched, splendid moment when many men were great and he was greater still. He is foremost because his contemporaries made him foremost, conceded his primacy, and conferred their power and their honor on him. In short, Abraham Lincoln stands alone in history largely because in life he stood among the people. Only through them, the inhabitants of a wide, broken, angry land, is it possible to find him. Their responses to him and his to them, their anguish and his sympathies, their aspirations and his endeavors, their reaching out and his upholding of them, are the strong roots from which his towering spirit grows.

It is these elements which give such transcendent importance to the White House papers, for they reflect not the wooden walls which once confined him, but the roads he traveled and the lives he reached. Behind were preparation and experience, the drudgery and the overcoming, the firm progression and the little victories; here was struggle and evocation, the heat of issue and the hazard of ruin, and here was where Mr. Lincoln received his testing and his proving.

Because they had the papers, Nicolay and Hay could write their formal history; and partly because he had their history, and because he had a freedom from deadlines, and a great heart, and a deep, wise, generous, interpretative understanding, and a power and felicity of expression, Carl Sandburg could describe the war years. Thus from the papers have come two monumental, imperishable works, radically different, but somehow inseparably associated. The literature of Lincoln has grown into thousands of volumes, and there are thousands of other monographs unhappily or happily buried in periodicals, newspapers, and public documents. While many are notable for original reseach, and many have made fresh and important contributions, nearly all are dependent in some degree upon the papers as they were filtered through the hands of the secretarial biographers. Yet to understand the potentials of the papers it is necessary always to take into account the fact that comprehensive and inclusive as their work was, John Nicolay and John Hay followed a scheme or pattern of their own devising, that they were obliged to condense and compress, that many materials were, in consequence, inappropriate to their purpose, that they made their individual accents and emphases, that they were occasionally restrained by Robert Lincoln's taste and judgment and hobbled by their own unconscious inhibitions; in short, that they were forced to select and choose. It is such considerations as these that make the question of integrity of the papers so pressing.

It has been charged (and the charges have been repeated) that they were purged before they were brought to the Library. From time to time Robert Lincoln had mentioned an intention to do away with them altogether. Young was reported to have made conflicting statements. It was known that some documents were withdrawn by Robert Lincoln for use as gifts. Some of these removals have already been mentioned; to them may be added: a letter of March 9, 1864 to Ulysses S. Grant, presenting his commission as Lieutenant General, accompanied by a pencil draft of General Grant's acceptance, which was given to General F. D. Grant on February 10, 1909; and a letter of September 12, 1864, to General Grant suggesting a concentration at Sheridan's Camp to enable him to make a strike, which was sent to N. E. Merrill, of East Walpole, Massachusetts, for the Department of History, Phillips Academy, Exeter, New Hampshire, on March 9, 1909. But only once did Robert Lincoln take a paper from the deposit in the Library. On May 14, 1919, within a week of their delivery, he came in person to secure the draft of an address to Mr. Molina, Minister from Nicaragua. That was all, although shortly before his death he was contemplating an exchange of manuscripts for Abraham Lincoln's watch chain which had come into the possession of a private collector. Added together these inroads cannot be considered serious.

But Robert Lincoln always insisted that he must submit the papers to a sifting. Did he carry out that intention? Perhaps he may have had some assistance from John G. Nicolay, or, again, he may have done the work himself at any time in the fourteen years between 1905 and 1919 when the papers were in his custody. It should be remembered, however, that he had only proposed to "glean out what is useless and classify the remainder in some sort." Such weeding would have been unfortunate, but it would not necessarily have impaired the usefulness and dependability of the collection. It should be remembered also that he recognized the existence of "many documents . . . necessary to the history . . . which would be damaging to men now living." He had taken pains to protect the sensibilities of the living, perhaps for the very reason that he might preserve the necessary documents.

If he had, on the contrary, as Young suggested and Hertz alleged, burned some papers burdened with scandalous content, why did he make the deposit conditioned upon the information being kept from the public, and why did he require in his deed of gift that the papers should be withheld for twenty-one years from the date of his death in order to prevent offense to the "immediate ancestors of persons now living"? If he had "purified" or "purged" the papers, there would have been no reason whatever for the imposition of secrecy. It seems unlikely that he did anything of the kind.

There are those who believe that Robert Lincoln impounded the papers in order to keep them from Albert J. Beveridge. There is a story which emanates from a person then close to Mr. Lincoln that he was so fiercely determined to prevent Beveridge from seeing them that he consulted actuaries as to the senator's life expectancy before he fixed upon the period of cloture. It is said that his adamant refusal to risk access on the part of one of the most gifted, learned, scientific, and careful biographers in the history of our literature was because he had heard that the senator had secured the use of the Herndon papers, which implied, in his view, that the senator's work would be tainted, tawdry, and grotesque.

Certainly Beveridge did everything he could to break down Robert Lincoln's resistance, and let it be known that he would resort to "dynamite, or chloroform, soothing syrup, or quinine, cocaine, or T.N.T." to get hold of the papers. His direct letters went unanswered. Meanwhile he worked with such sources as he could find.

Rebuffed or ignored, he sought the intermediation of others, among them Dr. Butler, Henry White, and Worthington Chauncey Ford, then of the Massachusetts Historical Society. Their efforts on his behalf were in vain.

Eventually Robert Lincoln sent a flat refusal to Senator Beveridge. It may have been more than a coincidence that it was written on the same day that he signed the deed of gift, decreeing that the papers should be locked away for a generation. If they had been purged, emasculated, whittled down to gentle innocence it would not have made any difference if everyone had seen them. When at last they would be opened they would, ironically, be shelved not far from the Herndon and the Beveridge papers.

This is the evidence on which the impression is based that the Lincoln papers in the Library of Congress are substantially intact. For years they were secured in three heavy safes. During World War II the Gettysburg Address and the Second Inaugural found refuge in the Bullion Depository at Fort Knox, Kentucky. But the corpus of the Lincoln papers sought safety from air attack in the vault of the Alderman Library at the University of Virginia. As the time for their opening approached, Dr. C. Percy Powell, assisted by Mrs. Helen D. Bullock, brought to conclusion the index which Mr. Fitzpatrick had only begun. It contained 38,403 entries. The separate documents once estimated at ten thousand were twice that number. They were bound in 194 sturdy blue buckram folios with red leather labels on their spines. Every paper with its envelope was microfilmed to prevent the possibility of loss. Secrecy was perfectly kept. Those few who worked with the collection were enjoined not to take even mental notes.

On the eve of the opening a congenial company met for dinner and to await the stroke of midnight. The talk was good. Carl Sandburg strummed his guitar and sang songs out of America's past. He spoke, as did Paul Angle, Jay Monaghan, James Randall, Lauriston Bullard, Ralph Newman, Frederick Meserve, William Townsend, Colton Storm, Louis Warren, Alfred Stern, John Washington, Robert Kincaid, General Ulysses S. Grant III, Gerald McMurtry, Harry Lytle, George Dondero, and the others. Miss Nicolay could not be present, nor Herbert Putnam now Librarian Emeritus, nor Oliver Barrett, but the rest were there, listening, recalling meetings with Robert Lincoln, and honoring him for his gift to all of the people. There was excitement in the quiet voices of those gentle students. Judge James W. Bollinger stood at his place, holding his cane above his head. "Not since that morning in the Petersen House," he said, "have so many men who love Lincoln been gathered together in one room." It was so; this was part of history, part of the Lincoln experience.

A little before twelve the party walked through the sultry night to the marble building across the street and there, on the third floor, watched while the doors were slowly, fumblingly opened and the Lincoln papers after eighty-two years came first to light. For the witnesses it was an unforgettable moment. Cameramen's flashlights exploded, there was the whir of newsreels in the making, a radio announcer's voice was heard above the noises people make when deeply stirred. Luther Harris Evans, Librarian of Congress, solemnly intoned the provisions of the Deed of Gift.

Back in the Main Building scores of the Library staff worked through the night, mounting exhibits, preparing press releases, typing cards and cutting stencils, conferring, interviewing, readying. At noon, on July 26, when the press was admitted, fatigue was on the faces of the journalists. For them, too, it had been a hard week. Some had been writing two stories a day, but it was the most completely covered public event the capital had ever known. Every news service designated special representatives, syndicates retained the expert services of specialists, all of the major networks carried the intelligence through the air and into the homes of Americans. The pictorial and iconographic documentation was exhaustive and exhausting. When the fabulous resources of the collection became assured, the spirits of these earnest and able servants of communication lifted and wiped away concern. It had been worth waiting for. Here, for the first time, was Abraham Lincoln three-dimensioned, whole, intelligible. They hurried to telephones, ground cameras, sent messages across the ether.

The formal ceremony took place at four o'clock. Near the platform sat a grandson. The Librarian said:

We observe a legal convention, property is transferred, a deed is validated. . . . We keep an engagement with the past. It is, in other words, a time for sentiment and searching. Because this is so, our first duty must be to avoid delusion. For some, brittle impatience, curiosity, and suspicion are shattered, and now are either satisfied, or disappointed, or destroyed. For others, expectation is realized, aspiration is fulfilled, discovery is at hand. A bandage is removed from ancient hurts, healed by benignant and unknowing time, but only at last quite understood. Here is a touchstone of history, albeit a touchstone of limited powers and ruthless mysteries.

But the listening people knew that a part of Mr. Lincoln had come alive again and that in this place his sole surviving child would still survive.

PART TWO

The Papers

W HEN THE LINCOLN PAPERS WERE OPENED ON JULY 26, 1947, IT
was ascertained that the collection was nearly twice as large as
previously had been anticipated. In it are more than eighteen thousand
individual documents, consisting of nearly forty-two thousand leaves,
bound up in nearly two hundred buckram folio volumes, and indexed by
approximately thirty-eight thousand entries for the names of correspondents. Exclusive of endorsements on incoming letters, of which no
enumeration has been made, and for which no satisfactory estimate is
feasible, there are about nine hundred Abraham Lincoln holographs; that
is to say, about nine hundred separate memoranda, copies of letters, drafts
of speeches, proclamations, official messages, et cetera, written wholly in
Mr. Lincoln's hand. In some, Mr. Lincoln dissolves into the character of a
ghost writer, for a governor of the sovereign state of Illinois, for his cabinet ministers, for his private secretaries; and very occasionally there are
letters exchanged by others which he himself copied for his own files.
The preponderance of these have been printed in the several editions of
his collected works, and although they possess a considerable interest by
reason of textual variations from their published versions, they lack the
freshness and therefore the importance of the letters which were addressed to him. Unless some special object is to be served, unless no record
of earlier appearance has been found, or unless they are necessary to provide background and explanation, such holographs will not be presented
in this volume. For the outstanding contribution of the Lincoln papers
comes from the materials which were addressed *to* him. Hitherto seen
only by John G. Nicolay and John Hay, and only very sparingly repro-

duced by them, these are the papers which give background, solidity, substance to his own writings; and from them it is possible for the first time fully to understand the meaning of his responses. They illumine episodes, alter older concepts, shift emphases and accents, prove the power of his personality, trace the development of his character and career. They reflect all conditions of the society of his time; many come from distinguished and exalted personages in the executive branch of government; others from congressmen, senators, and robed justices of the courts; others from military and naval leaders and subalterns; others from swaggering or influential politicians, party bosses, ward heelers; others from editors, clergymen, lawyers, diplomats, physicians, businessmen, organizations of all sorts for all sorts of purposes. But preponderantly Mr. Lincoln's correspondents were composed of the laity, that diverse, unclassifiable, resourceful, self-assured, and informed group which constituted the American public. Of this last category, many were lowly, illiterate, frequently impudent and obtuse, but they had needs, opinions, tragedies, expectations, humor; they knew what they required, and they knew that Mr. Lincoln was in Washington to serve them. Between them and him there existed an intimacy which only a man of the people and men of the people fully can exchange. Therein was the source, the strength, the explanation of his life, and therein is its most eloquent expression for us.

The present organization of the papers, in accordance with usual practice governing the arrangement of manuscript collections, is strictly chronological. An effort (usually successful) has been made by the indexers to establish dates where dates are lacking, but where they are supplied they have been accepted, even in those instances where internal evidence proves them wrong. Such lapses are ordinarily encountered during the early weeks of any January, when Mr. Lincoln's correspondents were most likely to forget a change of year. This arbitrary acquiescence in a writer's frailty occasionally produces problems, for there are cases where a series of letters on a specific and temporally circumscribed subject appear in volumes widely removed from one another, and the materials can be recovered and assembled only by the most assiduous "page-by-page" examination.

Another anomaly of the procedure is the separation of enclosures from the communications which once "covered" them. This results in the appearance of documents without relevancy or explanation, and, what is still more unfortunate, frequently defeats the complete understanding which otherwise they might convey.

As a consequence, in compiling these selections an effort has been made to avoid such pitfalls and to bring together the related examples in such ways as seem most likely to render them intelligible. Otherwise the order is, of course, the order imposed by time.

To this one further exception has been made at the beginning. There exist in the collection a few documents purely retrospective in character, representing a period in Mr. Lincoln's early life not reflected by contemporaneous records among the papers. Because they possess a unity of content, they afford a background, an introduction, to the selections which follow them, and permit their successors generally to speak for themselves, without elaborate apparatus, interpretation, or the nuisance of footnotes.

John G. Nicolay, in a letter to Jesse W. Weik, dated February 13, 1895, recalled that

The Autobiography . . . was written by Mr. Lincoln within a week or two after his first nomination. The request for it came from friends in Columbus, Ohio, who placed it with other material in the hands of W.[illiam] D.[ean] Howells, and he wrote a campaign biography from it . . . which together with several of Mr. Lincoln's speeches were printed in an ordinary campaign volume . . . Follett, Foster & Co. being publishers—the same firm that published the Lincoln-Douglas debates.

The MS. copy sent to Columbus was made by myself, being among my first work as Mr. Lincoln's private secretary. Mr. Lincoln's original autograph MS., which is now in my possession, was retained to make other copies from.

This sketch, one of several written by Mr. Lincoln at various times, has been frequently reprinted from the text as it appeared in the *Complete Works*. The "original autograph MS." survives among the Lincoln papers. Collation with the published version reveals discrepancies in abbreviation, punctuation, capitalization, underscoring, spelling (particularly in the case of place names), the form of words; and the further fact that in one place a line and in another a whole episode ("the ludicrous incident of sewing up the hog's eyes," which Robert Lincoln found distasteful) have been omitted. It is here transcribed accurately, with Abraham Lincoln's cancels italicized within brackets.

Abraham Lincoln was born Feb. 12. 1809, then in Hardin, now in the more recently formed county of Larue, Kentucky—His father, Thomas, & grand-father, Abraham, were born in Rockingham county Virginia, whither their ancestors had come from Berks County Pennsylvania—His lineage has been traced no further back than this—

The family were originally quakers, though in later times they have fallen away from the peculiar habits of that people—The grandfather Abraham, had four brothers—Isaac, Jacob, John & Thomas—So far as known, the descendants of Jacob and John are still in Virginia—Isaac went to a place near where Virginia, North Carolina, and Tennessee, join; and his descendants are in that region—Thomas came to Kentucky, and after many years, died there, whence his descendants went to Missouri—Abraham, grandfather of the subject of this sketch, came to Kentucky, and was killed by indians about the year 1784—He left a widow, three sons and two daughters—The eldest son, Mordecai, remained in Kentucky till late in life, when he removed to Hancock County Illinois, where soon after he died, and where several of his descendants still reside—The second son, Josiah, removed at an early age to a place on Blue River, now within Harrison county, Indiana; but no recent information of him, or his family, has been obtained—The eldest sister, Mary, married Ralph Crume and some of her descendants are now known to be in Breckenridge county Kentucky—The second sister, Nancy, married William Brumfield, and her family are not known to have left Kentucky, but there is no recent information from them—Thomas, the youngest son, and father of the present subject, by the early death of his father, and very narrow circumstances of his mother, even in childhood was a wandering laboring boy, and grew up litterally without education—He never did more in the way of writing than to bunglingly sign his own name—Before he was grown, he passed one year as a hired hand with his uncle Isaac on Watag, [i.e., Watauga], a branch of the Holsteen [i.e., Holston] river—Getting back into Kentucky, and having reached his 28th year, he married Nancy Hanks—mother of the present subject—in the year 1806. She also was born in Virginia; and relatives of hers of the name of Hanks, and of other names, now reside in Coles, in Macon, and in Adams counties, Illinois, and also in Iowa—The present subject has no brother or sister of the whole or half blood—He had a sister, older than himself, who was grown and married, but died many years ago, leaving no child. Also a brother, younger than himself, who died in infancy—Before leaving Kentucky he and his sister were sent [to] for short periods, to A. B. C. schools, the first kept by Zachariah Riney, and the second by Caleb Hazel. [In his] At this time his father resided on Knob. Creek, on the road from Bardstown Ky. to Nashville Tenn. at a point three, or three and a half miles South or South-West of Atherton's ferry on the Rolling Fork—From this place he removed to what is now Spencer County Indiana, in the autumn of 1816—A. then being in his eighth year—This removal was partly on account of slavery; but chiefly on account of the difficulty in land titles in Ky—He settled in an unbroken forest; and the clearing away of surplus [wooa] wood was the great task a head. A. though very young, was large of his age, and had an axe put into his hands at once; and from then till within his twentythird year, he was almost constantly handling that most useful instrument—less, of course, in plowing and harvesting seasons—At this place A took an early start as a hunter, which was never much [inf] improved afterwards—A few days before the completion of his eighth year, in the absence of his father, a flock of wild turkeys approached the new log-cabin, and A with a rifle gun, standing inside, shot through a crack, and killed one of them—He has never since pulled a trigger on any larger game—In the autumn of 1818 his mother died; and a year afterwards his father married Mrs. Sally Johnston, at Elizabeth-Town, Ky—a widow, with three children of [his] her first marriage. She proved a good and kind mother to A. and is still living in Coles Co. Illinois—There were no children of this second marriage—His father's residence continued at the same place in Indiana, till 1830—While here A. went to A. B. C. schools by littles, kept successively by Andrew Crawford,— Sweeney, and Azel W. Dorsey—He does not remember any other —The family of Mr. Dorsey now reside in Schuyler Co. Illinois—A. now thinks that the agregate of all his schooling did not amount to one year—He was never in a College or Academy as a student; and never inside of a College or Accademy building till since he had a law-license—What he has in the way of education, he has picked up—After he was twenty three, and had separated from his father, he studied English grammar, imperfectly of course, but so as to speak and write as well as he now [done] does—He studied and nearly mastered the Six-books of Euclid, since he was a member of Congress—He regrets his want of education, and does what he can to supply the want—In his tenth year he was kicked by a horse,

and apparently killed for a time—When he was nineteen, still residing in Indiana, he made his first trip upon a flat-boat to New-
Orleans—He was a hired hand merely; and he and a son of the
owner, without other assistance, made the trip—The nature of part
of the [*load*] cargo-load, as it was called—made it necessary for
them to linger and trade along the Sugar Coast—and one night they
were attacked by seven negroes with intent to kill and rob them.
They were hurt some in the melee, but succeeded in driving the
negroes from the boat and then "cut cable" "weighed anchor" and
left—

March 1st 1830—A. having just completed his 21st year, his father
and family, with the families of the two daughters and sons-in-law,
of his step-mother, left the old homestead in Indiana, and came to
Illinois—Their mode of conveyance was waggons drawn by ox teams,
& A drove one of the teams—They reached the County of Macon,
and stopped there some time within the same month of March. His
father and family settled a new place on the North side of the
Sangamon river, at the junction of the timber-land and prairie, about
ten miles Westerly from Decatur—Here they built a log-cabin, into
which they removed, and made sufficient of rails to fence ten acres
of ground, fenced and broke the ground, and raised a crop of sown
corn upon it the same year—These are, or are supposed to be, the
rails about which so much is being said just now, though these are
far from being the first, or only rails ever made by A. The sons-in-
law were temporarily settled at other places in the County—In the
autumn all hands were greatly afflicted with Ague and fever, to
which they had not been used, and by which they were greatly
discouraged—so much so that they determined on leaving the
County—They remained however, through the succeeding winter,
which was the winter of the very celebrated "deep snow" of Illinois—During that winter, A. together with his step-mother's son,
John D. Johnston, and John Hanks, yet residing in Macon County,
hired themselves to one Denton Offutt, to take a flat boat from
Beardstown Illinois to New-Orleans; and for that purpose, were to
join him—Offut [sic]—at Springfield, Ill. so soon as the snow should
go off—When it did go off which was about the 1st of March 1831—
the county was so flooded, as to make traveling by land impracti-

cable; to obviate which difficulty the [sic] purchased a large canoe and came down the Sangamon river in it—This is the time and the manner of A's first entrance into Sangamon County—They found Offutt at Springfield, but learned from him that he had failed in getting a boat at Beardstown—This lead [sic] to their hiring themselves to him at $12 per month each; and getting the timber out of the trees and building a boat at old Sangamon Town on the Sangamon river, seven miles N.W. of Springfield, which boat they took to New-Orleans, substantially upon the old contract—It was in connection with this boat that occurred the ludicrous incident of sewing up the hogs eyes—Offutt bought thirty odd large fat live hogs, but found difficulty in driving them from where [he] purchased them to the boat, and thereupon conceived the whim that he could sew up their eyes and drive them where he pleased—No sooner thought of than decided, he put his hands including A. at the job, which they completed—all but the driving—In their blind condition they could not be driven out of the lot or field they were in. This expedient failing, they were tied and hauled on carts to the boat—It was near the Sangamon River, within what is now Menard County—

During the boat enterprize acquaintance with Offutt, who was previously an entire stranger, he conceived a liking for A. and believing he could turn him to accounnt, he contracted with him to act as Clerk for him, on his return from New Orleans, in charge of a store and Mill at New Salem—then in Sangamon, now in Menard County—Hanks had not gone to New-Orleans, but having a family, and being likely to be detained from home longer than at first expected, had turned back from S.. Louis—He is the same John Hanks who now engineers the "rail enterprize" at Decatur; and is a first cousin to A's mother—A's father, with his own family & others mentioned, had, in [purf] pursuance of their intention, removed from Macon to Coles County—John D. Johnston, the step-mother's son, went to them; and A. stopped indefinitely, and, for the first time, as it were, by himself, at New-Salem, before mentioned—This was in July 1831—Here he rapidly made acquaintances and friends—In less than a year Offutt's business was failing—had almost failed, —When the Black Hawk war of 1832—broke out—A. joined a volunteer Company, and to his own surprize, was elected Captain of it—

He says he has not since had any success in life which gave him so much satisfaction—He went the campaign, served near three months, met [*some*] the ordinary hardships of such an expedition, but was in no battle—He now owns in Iowa, the land upon which his own warrants for this service, were located. Returning from the Campaign, and encouraged by his great popularity among his immediate neighbors, he, the same year, ran for the Legislature and was beaten—his own precinct, however, casting its votes 277 for and 7. against him—And this too while he was an avowed Clay man, and the precinct the autumn afterwards, giving a majority of 115 to Genl Jackson over Mr. Clay—This was the only time A was ever beaten in a direct vote of the people—He was now without means and out of business, but was anxious to remain with his friends who had treated him with so much generosity, expecially as he had nothing elsewhere to go to—He studied what he should do—thought of learning the black-smith trade—thought of trying to study law—rather thought he could not succeed at that without a better education. Before long, strangely enough, a man offered to sell and did sell, to A. and another as poor as himself, an old stock of goods, upon credit—They opened as merchants; and he says that was *the* store—Of course they did nothing but get deeper and deeper in debt—He was appointed Post-Master at New-Salem—the office being too insignificant, to make his politics an objection—The store winked out—The Surveyor of Sangamon, offered to depute to A that portion of his work which was within his part of the county—He accepted, procured a compass and chain, studied Flint, and Gibson a little, and went at it—This procured bread, and kept soul and body together—The election of 1834 came, and he was then elected to the Legislature by the highest vote cast for any candidate—Major John T. Stuart, then in full practice of the law, was also elected. During the canvass, in a private conversation he encouraged A. [to] study law—After the election he borrowed books of Stuart, took them home with him, and went at it in good earnest—He studied with nobody—He still mixed in the surveying to pay board and clothing bills—When the Legislature met, the law books were dropped, but were taken up again at the end of the session. He was re-elected in 1836. 1838. and 1840—In the autumn of 1836 he [*was licensed*] obtained a law licence, and on April 15. 1837 removed to Springfield, and commenced the practice, his old friend Stuart taking him into partnership—March 3rd 1837, by a protest entered upon the Ills. House Journal of that date, at pages 817.818. A. with Dan Stone, another representative of Sangamon, briefly defined his position on the slavery question; and so far as it goes, it was then the same that it is now. The protest is as follows—(Here insert it) In 1838. & 1840 Mr. L's party in the Legislature voted for him as Speaker; but being in the minority, he was not elected—After 1840 he declined a re-election to the Legislature—He was on the Harrison electoral ticket in 1840, and on that of Clay in 1844. and spent much time and labor in both those canvasses—In Nov. 1842 he was married to Mary, daughter of Robert S. Todd, of Lexington, Kentucky—They have three living children, all sons—one born in 1843, one in 1850, and one in 1853—They lost one, who was born in 1846. In 1846. he was elected to the lower House of Congress, and served one term only commencing in Dec. 1847 and ending with the inauguration of General Taylor, in March 1849—[In 1852] All the battles of the Mexican war had been fought before Mr. L. took his seat in Congress, but the American army was still in Mexico, and the treaty of peace was not fully and formally ratified till the June afterwards—Much has been said of his course in Congress in regard to this war—A careful examination of the Journals [sh.] and Congressional Globe shows, that he voted for all the supply measures which came up [while he was there], and for all the measures in any way favorable to the Officers, soldiers, and their families, who conducted the war through; with this exception that some of the measures passed without yeas and nays, leaving no record as to how particular men voted—The Journals and Globe also show him voting that the war was unnecessarily and unconstitutionally [commenced] begun by the President of the United States—This is the language of Mr. Ashmun's amendment, for which Mr. L. and nearly or quite all, other whigs of the H.R. voted—

Mr. L's reasons for the opinion expressed by this vote were briefly [this] that the President had sent Genl. Taylor into an inhabited part of the country belonging to Mexico, and not to the U. S. and thereby had provoked the first act of hostility—in fact the commencement of the war; that the place, being the country bordering on the East bank of the Rio Grande, was inhabited by native Mexicans, born there under the Mexican government; and had never submitted to, nor been conquered by Texas, or the U. S. nor transferred to either by treaty—that although Texas claimed the Rio Grande as her boundary, Mexico had never recognized it, the people on the ground had never [enforced, and] recognized it, and neither Texas nor the U. S. had ever enforced it—that there was a broad desert between that, and the country over which Texas had actual control —that the country where hostilities commenced, having once belonged to Mexico, must remain so, until it was somehow legally transferred, which had never been done.

Mr. L. thought the act of sending [the troop] an armed force [to the] among the Mexicans, was *unnecessary,* inasmuch as Mexico was in no way molesting, or menacing the U. S. or the people thereof; and that it was *unconstitutional,* because the power of levying war is vested in Congress, and not in the President. He thought the principal motive for the act, was to divert public attention from the surrender of "Fifty-four, forty, or fight" to Great Brittain, on the Oregon boundary question.

Mr. L. was not a candidate for re-election—This was determined upon and declared before he went to Washington, in accordance with an understanding among whig friends by which Col. Hardin, and Col. Baker had each previously served a single term in the same District.

In 1848, during his term in Congress, he advocated Gen. Taylor's nomination for the Presidency, in opposition to all others, and also took an active part for his election, after his nomination—speaking a few times in Maryland, near Washington, several times in Massachusetts, and canvassing quite fully his own district in [th] Illinois, which was followed by a majority in the district of over 1500 for Gen. Taylor—

Upon his return from Congress he went to the practice of the law with greater earnestness than ever before—In 1852 he was upon the Scott electoral ticket, and did something in the way of canvassing; but owing to the hopelessness of the cause in Illinois, he did less than in previous presidential canvasses.

In 1854. his profession had almost superseded the thought of politics in his mind, when the repeal of the Missouri compromise aroused him as he had never been before.

In the autumn of that year he took the stump with no broader practical aim or object than to secure, if possible, the re-election of Hon. Richard Yates to Congress—His speeches at once attracted a more marked attention than they had ever before done—As the canvass proceeded, he was drawn to different parts of the state, outside of Mr. Yates' district—He did not abandon the law, but gave his attention, by turns, to that and politics—The State agricultural fair was at Springfield that year, and Douglas was [*anounce*] announced to speak there.

In the campaign of 1856. Mr. L. made over fifty speeches, no one of which, so far as he remembers, was put in print—One of them was made at Galena; but Mr. L. has no recollection of any part of it being printed; nor does he remember whether in that speech he said anything about a Supreme Court decision—He may have spoken upon that subject; and some of the newspapers may have reported him as saying what is now ascribed to him; but he thinks he could not have expressed himself as represented.—

———◦◦———

When William Dean Howells was commissioned in May 1860 to prepare a biography of Mr. Lincoln, he himself did not go to Springfield. In his stead went James Quay Howard, a young law student, who interviewed many of Mr. Lincoln's oldest friends, especially those who had known him as a youth in the vanished village of New Salem. As a result, Mr. Howells's treatment of that period, to which he devoted one third of his book, is regarded by modern students as "trustworthy" and "particularly fortunate." But Mr. Howells's rhetorical text is a kind of palimpsest superimposed upon Mr. Howard's most informal notes which now have been discovered among the Lincoln papers. They are staccato, even telegraphic in style, sometimes as repetitious as hammer strokes, as shapeless in themselves as bits of masonry which chisel removes from marble block, but the image they leave is faithful, picturesque, and moving.

Here they are:

LINCOLN'S COURSE FROM 1829 TO 1846

George Close who *split rails* with Lincoln, says L came from Indiana to Macon Co. Ill. in fall of 1829—Was there working by Clay's works, chopping wood, splitting rails, and going about wherever he could get work. I helped him make rails for James Hanks and William Miller—made about 1000 together. Lincoln *had nothing only plenty of friends*—He helped to put up first house in Decatur—Gen. W. L. D. Ewing and a man named Posey were candidates for legislature in 1829—came to Decatur to make speeches—As Posey did not treat we persuaded L to get up and abuse him—said he would if I would not laugh at him—was frightened but got warmed up and made the best speech of the day—Did not abuse Posey but spoke well of both men—pictured out the future of Ill. When he got through Ewing said "he was a bright one." His pants were made of *flax and low,* cut tight at the ankle—his knees were both out. Was the roughest looking man I ever saw—poor boy, but welcome to everybody's house—Visited some friends in Mason Co. their table was hewn out of a log and had but three legs—made use of his long leg to hold up the table. Got from 25 to 30 cts. per hundred for splitting rails—never got any money—was paid in socks, Jeans, etc. Bargain with Mrs. Nancy Miller was this—was to maul 400 rails for each yard of brown Jeans dyed with white walnut bark, until he got enough to make a pair of pants.

God never made a finer man than Abraham Lincoln! Need not be with a man more than an hour to gain his good will. Hard time to get work—All a man could do was to keep himself in clothes—Walked 5, 6 and 7 miles to his day's works. Always had something nice and interesting to talk about. Started from Decatur with a drove of hogs owned by Denton Offutt. Got 7 or 8 dolls. per month—Drove to head waters of Sangamon River to find and pack them.

His favorite paper was the "Louisville Journal," which he for many years studied—and paid for when he had not money enough to dress decently—First political speech he ever made—at the north end of where Petersburgh now stands—Spoke on the general issues between the whigs and democrats, at the time. Although party feeling was high and Lincoln was a strong Adams man, in the New Salem precinct he got one more vote than both the Jackson and the Adams candidates for Congress, put together. This was in 1832. Official vote as shown by poll book in Clerk's office in Springfield is as follows

For Congress
$\begin{cases} \text{Jonathan H. Pugh} & 179 \\ \\ \text{Joseph Duncan} & 97 \end{cases}$

A Lincoln for Legislature   277

At the election in 1834 his majority was almost equally decisive—This was the last time he was the candidate while living at New Salem—A candidate named Taylor whom L thought unqualified, thought he could make Lincoln vote for him, by going to the polls with L. and reading aloud his ticket which was for Lincoln—but L in the same open manner voted for Taylor's opponent—Truth and honesty have made him what he is.

HON. WILLIAM BUTLER, TREAS OF STATE—

First time I saw Lincoln was when he came down Sangamon River from Macon Co. in a canoe—He was as ruff a specimen of humanity as could be found—His legs were bare for six inches between bottom of pants and top of socks—Sawed the planks for flat boat with whip saw—Happened to be traveling with L one day—got to telling me about how he was in debt as a surety for another man; said when he saw a man in distress could not help going his security—asked him how much he owed—told me $400. Asked him what he would do if he had money—Said he would first pay his debts, and then would like to study law—but did not see how he could do it, as he had no books or influential friends—said that every body wished him well—but he never could ask a man for a favor—I saw that he was an honest and worthy young man, and took him into my family and for three years treated him the same as my son—I paid his debt of $400, which L was not aware of till almost a year afterwards—Got him books and clothes and encouraged him in study of law.

diffidence and generosity were the causes of his failing to accumulate any thing during early life—Was also unprepossessing in appearance—never would push himself forward—L has tried again and again to pay me but I never would receive any thing. He came to me with the money a few years ago. I told him not to mention the subject again if he did not wish to offend me. Has been very grateful—

The following which is the beginning of a letter found in Sangamon Journal of June 15th, shows Mr. L's frankness—

New Salem, June 13, 1836.

To the Editor of the Journal:

In your paper of last Saturday, I see a communication over the signature of "many voters," in which the candidates who are announced in the Journal, are called upon to "show their hands." Agreed. Here's mine!

Cumberland

He then states his position which was substantially that of the Whig party Was elected to Congress in 1846, by 1400 majority over Peter Cartwright

WILLIAM G. GREEN

Met Lincoln at New Salem 1830, was Capt. of Flatboat—Boat belonged to Denton Offutt—was standing on mill dam trying to pry boat off—pant rolled up about a ft. dressed very ruff—blue Jeans breeches, a hickory shirt—alternate stripes of white and blue—made of cotton, buckeye chip hat—cost a "bit." Offutt had started from region above Decatur, Macon Co. 80 miles above Salem—got aground at mill dam—Offutt rented mill to grind produce—rented old store house put goods in—Lincoln as clerk at 15 dols. per month —2 or 3 mos. after he landed, said he would study grammar—good practical grammarian in three weeks—Said to me Bill if that is what they call a science I'll subdue another—Asked about authors on Surveying told him Stuart's was good—borrowed it—Said he, If I thought the law was as easy as these, I would commence it—wanted to get hold of something that was knotty—6 or 8 mos. after he came boarded with John Camron, Pres preacher—1.00 per week—Either at his books, wrestling, or running foot races, did it to be agreeable with the people—*Richland,* place where volunteer company met. Kirk Patrick—man L worked for very prominent, influential man, candidate for Capt. At least three fourths went to L. Patrick overhearing, L quite badly treated when he worked for K. Patrick. Was pleased to be elected Captain.

Clerk for Offutt one year. L and Berry bought a Grocery Store, tea, coffee, sugar, powder, lead, etc. Reuben Radford had this store— "Clary's Grove Boys" had broken R's windows—Value of store 525 dolls. I was to pay Radford 400. L said he would give $125 for bargain—L had not a dollar, had used all to buy a compass and few books. L paid his half of notes when fell due in 6 mos. I was surety on L and Berry's notes to Radford. This debt hung over L and me for some years as Berry had failed—we called it the national debt— I at length paid the whole debt. About five years later L wrote to me in Tenn. that he was equitably and legally bound to pay all Radford's claim and he was now for the first time able to refund— L paid me principal and interest in full. L would have me see his father, was cleverest homespun man I ever saw—could tell more good anecdotes than "Abe." L used grape vine for surveyor's chain. Always on side of justice, with the weak ever as brave a man as ever lived Indian came to our camp, all said they must kill him. L opposed it—said barbarians would not kill a prisoner—Some others said L was cowardly—L said try me—Swore if Indian was slaughtered must be done over his dead body. Asked them to come out and fight him, if they thought he was cowardly. Indians life was saved. Popular as an officer in Campaign—also on account of his athletic powers—But one man could throw him down—to wit Thompson. Marched first to Rock Island—was disbanded at Ottawa —Lincoln volunteered and went on in active service under Gen. Dodge—out about 4 mos altogether—L I do not think ever drank a quart of liquor in his life—drank out of 40 gal. barrell—Cut Herndon off at the knees in debate at Petersburgh—H called L an interloper, L said when he had been a candidate as often as Herndon he would quit—Had a horse for political campaign, but sold it for compass and walked to legislature at *Vandalia* about 100 miles— L favored? removal capital from Vandalia—1836? L became partner of Judge Logan the leading lawyer of Springfield. Magistrates were afraid to issue process against "Clary's Grove Boys." Said in contest with Jack Armstrong, I am sorry that you bet the money, I do not believe that there is a man on earth that can throw me now. Jack after they had worked for a long time, caught him by leg and got better of him. L said if they wanted to wrestle fair he was ready, but if they wanted to fight he would try that——Jack quashed—called it drawn. Son of Armstrong he volunteered to defend and cleared without a cent of compensation—Long nine elected in 1834—

Lincoln hewed timbers for flatboat 8 miles N. W. of Springfield at Sangamon town 1829—St. Gama—John Rahl among the wealthiest in S. made the pins for boat—Whenever he could find a young man he put him on right course, encouraged morality integrity and honesty—all that have looked up to him as an oracle have succeeded well—best surveyor in the country—Was always reading Burns & Shakespeare. Knew all of Burns by heart—Was as great when a surveyor or flatboatman in his circle as he is now in a higher one—Was the center of attraction on all occasions—Was always appointed one of Judges when at horse race and was never objected to by either party. When I was at Illinois College I brought home with me, one vacation, my young friend Dick Yates, present Republican candidate for governor, and some other boys. In order that they might enjoy their visit, I proposed that we would go up to New Salem and see a talented and interesting young man by the name of Lincoln—When we approached I was mortified to find that Abe was lying stretched out flat on his back on a cellar door reading a paper— I introduced him and he appeared so awkward and ruff, that I was afraid my college friends would be ashamed of him—We made him go down to dinner with us—At the table he upset his large bowl of milk and when my mother was trying to apologise for the accident L remarked that he would try and not let it trouble him hereafter—

Mr James Rutledge please to pay the bearer David P Nelson thirty dollars and this shall be your receipt for the same

March 8th 1832 —

A Lincoln for D Offutt

Ann M Rutledge

ENGLISH GRAMMAR,
IN
FAMILIAR LECTURES;

ACCOMPANIED BY A

COMPENDIUM;

EMBRACING

A NEW SYSTEMATICK ORDER OF PARSING,

A NEW SYSTEM OF PUNCTUATION, EXERCISES IN FALSE SYNTAX,

AND

A KEY TO THE EXERCISES:

DESIGNED

FOR THE USE OF SCHOOLS AND PRIVATE LEARNERS

BY SAMUEL KIRKHAM

SIXTH EDITION,
ENLARGED AND MUCH IMPROVED.

CINCINNATI,
PUBLISHED BY N & G GUILFORD, AT THEIR BOOK
FR. M'LEAN'S HEAD, 14, LOWER MARKET STILL.)
W. M. & O. FARNSWORTH, JR. PRINTERS
1828.

A TEXTBOOK WHICH LINCOLN STUDIED

This is Ann Rutledge's copy of Samuel Kirkham's *English Grammar*. Mounted on the inside front cover is an assignment from Denton Offut to David P. Nelson of thirty dollars owing from Ann's father, James Rutledge, and signed by Abraham Lincoln as agent. Reproduced from the original in the Library of Congress

I first bought Grocery Store of Radford, then sold to Lincoln & Berry—When Berry fizzled out I helped L close up the business—I knew I would have Berry's part of note to pay—

WILLIAM G. GREEN

Explanation of way L went into Grocery business is this—I rode up to Radford's one day soon after "Clary's Grove Boys" had broken his windows R said he was determined to sell out—I at random offered him $400 for whole stock—Said he would take it—Lincoln came in next day—proposed that we should take an inventory and see what kind of a bargain I had made. Did so and found the "traps" were worth $600—L was then out of employment, said he would give me $125 for my bargain. Proposed that they (L and Berry) should take my place—i. e. give their notes to Radford and I withdraw mine—R. would not do this without I would be surety— L kept store on his own hook about 9 mos. Berry was very trifling and failed—I went in with L and helped him close up the business— I knew nothing about law, and supposed it was my duty to pay Berry's half of notes and was surprised 5 or six years afterwards when I had gone to Tennessee to live, that he was now ready to pay me what I had paid for his partner Berry.

MENTOR GRAHAM

When L was about 22 said he believed he must study Grammar— one could not be obtained in neighborhood—walked for 8 miles and borrowed Kirkhams old Grammar. In 1827 he made *the rails*—Was clerking for Offutt in New Salem, in Dry Goods Store about one year—Well liked by every body—What he said every one relied on— Was surety for Berry—his compass chain, etc. were sold on execution—James Short *bought them and gave them back to him.* Lincoln tells the story on himself that when his flatboat got full of water he bored a hole in the bottom and let the water out. Explanation is that the boat was fast on the mill dam and the end over the dam being lowest the water ran to that end—

When I first saw Lincoln he was lying on a trundle bed rocking a cradle with his foot—was almost covered with papers and books— There was one half foot space between bottom of pants and top of socks.

L. M. GREEN A LAWYER OF PETERSBURGH

Offutt said L had been so faithful that he would make him his chief clerk—

Walked 6 miles to debating Club in '31 and '32 Every time I went to Salem he took me out on the hill and got me to explain to him *Kirkham*—Said to me one day that all his folks seemed to have good sense but none of them had become distinguished, and he believed it was for him to become so—had talked with men who had the reputation of being great men, but could not see that they differed from other men—I never knew him in one instance to deviate from the strictest principles of integrity and morality.

Read every thing he could get hold of—What was difficult to most persons seemed open to him—John Calhoun, late of Kansas being County surveyor appointed L deputy—Was a good surveyor —found as many old corners as any one—Was Post Master one year— He always made a good speech—First political speech made every one warm for him—L made a speech in 1834 which carried the people away—Many then said he would be Governor.

ROIL CLARY

Goods for store were hauled from Beardstown. Jack Armstrong legged Lincoln—Jack said before his death that he threw L but did not do it fairly—He won us by his bearing and boldness—Jack and

[Lincoln] were the warmest friends during life—Jack whipped a man for abusing L. Was but one man in army that could throw L down—he was Thompson, and by his superior science could throw every body—L tried to make Jack Armstrong door keeper of House— Was elected from New Salem but once.

DR STEVENSON OF MENARD CO.

Lincoln surveyed town of Petersburgh, County Seat of Menard Co. formerly Sangamon Co. Sawed half day with Cross cut-saw against four men who were trying to make him *give out*. L said he never worked harder—A friend of mine once met a part of *long nine* and other members of legislature coming from Vandalia at end of session—Were all on horse back but L who kept up with them on foot, being too poor to keep a horse—L complained of cold: one of long nine said it was no wonder for there was so much of him on ground—Gov. of Indiana, being in company with Offutt and Lincoln awhile, told Offutt that that young man had talent enough in him to make a president—

DR. JOHN ALLEN

Lincoln was appointed Post Master at New Salem in 1832, by Pres. Jackson. Was almost the only man then there who could make out the returns. Never saw a man better pleased. Will not be so well pleased, if he is elected President of the U. S. Was because, as he said, he would then have access to all the News papers—never yet being able to get the half that he wanted before. First speech L made in that region was at a country debating club which met in an old stone house. Did pretty well—Used to walk 6 miles to attend another debating Society, and "practice polemics" as they said. These "polemics" were equal some times to the best farces played in theatre. With but a rare exception Clubs were composed of men of no education whatever. While P. M. was appointed Deputy Surveyor—Surveyed from 1832–1834 pretty steadily—Came to New Salem in Spring of 1831—Spring of '32 went to Black Hawk War—

Man who was a candidate for Captain against L. he had formerly worked for but had fallen out with him and left him because he was so *tyrannical*. Way Capt was chosen was that the candidates stood out alone and the men walked to the man that they chose to be their leader. At least three out of every four went to Lincoln at once, when it was found that he was the choice they kept coming over to him from until his opponent was left standing almost alone. He was the most influential man in neighborhood and I felt badly to see him cut so.

HENRY McHENRY

I went to L with a case to prosecute—would not take it because he said I was not strictly in the right—Could give the other party a great deal of trouble and perhaps beat him but had better let suit alone. In 1833, I think went to Springfield and bought at an auction a copy of Blackstone. When he began to study law he would go day after day for weeks and sit under an oak tree on hill near Salem, and read—moved round tree to keep in shade—was so absorbed that people said he was crazy—Sometimes did not notice people when he met them—Had a case on hands for me for three years, and took it through three courts to Supreme Court and only charged me $75. When he rised to speak there was always profound silence—Never knew him to swear or drink a drop of liquor in his life. Was always on the side of the weak.

L. M. Smith who was in L company says he thinks L finally got every vote for Captain—If I should mention any one thing as eminently peculiar of Lincoln, it would be that during an acquaintance of 30 years, I never heard him state or contend for any thing he did not believe—Denton Offutt once said that he thought L had a better mind than any man in the U. S.

HON. JOHN T. STUART

We got back from Black Hawk war ten days before election—L's friends had proposed him for legislature—

There are no sticking points in his history—Groth was steady, gradual and constant—L not so ready or ingenious as Douglas—first impressions not reliable—when he has time to reflect is a very safe man—

Better at defending and improving existing sytsems than in originating—Does not believe in reforming so much as perfecting—

I believe if elected Pres. he will have a *purer administration* than there has ever been in our Country—Mind of a metaphysical and philosophical order—His knowledge of the languages is limited but in other respects I consider a man of very general and varied knowledge—Has made Geology and other sciences a special study—Has an inventive faculty—Is always studying into the nature of things. Oldest boy 17—Wife is a woman of fine intellect very ambitious—Sincerity his *forte* before a jury—excels in whatever requires close reasoning—

[June, 1834]

To the county commissioners court of the county of Sangamon at its June term 1834.

We the undersigned being appointed to view and locate a road. Begining at Musick's ferry on Salt creek. (Via) New Salem to the county line in the direction to Jacksonville—respectfully report—that we have performed the duties of said view and located as required by law and that we have made the location on good ground and believe the establishment of the same to be necessary and proper—

The enclosed map gives the courses and distances as required by law

Michael Killion
Hugh Armstrong
A. Lincoln

From March 4, 1847, until March 3, 1849, Mr. Lincoln was a Whig member of the House of Representatives, in the Congress of the United States. From the standpoint of insight into his own character, the material for that period, as represented in the papers, is generally disappointing. His correspondence was principally concerned with securing or maintaining public office. Naturally, the appeals made to him ordinarily emanated from gentlemen belonging to his own party, but this was not always the case.

John Alexander McClernand, like Mr. Lincoln, was a native of Kentucky who had emigrated to Illinois, a lawyer, a veteran of the campaign against Black Hawk, a member of the same Congress, and years later was to become a prominent brigadier and major general of Volunteers in the war for the Union. But McClernand was a Democrat, a dissimilarity which did not deter him in 1847 from asking favors of one who espoused an opposing political cause. Witness the following letter:

PRIVATE

Mt. Vernon. Ill.
May 26. 1847.

My dr. sr.

I wish you to write to the Secretary of the Home Department stating your wish that he should not remove Braxton Parish from the Land Receiver's office at Shawneetown without first consulting you, and if it is determined on to make a [*removal*] change, I wish you to suspend the change until Mr. Parish's Commission expires. I make this as a personal request, going further for Mr. P. than I would for myself. I have been induced to [*do so*] make the request because Mr. P. lately left his home in Franklin Co. to hold the office; because he has incured [sic] considerable expense in relocating; in short because his removal now would *ruin* him pecuniarily. *You may count upon me under like circumstances* for *a similar favor;* or for a response in any way in my power. What you may write me in answer will be held in inviolable confidence. Drop me a line directed to Shawneetown.

Yours, &c.
J. A. McClernand

Hon. A. Lincoln.

As General Taylor's inauguration approached, loyal and "deserving" Whigs looked forward with hope and expectation to an improvement of their personal fortunes. It was in this atmosphere that Joshua F. Speed, one of Mr. Lincoln's most steadfast and confidential friends, wrote to him on February 13, 1849. When Mr. Lincoln replied a week later he reported: "I am flattered to learn that Mr. Crittenden has any recollection of me which is not unfavorable; and for the manifestation of your kindness towards me, I sincerely thank you. Still there is nothing about me which would authorize me to think of a first-class office; and a second-class one would not compensate me for being snarled at by others who want it for themselves. I believe that, so far as the Whigs in Congress are concerned, I could have the Genl. Land Office almost by common consent; but then Sweet, and Don: Morrison, and Browning, and Cyrus Edwards all want it. And what is worse, while I think I could easily take it myself, I fear I shall have trouble to get it for any other man in Illinois."

House Reps. 13 Feby 1849

Dear Lincoln,

I wish to write to you fully freely and in *strict confidence* of my action as negotiator in the matter which was the subject of your last letter to me—

I introduced the subject by drawing the Governor out first upon the talent, capacity, and standing of Douglas Breeze & others—

Having done this by way of directing his attention to Illinois men —I elicited without exciting distrust an opinion from him as to the capacity of Hardin Baker & yourself—

Do not communicate it to B. for it may prejudice him against the Governor—But in my opinion you stand higher in his estimation than he—Bakers moral weight is not as great as it should be—His career is regarded as erratic—and he is not thought to possess those patient, plodding, business qualifications so necessary to make a first rate Cabinet Officer—

I do not however believe that Crittenden will exert much influence —he has more confidence in Taylors judgment of men than in his own—He will I think take a place in the Cabinet himself—and beyond this, in the formation of the Cabinet I do not think he will go—

So much for my mission in behalf of our friend—

Now for yourself—If you desire any thing—Bob Todd has as much influence with Crittenden as any one here—

Do not throw cold water on B's hopes by communicating any thing here written—I hope he may succeed—and as I said before I do not believe Crittenden will aid at all in the formation of the Cabinet—

Your friend
J. F. Speed

———— • ————

Even his wife's family looked to Congressman Lincoln to find a place for one of its members who had fallen on hard times. Hence these letters from Mrs. Lincoln's father Robert Smith Todd, her uncle David Todd, and her cousin Anne E. [Todd] Campbell.

Frankfort Feb. 20. 1849

Dear Sir

I take the liberty of enclosing you a letter from my brother David of Missouri, soliciting at the hands of Genl. Taylor an appointment for his son in law Mr. Campbell, accompanied by one from Mr. Crittenden. David & myself are acquainted personally with the Genl. & Mr. Crittenden is our friend.

Please use your influence to get this matter done by the use of the enclosed papers or such as you choose.

Govr. Metcalfe & Mr. Underwood, will I am sure aid you and desire you would in my name solicit their Co operation—I have been quite unwell for a few days and worn down with legislative labours, which are any thing but agreeable to me. We are all very well, except myself.

Respectfully
Yours
R. S. Todd

❀
❀　❀
❀

[This is endorsed by Lincoln:] Recommendation sent to Home Dept.

Columbia Mo. 3. Feby. 1849.

Dear Robert:

I take the liberty of enclosing you a proposed recommendation of my son in law Mr. Thomas M. Campbell of Boonville in this State, for an appointment as a clerk in some of the departments at Washington, under the incoming administration. He is in dependant in circumstances owing to a failure in mercantile concerns, a few years back, as is universally believed by over confidence in a manager of his concerns who stripped him—and is revelling upon his means. His energy has supported himself and family, and can yet do so— but a situation now desired, would place him in a more comfortable situation. Those, who are in the West, have been for years placed by the action of the General as well as State governments, in perfect dependance, without the least aid from official station; and it is only by the elective power for small offices, that, any, opposing the democracy can obtain the least favor. It is thus, now, in the five States adjoining, Arkansas, Missouri, Iowa, Wisconsin & Illinois. I venture to say that in neither is an office held under State or U. S. appointment, by a Whig: and you know Mr. Lincoln is the only Whig member of Congress from either. Should things so continue, or if the new administration, for want of information, or other cause, remain indifferent to our condition, we should remain the lowest *serfs* of party in the Union. We have never yielded a contest for our principles, and from the causes stated a better set of Whigs, and better qualified for office, exist no where, than in the West. I rather offer these remarks as an excuse for troubling you with the application named than for any other. Mr. Campbell was raised in Philadelphia, his father Mr. Q. Campbell is alive, and he will receive aid from his friends in that quarter. I desire also to aid him, if I can; and recommend him as a well informed, intelligent man, about 40 years old, with a small family to support, of unquestioned integrity and good morals.

I desire [to] you to present my wishes, with the recommendation to Mr. Crittenden, and obtain a letter from him or an endorsement on mine, as he may desire—and that your own be added in some form—and that you by letters to Govr. Metcalf and Judge Underwood, request their letters or recommendations to the proper department, and enclose the whole to Mr. Lincoln, with a request that he add his efforts, and place them before the departments after the inauguration. You will greatly oblige me in this matter, if you will take the interest in it, that I solicit, for I feel myself, rather presuming too much, to act more open in it, (had I power to effect any thing, which I confess I have not.)

My family are in good health: my oldest son for 18 mos. has been in Louisiana, (at Bastrop) practicing law successfully; my other (a physician) follows him next month. Of them, I have no fears—for they are strictly moral, persevering, and qualified in their professions—with ideas of strict economy, which they practise upon. My youngest daughter is finishing school. Saml. B. Todd enjoys better health than usual, his family are well—so with R. North's family—I farm a little, and peddle the law out, and make a living—and enjoying health, feel contented.

Let me hear oftener from you

Affectionately David Todd.

Columbia April 29th/49

Dear Sir

More than a month since my father received a letter from Uncle R. S. Todd of Lexington in which he mentioned having enclosed to you a letter from Gov Crittenden to Gen Taylor in behalf of my husband who is an applicant for a small office in Washington. He left home about a month since. I received a letter from him last evening from Washington in which he expresses great disappointment in not finding the letter. He supposed you would have left it, directed to him, and requested me to write you, requesting the favor of writing to him at Philadelphia immediately if you had received such a letter; if so where it could be found. Please direct to Thomas M. Campbell Care of Quentin Campbell. Let me also solicit the favor on the score of both old acquaintance and relationship your influence in behalf of my husband, a letter from you to any of your influential friends at Washington would be highly acceptable and very gratefully received by him. He has some warm Eastern friends, among them Mr. J Ingersol who mentioned to Mr. C. being acquainted with you. Your wife is acquainted with my husband, and I hope thinks him very clever. You I hope will be influenced by her and myself to have the same opinion. Were you to know him I am sure you would. Please remember me most affectionately to Mary. I should be delighted to once more see my dear relatives at Springfield. They are and ever will be among my highest and dearest memories. Be kind enough to remember me to all of them and excuse in me the trouble I have given you and believe me sincerely your

friend and cousin
Ann E. Campbell

Should you have forgotten, ask Mary who I am?

From February 14 to June 21 the Honorable Abraham Lincoln, of Illinois, was preoccupied with the question of appointment to the commissionership of the General Land Office. At first he endorsed the candidacy of Cyrus Edwards, while his colleague, Edward D. Baker, urged the choice of Don Morrison. It soon became apparent that unless they could agree upon a recommendation the desirable post might be lost to Illinois. When he returned to Springfield, friends urged Mr. Lincoln himself to seek the place, and in April he yielded to their solicitations provided the cause of Edwards and Morrison became hopeless. Meanwhile, Justin Butterfield, a Chicago lawyer, had entered the lists. A friend of Henry Clay and Daniel Webster, a wit, an eloquent orator, and a competent lawyer, Mr. Butterfield was acceptable to President Taylor's advisers, but among Mr. Lincoln's partisans he was not considered to have labored with sufficient earnestness for the principles of Whiggery to merit any consideration whatever. Eventually the competition narrowed to a struggle between Mr. Lincoln and Mr. Butterfield, and Cyrus Edwards became convinced that Mr. Lincoln had been guilty of duplicity in the half-hearted manner whereby he had represented his interests. Rivalry was intense. When at last Mr. Lincoln learned that Mr. Butterfield had defeated him, he was so grieved and hurt and embarrassed that he threw himself on his bed and lay there for more than an hour.

Among the first to urge Mr. Lincoln to seek the commissionership was the redoubtable Judge David Davis, of the Eighth Illinois Circuit.

Bloomington Ills.
Febry. 21st 1849

[*My*] *Dear Lincoln*
Your letter of Feb 12 is just received—What you state shows the infirmity of human nature—all the men who are writing to you are thinking about themselves—and they suppose that you have no need of their aid—

[*If I was in*] My advice is worth nothing. Still were I in your place, could I Get it, I would take the Land Office—

[*If so*] It is a mistake that you would necessarily [*leave*] finally surrender the Law—Shd a change of administration take place, I know you well enough to know that you could readily go back to the Law, and get in the Circuit & in the Supreme Court as good a practice as you want—

The practice of law in Illinois at present promises you but poor remuneration for the Labor—

Except in the large commercial plans of the State, the practice will always be poor—or rather, as long as you & I take any active interest in affairs.

In haste Yr friend
D. Davis

P. S.—
Duncan is going to California and it is said has resigned his Post Office—

The almost universal sentiment of the town is in favor of the appointment to the Post Office of Mr. Hazo Parsons, a worthy man who is honest, lame, poor, old, capable, & has a large & helpless family—

I believe there were some papers got up for him and sent to you while I was in Springfield.

If Duncan resigns, you had better have him Parsons appointed before you leave—The town universally wants him—

You would oblige your friends here by going to the Post office Department after the new Post Master General is in office, & having this appointment made at once—The town has been cursed with Duncan long enough—They dont want him any longer than they can help—I am just advised that a large petition for Parsons has been sent to you & Wentworth—

Yr friend
D Davis

By the close of his term in Congress (he was not a candidate for re-election) Mr. Lincoln had attained a prestige sufficient to warrant New England in trying to claim his ancestors. Indeed Mr. Lincoln, whose catchword endorsements on envelopes classified his correspondence at various times by such terms as "doctrine," "morality," "foolishness," "appointments," "union," "about California," "Sumter," "Baker's Backers," "In Cabinet," "Greeley," "private and important," "Needs no answer," "villainous articles," also included "family."

His replies to Mr. Solomon Lincoln's several inquiries are not published in the *Complete Works*, but extracts from them appear in *Notes on the Lincoln Families of Massachusetts with Some Account of the Family of Abraham Lincoln, Late President of the U. States*, by Solomon Lincoln, of Hingham; Boston, David Clapp & Son, 1865.

Hingham, Mass Feb 26. 1849.

Hon. Abraham Lincoln,
Dear Sir,

In a letter which I had the pleasure of receiving from you nearly a year since, you gave me some information of your ancestry and relatives, and mentioned that you would make inquiry of Govr. McDowell as to the existence of any of the name of *Lincoln* in his District.

Feeling a strong desire to perfect an account of all the Lincolns I venture to renew my application to you to learn whether Gov. McDowell is able to refer me to any person in his District from whom I could probably obtain any information on the subject, or will he permit me to address him. The names which you gave Abraham, Isaac, Jacob, Mordecai &c. are all family names here and I hope yet to link you to a New England ancestry.

I suppose you will in a few days leave Washington—and hence my desire to mention the subject to you before you shall lose the opportunity of seeing Gov McDowell.

If upon your return home, or at any time you should be able to devote a little time to aid my investigations, I should be pleased to learn whether—

1. Your grandfathers brothers Isaac, Jacob, Thomas & John emigrated to Kentucky?

2 If they or either of them did so emigrate—to what places in Kentucky did they emigrate & did they leave descendants?

3 Did your Uncles Mordecai & Josiah live to be heads of families?

4 If they did—have they descendants & where?

I find on reference to your letter of 24 March 1848—that your Uncle Mordecai had three sons viz.—Abraham James and Mordecai—

5 Did *they* settle in the West?

I cannot expect of course to intrude these matters upon you amid the bustle of the close of the Session—but I thought from your kind expressions of a willingness to aid me that you might have an opportunity to see Gov McDowell before your departure from Washington & to communicate to me the result.

If I shall be able to complete my investigations, it will afford me very great pleasure to communicate to you full information on the subject at any time hereafter—and if I shall be permitted to know your address I may be glad to avail myself of the opportunity to address you again—

It was a subject of regret to me when you were in this part of the country that I was so situated that I could not do myself the honor of seeking your personal acquaintance—It will be a great gratification to me if you shall be able to find opportunity to reply to such parts of this letter as may be in your power

I remain with great respect
Very truly your obt. servt.
Solomon Lincoln

It seems likely that Mr. Lincoln, while in Washington, gained a reputation and an audience as a raconteur of earthy fables. At least that is the impression derived from the following letter written by Moses Hampton who had served with him in the Thirtieth Congress.

Pittsburgh
March. 30. 1849

Hon Abm Lincoln
    Dear Sir

Do you remember the story of the old Virginian stropping his razor on a certain *member* of a young negro's body which you told and connected it with my mission to Brazil—Now my good fellow, I am "arter" that same Mission, and my object in writing to you just now is to ask the favor that you will address a letter to Gen Taylor or Mr. Clayton on that subject—and you may *spice* it just as highly as you please, I have made up my mind to *stand* it—I want that appointment and *must have it*—Will you have the goodness to procure a letter from Col Baker, who is well and favorably known to Gen Taylor—Any influence you may feel disposed to exert, shall be repaid with compound interest, if ever in my power to do so—

I want this application to be like your story of the old womans *fish*—get *larger*, the more it is handled—

Let me hear from you soon—

Very truly
Your friend &c
M. Hampton

Springfield April 6th 1849

Hon A. Lincoln
    Dear Sir

Regarding it as of great importance to the interests of Illinois to have the Commissioner of the Genl Land Office given to one of our own Citizens; and being Satisfied from what we learn from Washington, that you are the only man in the State that can secure the Appointment, it is our earnest desire that you should without delay press your claims upon Genl. Taylor for the Office.

If you will consent to do so, it will afford us great pleasure to use our influence to promote your success; while at the same time we will take care that no misapprehensions on the part of your friends who are now Soliciting the appointment, shall render you in their estimation obnoxious to the suspicion of having acted in bad faith towards them personally—

Your early attention to the Subject is in our opinion [*is*] of great importance in the present posture of affairs—

Please inform us at your Earliest Convenience your determination

Very Respectfully
Your Friends
A. G. Henry
W. B. Warren
Wm. Pope
John T. Stuart
Simeon Francis

Springfield Ills. April 7. 1849

Gentlemen:

In answer to your note concerning the General Land Office I have to say that, if the office can be secured to Illinois by my consent to accept it, and not otherwise, I give that consent—Some months since I gave my word to secure the appointment to that office of Mr. Cyrus Edwards, if in my power in case of a vacancy; and more recently I stipulated with Col. Baker that if Mr. Edwards and Col. J. L. D. Morrison could arrange with each other for one of them to withdraw, we would jointly recommend the other—In relation to these pledges, I must not only be chaste but above suspicion—If the office shall be tendered to me, I must be permitted to say "Give it to Mr. Edwards, or, if so agreed by them, to Col. Morrison, and I decline it; if not, I accept"—With this understanding you are at liberty to procure me the offer of the appointment if you can; and I shall feel complimented by your effort, and still more by its success—It should not be overlooked that Col. Baker's position entitles him to a large share of control in this matter; however, one of your number, Col. Warren, knows that Baker has at all times been ready to recommend me, if I would consent—It must also be understood that if at any time previous to an appointment being made, I shall learn that Mr. Edwards & Col. Morrison have agreed, I shall at once carry out my stipulation with Col. Baker as above stated—

Yours truly
A. Lincoln

Col. W. B. Warren, & others.

When Mr. Lincoln was competing for the Land Office commissionership, he was kept informed of the posture of affairs in Washington by Josiah M. Lucas who then held a somewhat precarious position in that bureau. Mr. Lucas was a citizen of Jacksonville, Illinois, who at one time owned and edited the *Illinoisan,* served as recorder of Morgan County, and whose federal offices included the postmastership of the House of Representatives and the Consulate at Tunstall, England.

Washington April 12/49

Dear Sir

If I may be permitted to trespass upon your time and patience a few minutes while I urge upon you the necessity of action as regards the Commissioner of the Genl. Land Office. Notwithstanding you may have an understanding with Ewing (I do not know that you have) admitting that you may have—Still I believe there is danger. I do know that Butterfield is trying his best for the place, although not here in person, he is operating through friends—I know further that he is telegraphing persons here, [*second*], who are in power second to Cabinet stations to leave nothing undone &c. Perhaps you are aware that several of the Cabinet are for him, for *something*, and Ewing, I have reason to think is his friend. Some fellow once wrote that pledges made by politicians were written in sand, or [*in the way*] and I think myself few are to be trusted—the fidelity of some I have proved—therefore, I would urge you to do something and that soon—delays are dangerous—and nothing is well done, 'till 'tis done; I do think that you could get the appointment—and every whig in Illinois with few exceptions—would say *amen*—I can't understand Baker—[*far*] for the life of me—I disliked the idea of his throwing cold water on your case when all the Illinoians here wanted you to get the place. If there cannot be an *early* arrangement between Gov Edwards & Morrison—[*the*] neither will get it, Butterfield may get it, but there is much danger of the State loosing it, as Alabama, Florida & Mississippi are claiming it. If you dont get it try and get Morrison to go in for Edwards—Do something quick—any body but Butterfield, however—he would be a mere tool, without any will of his own.

There is no little confusion here, yet, with regard to the offices. The fine building of the sons of temperance burned last night—I hope that you will write me soon.

I would like, through you, to get some prominence, with old Ewing, and Col Warren, the 2d Assistant P. M. G.—I could, perhaps, be of service to our friends in Illinois, a letter to them would set the thing right, perhaps, they will be sometimes, no doubt at a loss, and would like to have at times a Whig to consult from [*that*] our State—

Respectfully yours &c
J. M. Lucas

N. B. Tell Francis to send me his "journal"

J. M. L.

———•———

Z. C. Robbins, who in April 1849 wrote to inventor Lincoln about a device for lifting steamboats and other vessels over shoals, was a Washington "patent agent."

Washington D. C. April 13th 1849

My Dear Sir

It affords me much pleasure to inform you that I have obtained a favorable decision on your application for a patent for your improved manner of combining expansible buoys with a vessel, and operating the same. The patent will be issued in about a month.

Wishing you prosperity and happiness, I remain Truly Yours

Z. C. Robbins

Hon. A. Lincoln

Washington April 15. 1849

Dear Sir

Excuse me for again troubling you with [any] another letter but believing it to be my duty I take the responsibility. Since my last letter things have come to my knowledge which convince me almost beyond a dobt that the strongest efforts are making to make Butterfield the Commissioner. I do know *positively* that a strong [*eastern*] *Eastern influence* is at work for him and I further know that Lyle Smith was telegraphed to come on here, and that he is here urging his appointment in every conceivable shape—and that it is with Butterfield's knowledge and solicitation that he does it—[*and that*] I have *good reasons* for believing that Truman Smith and Danl. Webster are backing Butterfield—Do [*do*] not call me an alarmist—but, Sir, I ask you if it does not look squally. Things are moved here by *personal importunity*—And allow me to inform you, that in my humble opinion, unless something is done by *you—you*, Sir, the aforesaid Butterfield will succeed. The reason why I emphasize the word *you* is, because *you* possess an influence *here*—Baker has little, or no influence, and the *wind* has been taken out of his sails, until they *flop*. You may doubt me but I believe I am right in my prediction.—Butterfield, you know was asking to be Soliciter—that place, I am credibly informed is to be given to a man in Alabama—I know that Butterfield told Judge Young that he was not after his place, but that he was anxious for him to remain—now why, this double dealing—

You know too, that he opposed Williams, and that he previously disavowed any intention to do so—I for one, and I know that it is the [choice] desire of the Whigs, that you should be the man—and I must confess I feel much Solicitude in your behalf—I fear that friend Edwards stands no chance—Morrison is out of the question, [I think]—You, I think, can [fool] foil Mr. B. If you intend to make an effort, I should like to be apprised of it. You can confide in me, [having] I [hope] ask that what I here write will be considered confidential—for should Butterfield be the Commissioner, [it] I shall, of course, be at his mercy, nothing, however, exists between us but friendship,—but individually, I prefer someone else—and I do Know that he would not be the choice of the Whigs of Illinois. Baker has, from cause, injured himself, and has no influence, I regret this very much.

Bond will be Marshal,—Prentice's commission has been annulled—on account of being behind with the Government. I could inform you of certain rumors about [places] appointments &c but will decline, as it may not be interesting.

Yours in haste
J. M. Lucas

Washington May 7. 1849

Dear Sir

I have received your favors,—I get my information from a semi official source, that Judge Young will be removed [by] between this and the end of the fiscal year. I believe that, could you be present in Washington that you could defeat Butterfield—I come pretty nigh knowing it. As it regards Morrison, he is out of the question—and it is nonsense for him to think about it—I verily believe that you could get it—and if my old friend Edwards was [out] off the track your chance is the best of any—because Collamer is for you and so is old Rough & tumble—My advice is that you come on *immediately* [to] and work for Edwards as long as there *is hope for him* with the *written* understanding with Edwards that, provided, he cannot succeed, for him to transfer his strength to you—This done my [word] opinion is that the thing will go [as] right—I feel it in my bones, and when that *sign* is right, I am seldom mistaken. I know that you are under obligations to Edwards, but I know enough of that good old gentleman, that he is reasonable, and will do what is right—by the by, no man has a higher regard for Cyrus Edwards than myself.

If you will have an *immediate* understanding with Edwards to the effect suggested and come on here *with all possible dispatch*—I am next to certain the thing will work—there is no mistake about it. Let Browning, D. Davis, Woodson, Yates, Williams, and such leading Whigs as you know immediately address the President. If the thing is pushed *immediately,* the thing is settled right—otherwise old Butternuts gets it—Who in the thunder wants him? I am ready to swear that Illinois does not—and if I could be in Illinois 3 weeks I could defeat him if the voice of the Whigs there are to be regarded.

We are all for you here—as soon as a fellow comes here from Illinois or Missouri *I set him*—I have got the boys together on several occasions and they are all for you to a man—and it is a strong game, and Ewing feels it sensibly. I hope you got Davis' letter—he has written a strong *editorial and sent home*—I hope it will have its effect —*By all means come on*—Young has written you. Send me the letter to [Ya] Ewing, Taylor, Warren & Collamer &c &c I can help my friends better. As to myself I do not know whether I am entirely safe or not—I think, however, my chances for permanency is good. Any help you can throw in will be thankfully received.

Please write me immediately—I will write Dr. Henry in a few days—

Your friend
J. M. Lucas

--- • ---

Judge Richard Montgomery Young, the retiring commissioner of the General Land Office (he was a Democrat who owed his appointment to President Polk) hoped that Mr. Lincoln might succeed him. "Mr. B. of C." was, of course, Mr. Butterfield of Chicago.

(STRICTLY CONFIDENTIAL)

Washington City, May 7. 1849.

My Dear Sir

As the time is fast approaching when it is thought some one may be selected as my successor; and as I feel much concern for the welfare of those who will be left behind me, in this office, with whom I have been in daily intercourse now for upwards of two years, I have thought it would not be amiss to address you a line at the present juncture, so that you may peradventure (as Judge Scates would say) by timely interference prevent, what otherwise may happen—that is the appointment of some one who would not be acceptable—You know what I said to Mr. Ewing in regard to the Successorship—and why not lay modesty aside and strike for yourself—From what I can learn Mr. B. of C.—contrary to what he said to me when you was here, and after having lost the Solicitorship of the Treasury, is now playing a strong game for the Land office—Some think he will succeed—Now cant you prevent, by urging the claims of one A. Lincoln —who I am sure, would be more acceptable here than any Whig in Illinois? What say you—Whatever you do, it will be well for it to be done quickly—and I am very sure that you can succeed better with this man Lincoln than any person else—

Your friend
R. M. Young

Hon. A. Lincoln
Springfield Ill.

I understood from Judge Collamer, some week or two ago that he would prefer this Mr. Lincoln, he thought—He at the same time asked me what I thought of this Mr. B. of C.—

Washington May 10/49

Dear Sir

If you are not worn out with my letters you can read this—Chambers of the Republican is here and he informs that he has been informed by letter from St. Louis, that Cyrus Edwards has withdrawn in your favor—I hope it is so. Chambers, inclines towards Morrison, but says between you and him—he has no preference—he is decidedly, however, against Butterworth—and says he won't do at all. Mr. Chambers, showed me a letter purporting to be the proceedings of a meeting held at the Court house of Randolph County which urges the appointment of Morrison—I judge the Court of that County was in cession, and a few loafers, having little else to do, got up the thing. The proceedings contained no doubt all the names that endorsed it, the number is five with Col Servants at its head, the letter was written by Servants. I noticed that one of the signatures was a written thus "————— Edwards, of Perry County." Now I still am of the opinion, from all that I can learn, that you can get the appointment. I would give it as my opinion if it is worth any thing—viz. *Come on immediately,* bring with you all the strength you can—of course you know all about such things and will please excuse me for my zeal in your behalf may be plead as the excuse I am thinking that I will get [*up*] those from the West here present to write letters to the President in your behalf. I don't see that it can have any bad effect, if properly [*manaj*] managed.

Judge Young, I am certain will resign—at least he told me that he would not hold the office—my impressions are that the cabinet are treating him cavalierly and are making the place *too hot* for him. I think a great deal of Young and it is wrong to abuse so good a man. I assure you there is not a moment to loose and if you do any thing, *let it be done quickly.* Pocket your *modesty,* as the preacher did his religion until you thrash *Butterworth.* I just know you can do it, if you will come on—

Your friend
J. M. Lucas

Washington May [*10*] *9/49*

Sir

This is the second letter which I have written you to-day—I found out the following when too late to take No. 1 out of the office so I send after it No. 2.

I have just learned from Chambers that Ewing *insists* upon Butterfield—and that he is *his man*—[*he us*] Ewing used this language viz. "That he anticipated much trouble in land titles—and that as the man was to come from Illinois," that he chooses Butterfield for the reason that he is the most profound lawyer in the State, especially as a Land lawyer—this is his language—Morrison is writing to Chambers but C. told me he intended to write to Morrison to knight that he need not come on that Butterfield would get the appointment.

Now, Sir, you have the case before you, and I doubt not that you can see how the land lies. Taylor is for you, I think, and so is Collamer. Whatever you do, do quickly

Yours &c
Lucas

The orthographical idiosyncrasies of Colonel Augustus H. Chapman, who wrote of the serious illness of Thomas Lincoln, extended even to his rendering of Abraham Lincoln's foster brother's name: John D. Johnston. Colonel Chapman's wife Harriet was the daughter of Mr. Lincoln's cousin, Dennis Hanks, and once had stayed for more than a year and a half in the Lincoln home in Springfield, where she found Mrs. Lincoln extremely difficult to get along with.

Charleston Ills May 24th 1849

Mr. Lincoln

Sir at the special request of J. D. Johnsin I write you to inform you of the very Severe illness of your Father. He was atacken with a lesion of the Heart Some time Since & for the last few days Has been getting much Worse & at this time He is very Low indeed. He is very anxious to See you before He dies & I am told that His Cries for you for the last few days are truly Heart-Rendering. He wishes you to come & see Him instontly if you possibly can. If you are fearfull of Leaving your family on account of the Children & can bring them

With you we would be very Glad for you to bring them with you.
the Health of our place is excelent & Harriett & I would be very glad
to Have bring them with you as we are very comfortably fixed & will
do all we can to render your stay agreeable.

Yours in great Haste

A. H. Chapman

you need Have no fears of your Fathers Suffering for any thing
He may need as Harriett & I will See that He Has everything He
may need.

A. H. C.

Dennis Hanks once wrote of Thomas Lincoln that he "loved his Reli-
tives Do anything for them he could," but he doubted that Abraham returned his father's affection. He didn't know whether "Abe Loved his
farther Very well or Not," but added "I Dont think he Did." In any event
he seems not to have responded to this appeal from John D. Johnston.

friday morning Char. May 25th 1849

Dear Brother

I hast to inform you That father is yet a Live & that is all & he
Craves to See you all the time & he wonts you to Come if you ar able
to git hure, for you are his only Child that is of his own flush & blood
& it is nothing more than natere for him to crave to See you, he says
he has all most Despared of Seeing you, & he wonts you to prepare
to meet him in the unknown world, or in heven, for he thinks that
ower Savour Savour has a Crown of glory, prepared for *him* I wright
this with a bursting hart, I Came to town for the Docttor, & I won
you to make an effort Come, if your ar able to get hure, & he wonts
me to tell your wife that he Loves hure & wants hur to prepare to
meet him at ower Savours feet, we are all well, your Brother in hast

J. D. Johnston

As announced in Colonel Chapman's second letter, Thomas Lincoln recovered from this illness. He died January 17, 1851.

Charleston Ills May 28th 1849

Mr Lincoln

Sir on Friday last I wrote you at the request of J. D. Johnson which I suppose Has given you Considerable unecessary trouble on account of your Father. I was fearful at the time I wrote to you that I was giving you considerable unecessary uneasiness & So told Johnsin, but he said that it was not So. I wished him to wait untill Allison returned from your Fathers but he would not consent on the grounds that if He did not Send you a Letter then that he would not Have the Opportunity of writing until the present Mail. So I wrote you at his Earnest Solicitation & He had the Letter Mailed instontly. I now Have the pleasure of informing you that your Father is not only out of all Danger but that He is not afflicted with a Disease of the Heart as Dr. Allison Supposed all along but that his illness arose from an unusual amount of matter being confined in His Lungs which accasioned the Oppression of the Heart & Led Allison to Suppose this Disease was one of the Heart—Yesterday & to day He has raised a Large amount of Matter or fleghm from Lungs & is almost entirely Releaved & will doubtless be well in a Short time. I hope you will receave this before you get off for this place if you are intending to come here as I would be very Sorry indeed for my Last Letter to cause you to Leave any important business that you Might Have on Hands & that required your imediate attention. I hope you will forgive me for writing you as I did without Knowing what I was about & promise for the future to be more carefull Harriett Sends Her love to you all

Respectfully yours
A. H. Chapman

Springfield Ills. June 5. "49

Dear Sir

Would you as soon I should have the Genl. Land Office as any other Illinoian? A. Yes If you would, Write me to that effect at Washington where I shall be soon—No time to loose—

Yours in haste
                    A. Lincoln

I most sincerely wish you success.

                              D. E.

Taylorville. Christian Co.
June 6. 1849

Dear Lincoln—

I rec'd on Yesterday a letter from Dr. Henry telling of the trouble about the Land Office—& that you had gone to Washington, & desiring me get any Whigs hereabouts to join in a letter addressed to Genl. Taylor

I have written herewith a Letter which I enclose to you—& if it suits—& will do any good, of course deliver it—

The appointment of old Butterfield would be outrageous—The party in this State—if such is the policy—is flat—

Is it not strange—that the voice of Members of Congress from a State is not taken about appointments

                    Wishing you success
                              Your friend
                                   David Davis

Emerson signed the Letter with me—He was the only Whig Lawyer here out of Springfield—The untimely death of my poor friend Colton has overwhelmed me with grief—

COPY.

Springfield. June 8. 1849

Hon: N. Pope:
Dear Sir:

I do not *know* that it would, but I can well enough conceive it *might* embarrass you to *now* give a letter reccommending me for the General Land Office—Could you not, however, without embarrassment, or any impropriety, so far vindicate the truth of history, as to briefly state to me, in a letter, what you *did* say to me last spring on my arrival here from Washington, in relation to my becoming an applicant for that office? Having at last concluded to be an applicant, I have thought it is perhaps due me, to be [*able*] enabled to show the influences which brought me to the conclusion—among which influences the wishes and opinions you expressed were not the least—

Your Obt. Servt.
A. Lincoln

✿
✿ ✿
✿

[This copy is in Lincoln's holograph]

Springfield June 9th 1849

Dr Sir

Situated as we are it is unpleasant to my feeling and I presume equally so to yours to go to Washington upon such a mission as we are embarked in—I would wish to avoid the imputation which such a proceeding may subject us to among friends and enemies—I therefore propose for your consideration whether it would not be better for us both to remain at home: which I am willing to do, If you are —please send an answer by the bearer:

Respectfully
Your Obt Servt
J. Butterfield

Hon. A. Lincoln

JUNE 1849

Springfield. June 10/49

A Lincoln Esq—
  Dear friend.

I learn that Mr. B. has left this morning—for Chicago—and thence to Washington—City—I have no doubt of your success—still the true plan is to leave no stone unturned. Let me then advise you—not to delay any time on your way—reach the City as soon as possible—I have written several letters to my friends in the South requesting them to forward letters *direct* to Old Zack. They were put in the office this morning—I was told this morning that Butterfield is very much alarmed—it is *thought* by news he has rec'd from *Washington* —*Nil desperandum* is the motto of physicians in desperate cases of disease & I presume it will be Mr. B's in his case

Your friend truly
J. M. Davis

Mt. Carmel Wabash Co. Illinois
11th June 1849

James Brooks Esq—
  Dear Sir

Some remarks of yours occassioned by the appointment of the Marshall for New York has induced me to adress you on the subject of an appointment now pending at Washington. I believe it is conceded that the Com. of the Land Office is to be taken from this State. The appointment rest between two individuals Hon A. Lincoln late M. C. from this State & a Mr. Butterfield from Chicago. If the administration pays any regard to the wishes of the Whigs & more particularly the working Whigs Mr. L. will receive the appointment. Mr. Lincoln from the first organisation of our party in 1839. to this day has been active in the cause: was a candidate for Elector in /40 & /44: traversed the State from one end to the other, addressed the people in almost every County & with great effect. I speak but the universal sentiment of the Whigs when I say that he has contributed more to sustain the Whig cause than any other man

183

in the State. And while he has been thus active he has at all times retained the respect & confidence of the Democrats & probably there is no man in our ranks whose appointment would be more satisfactory to them than Mr. Lincolns. Mr. L. fitness in point of ability will not be denied. All of which together with his *general acquaintance* would make it a suitable & extremely popular appointment with all parties in this State.

On the other hand if Mr. Butterfield has ever aided the Whigs in any way I have yet to learn it. Indeed, I never heard of him as a Whig, never met him in Convention, never knew of his addressing the people at any time. But he may have done some service in the cause, yet it is so slight as not to be remarked. I have been familiar with all prominent political movements in this State from the first organisation of the party in 1839 to the present day: was present at the first convention in that year, a member of the one that formed the ticket in /44 & at others in /47 & /48. And in all that time [*from*] viz. from /39 to /49 in constant correspondence with Whigs in all parts of the State & while Mr. Lincoln was frequently referred to as addressing or about to address meetings I never heard Mr. Butterfield mentioned as in any way connected with our party. I do not wish to be understood as saying that Mr. B. is not a Whig. I presume he is: but being a gentleman of decided ability has taken good care to husband the talents given him for some other purpose than advancing the interest of the party to which he belonged.

I have taken the liberty addressing you on on this subject because I know you feel an anxious desire for the success of Whig principles: and hope if not inconsistent with your views will aid us *Working Whigs* in securing the appointment of Mr. Lincoln.

Mr. Lincoln is now in Washington City. For myself I refer you to my brother in Law R. H. Waller Esq. of your City

I am yours respectfully

Wm. T. Page

Buffalo June 13. 1849

My dear Sir.

Yours of the 5th inst. was rec'd. this morning.

I think i gave last winter to Mr. Butterfield of Chicago a letter recommending him for some place—it may have been Comr. of the G. L. Office for which I understand he is a candidate—and I cannot therefore consistently write for you such a letter as you desire.

I have known Mr. Butterfield for many years & have a high opinion of his competency & should hate therefore to do any thing which might seem to be opposed to the letter I gave him last winter.

In great haste
Very truly yours
N. K. Hall

The Hon
A. Lincoln
Wash'n

Chicago June 15 1849

My dear Sir,

I have heard that you are a candidate for the office of Land-Commr.—If so is there any way in which I can serve you? I neither have nor seek influence with "the powers that be"—believing the commodity rather troublesome than useful—yet for your sake I should be willing to have a little—helping your appointment would give me great pleasure 1st—because I know you would make an excellent public officer & 2dly.—on account of the personal feelings of kindness & esteem with which in common with all the Whigs of the 30th Congress I regard you

I am very truly &c
William D. Alt

Hon. Abm Lincoln
Dr. Sir

Your letter although dated June 4th did not reach until the 16th— Most assuredly I would not only as soon you should have the Genl.

Land Office as any other Illinoian, but if the appointment was in my power I would give it to you *immediately or sooner* if possible. I have written a *hasty* letter and directed it to the Secy. of the Home Departt. without knowing whether that is exactly right or not—But if it is such as you would be willing to show, its direction may not be very material. I wish you success.

> Very truly
> Yours &c.
> *Chester Butler*

Wilkes Barre June 18. 1849

> *Milton Pa. June 18. 1849*

Friend Lincoln

As I "would as leave," and a little leaver, see you in the General Land Office, "as any other Illinoian" I send you the enclosed. I recd. your letter yesterday, & answer at once as you say no time is to be lost. Go it strong! & do not permit any one to *check mate* you. I hope to hear of your success.

All well. I am now engaged in the dry details of the law, & expect to continue so.

> Yours truly
> *Jas. Pollock*

Dear Lincoln

I give you a letter with great pleasure. I had not only "as lief you should have the office as another Illinoisan" but a little "liefer."

I remember very well when a small band of Genl. Taylors friends (30 in number) at Washington, and you one of them, brought about his nomination: since then many have received the credit of that act who are in no way entitled to it, but about your action there is no mistake

> Truly yrs
> *Alexander Evans*
> Elkton Md. June 23. 1849

Disillusioned, mortified, and aggrieved by his failure to secure the Land Office appointment, Mr. Lincoln returned to Springfield and his practice. Gradually he resumed his place at the bar. He paid little attention to politics. And then, in the summer of 1854, something happened which marked the beginning of the most important period of his career. On May 30 President Franklin Pierce signed the Kansas-Nebraska Bill, which had been championed by Democratic Senator Stephen A. Douglas, of Illinois, and which repealed the Missouri Compromise. In accordance with the "popular sovereignty" doctrine of Senator Douglas, it would leave to the citizens of the area the right to determine whether it should be free or slave-holding territory. An immediate result was the redistribution of political forces. Mr. Lincoln did not at once announce his position, but in August he took the stump in behalf of the candidacy of Richard Yates for the House of Representatives on an "Anti-Nebraska" platform. A change came into the matter and manner of his speeches. They contained a new cogency, directness, shrewd analysis, which differed conspicuously from the broad humor and oratorical flourish which formerly had characterized them. More than that, he established himself as the leader of a cause and the most outspoken opponent of the theories so eloquently expounded by the "little giant," Senator Douglas. He continued to call himself a Whig but influences were at work which would bring him into the Republican party.

Abraham Jonas, who invited Mr. Lincoln to speak in Quincy (he delivered the address at Kendall's Hall on November 1) was an English Jew, and one of Mr. Lincoln's most loyal supporters.

Quincy Ills. Sep 16. 1854

A Lincoln Esq.
Springfield Ills.
   My Dr Sir
We are in the midst of what will probably be the warmest contest for Congress that we have ever had in this district—if the election was near at hand—Williams, I think would be elected beyond a doubt—This district is to be the great battle field, the defeat of Richardson at this time, would be the downfall of Douglas, Standing and occupying the same posittion on the Nebraska humbugs—every foul and unfair means will be brought to operate against Williams— Douglas is to be here and will [*speak*] in this and other counties of

the district—Williams has just left for Oquaka—it being court in
Henderson on Monday next—and has requested me to say to you,
that he, as well as *all the Whigs* here, would be much gratified if
you could make it convenient and pay us a visit, while the little
giant is here. It is believed by all who know you, that a reply from
you, would be more effective, than from any other—I trust you may
be able to pay us the visit and thereby create a debt of gratitude on
the part of the Whigs here, which they may at some time, have it in
their power, to repay with pleasure and with interest—we do not
exactly known when Douglas will be here—but you can consent to
come, we will let you know in time—I will thank you to answer
this as soon as convenient—and be assured that nothing will afford
greater pleasure to your personal friends and the Whigs generally
than your consent to visit us—and the Douglasites would as soon see
old Nick here as yourself—The present indications here are good—
This county will do better, or I am much mistaken, than it has done
for many years—Pike will give a decided majority for us—Brown will
do as well as on former occasions, although Singleton is doing all in
his power against us—we here favorably from all parts of the district
—and I think with your assistance, we can check mate them. Trusting to hear from you soon

> I remain Yrs truly
> *A Jonas*

One week after receiving the following invitation from Mr. Wilson,
Abraham Lincoln addressed a large gathering in Chicago's North Market
Hall, and the *Journal* commented: "The impression created by Mr. Lincoln
on all men, of all parties, was first, that he was an honest man, and second,
that he was a powerful speaker."

> *Journal Office Chicago*
> *Oct 20th 1854*

Friend Lincoln

Our folks up this way would be pleased if you could make it convenient to address them at some time you may name prior to the

Election. It would be most acceptable if you could make it convenient to be here for a day or two before speaking, to learn a little of the *Northern Light,* but be assured whenever you come you will receive a cheerful welcome.

Permit me to congratulate you on "the points" you made against the "Little giant," & particularly the one where the idea of the Whig Party [*was*] being dead was repudiated—It *told* up this way with good effect. Our folks want you to come & I think it would have a most excellent effect not only upon the present canvas, but for future action consequent upon the result.

Please let me know at as early a day as practicable if you can come & we will make all the necessary arrangements. How do you relish the Election returns?

Douglas came to town last night pretending to have the ague, & probably cannot be induced to speak here again. Gen. Cass is here & is announced to speak this evening but it will be to a very slim croud. Crittenden of Ky is also here & has been for several days, & I learn that *Houston* & *Bell* are expected soon. What the movement is, I dont know, perhaps it is all accidental, but it looks to me very much as if there was going to be a shift in the wind.

Our end of this State looks very well & the lowest figures I can make adds up well among the thousands, & from the best information I can gather, having a good opportunity of knowing the defeat of Shields is certain.

You would oblige me by an early reply.

Very truly yours
Richard L. Wilson

[The envelope is addressed Hon A. B. Lincoln Springfield Ills By Mr. Horace White]

Until November, when the results of the election became known, Mr. Lincoln had had no thought of becoming a candidate for the Senate, but once he was convinced that a Whig, "by possibility," might be elected, he announced to his friends: "I want the chance of being the man." He seems to have written many letters on the subject, beginning November 10.

Horace White, who suggested the possibility of a *coup d'état,* was then in his twentieth year, and a reporter for the Chicago *Journal.* He studied Mr. Lincoln's countenance, "so overspread with sadness" that he thought "Shakespeare's melancholy Jacques had been translated from the forest of Arden." Mr. White was later to become the editor of the Chicago *Tribune.*

Springfield, Oct. 25, 1854.

Mr. Lincoln:
    Dear Sir:

In regard to your visit to Chicago concerning which Mr. Wilson wrote to you, I am authorized to state that it is the farthest from [*our*] the wishes and [*intest*] intentions of our people to deprive Mr. Gates of your assistance in case he should need it.

To come at the point at once; (I don't know whether Mr. Wilson wrote to you about it or not) the Whigs are bound to elect a U. S. Senator in place of Shields. Chicago has five votes in the Legislature and influences a great many more in Northern Illinois. Part of our [*B*] Representatives in the next Assembly will be Whigs, part Free-Soilers & part Anti-Nebraska Democrats. These Democrats might bolt at the nomination of a Whig for the Senate. It would be unprecedented if they didn't. The idea is to have you go to Chicago and make a speech. You will have a crowd of from eight to ten or fifteen thousand and the result will be that the people will demand of their Representatives to elect a Whig Senator. What might be doubtful otherwise will thus be rendered certain. The time [*to*] necessary for this *coup d' etat* would not be more than three days at the most.

Of course it is all at your discretion.

Very respectfully
Horace White
Chicago "Journal"

Hon. A. Lincoln

Mr. Lincoln was mystified by the following letter from Ichabod Codding. He replied November 27:

". . . I have been perplexed some to understand why my name was placed on that committee. I was not consulted on the subject, nor was I apprised of the appointment until I discovered it by accident two or three weeks afterward. I suppose my opposition to the principle of slavery is as strong as that of any member of the Republican party; but I have also supposed that the extent to which I feel authorized to carry that opposition, practically, was not at all satisfactory to that party."

Chicago Nov. 13 1854

Hon. A Lincoln
    Dear Sir,

By request of those members of the Republican State Central Committee, residing in Chicago & vicinity, I hereby inform you that there will be a meeting of said committee in this City this week Friday (17th inst) at the office of J. E. Farnsworth opposite the Sherman House at 2 o clock P. M. Your attendance is requested.

Yours truly
I Codding

Elihu Benjamin Washburne, who reported so encouragingly on Mr. Lincoln's prospects, was a member of the National House of Representatives.

Galena Illinois
Nov. 14. 1854.

My dear Sir

My friend, the Hon George Gage, the Senator elect from Lake & McHenry Counties, came over and spent the day with me on Sunday last. We talked a good deal about U. S. Senator and I was gratified to find that he agreed with me that you should be the man if we could elect any body. I was upon the point of writing you this fact, when I received your letter of the 10th. last night to which I now hasten to reply. You are my choice above all others and any thing I can do to secure your success, shall be done. In this district we have now made a clean thing of it so far as the Legislature is concerned. Every single Senator and representative belongs to the Republican Party. I will just tell you who they are, where they live and what their political antecedents have been:

Senators.

Geo. Gage, Lake & McHenry Counties. Free-Soiler. Strong for you. Post-office, McHenry, McHenry Co., Ills.

Wait Talcott, Winnebago district. Abolitionist, but will be practicable. P. O. Rockton, Ills.

John H. Addams, Joe Daviess & Stephenson. Lives at Cedarville, Stephenson Co. He is an old Whig and will be for you without doubt.

Representatives

Joe Daviess & Carroll. Dr. W. A. Little, of Elizabeth in this County, and Porter Sargent of Savanna, Carroll Co. Both free-soil Whigs and I have no doubt will be for you.

Stephenson Co. Thomas J. Fraser, Freeport, whom you know. He is identified against Nebraska and with the Republicans, but where he will be on Senator I do not know. I *guess* he would like to be Speaker of the House. That is worth looking to.

Winnebago. Dr. Wm. Lyman, Rockford. Originally an old democrat, but a thorough republican. I cannot say how he will be, but I think "right on the main question."

Ogle. Prof. D. J. Pinkney of Mt. Morris—Whig and Republican & I think will be for you.

Boone & McHenry. Wesley Diggins, Chemung, and Rev Luther W. Lawrence, Belvidere—the former an old abolitionist and the latter an old Whig. I think they will be for you.

Lake. Hurlbut Swan, an old Whig free-soiler, who will go with Gage. His P. O. is Fremont Centre, Lake Co.

I have not yet seen sufficient returns to know how the Legislature will stand, but it seems to me if the anti-Nebraska men or republicans have a majority in both branches you ought to be able to go through. I should like to hear from you how matters stand in this regard.

I shall leave for Washington in some ten days.

My majority is 6000 over Jackson and 5000 over both him & Ferry. I am sorry that Dick was beaten.

Yours Truly
E. B. Washburne

Peoria Novr. 16th 1854

Dear Lincoln

Your favor of the 10th instant only came to hand last evening I embrace the first opportunity to reply

Our Election here terminated gloriously. We have elected Grove and Henderson in this Representative District And Dr Arnold to the Senate in this Senatorial District Dr. Boal is also Elected to the House from the Woodford Marshal & Putnam District All of whom are good Whigs and I think all are for you And you may rest assured that I will use all my powers with them and any others in your behalf.

But allow me to call your attention to a matter connected with the subject of your letter well worthy of your attention and perhaps immediate action You I see have been Elected as a member of the Legislature. Allow me to call your attention to the 7th Section of the 3rd Article of our new Constitution which makes you ineligible for the Senate of the U. S. Now if you decline accepting the seat in the legislature and so notify the Governor and have a new Election this will save your bacon I merely suggest this as worthy of your immediate consideration It has been talked of here amongst some of us as your being the Choice for Senator And the fact of your ineligibility has been mentioned which will have a tendency to injure your prospects unless it is removed immediately. Let me hear from you on the receipt of this letter on this point Are you not ineligible if you take your Seat? Can you not decline Serving before you take your Seat and have another Election and save yourself? Be sure to write me immediately

Again let me repeat I am for you against all others from any quarter and shall be glad to do what I can for you. I believe we will have an Anti Nebraska Majority in both houses Now as Whigs we must be liberal in the organization of the Senate & House in the disposal of the offices between Whigs & Anti Nebraska democrats if we want to get the U S Senator Is not this right These are my reasons

I hope to be in Springfield in December and shall probably be there when the legislature meets. I do not know of any office I want there unless it should be to bear expenses while log rolling for friends

But write me fully on receipt of this for I can do you good if the difficulty is removed suggested above

Yours
Respectfully
E. N. Powell

Knoxville Novr. 17/54

Hon A. Lincoln
    Dr Sir

Yours of the 10th Inst. finds me with more care on my Shoulders than I can well stagger under. The death of my Partner, soon after my Return from Washington, leaving my business so much at loose ends that I am compelled to labor night & day to get Ready to Return.

In this Section you are favorably Known, and I have no doubt would be generally preferred to others

Samuel W. Brown—*Galesburg* is elected in Knox

Babcock—*Canton* in Fulton

Thos. J. Henderson *Toulon* in Starke

? Lee—Rock Island
Dr. Robert Boal—Lacon
Henry Grove—Peoria
? Rice   Oquawka

Most of these I presume you Know nearly as well as I do.

The State Register concedes the Election of *Archer* which (aside from personal Regard for Yates) is a fair offset against Harris.

So far as I am *posted* we Shall doubtless have a Majority of Anti Neb. Members in the House—*but* I *fear* that Ranged on *old* Platforms the Locos *may* prevent the Election of a Whig Senator.

If in this Respect I should be happily disappointed, and Shields place is supplied by a Whig, I shall think better of our Sucker State than I ever expected to!

Yours Very truly
James Knox

Peoria Nov 18 1854.

Dear Sir

Your favor of 13th inst is now before me. Absence from home on a visit to Chicago prevented an earlier answer.

I have no objection to stating fully my views as to the United States Senatorship. I believe that a very large majority of the men who voted for me expect me to vote for you, that is they prefer you to any other person. I confess also that so far as I am acquainted with your political views I prefer you to any other person, but before committing myself fully, it would afford me pleasure to hear from you as to one or two matters further.

1. Are you eligible to the office under our constitution. My information is that you are a member elect to the House.

2. I understand you to be opposed to the extension of Slavery into Territory now free: I would expect you to maintain this position on all occasions.

3. At some time when it could be done in a proper spirit I should like to see Slavery abolished in the District of Columbia. In my

judgment the continuance of Slavery there works no benefit to the institution in the States. I disclaim all right on the part of the Federal Government to interfere with the institution of Slavery when it exists in the States, but the power of the Government over the District is allmost universally conceded and in a proper time & manner I would rejoice to see it abolished there. Would you vote for such a law. I don't ask to become an agitator nor to go for it as a matter of insult or invitation to the South but in your own quiet good humoured way relieve the nation of the disgrace of sanctioning slavery at the National capital. And if you cannot go for that would you go for submitting the question to the people of that District for settlement. If your views harmonize with mine then you are my man as at present admired. As to your views on national policy they accord with my own altogether You may put me down as pretty sure for Abe. Will you do me the favor to send me a copy of the rules of the last House. Who do you go for for Speaker. Do you know just how matters will stand with us so far as the two houses are concerned

Yours truly
H. Grove

Hon A. Lincoln

P. S. One word further I dont want you to commit yourself to any party or views. Think and act as becomes the Senator of Illinois & Lincoln, but dont lash us to Slavery in any way.

It will be remembered that Ward Hill Lamon was a law partner of Mr. Lincoln.

Danville Illinois
Nov. 21st 1854

A Lincoln Esq
    Dear Sir:
    Your favor of the 10th instant mailed at Clinton is at hand—Since its reception I have seen Dr. Courtney (our Representative-elect)

upon the subject to which your favor related; and he authorised me to say to you that he is *"unqualifiedly for you for the U. S. Senate—before any other man in the State"*—Our citizens here appear to look forward with a great deal of interest to the time that you will be a member of that Body—there appears to be but one feeling here upon the subject—At what time during the Session of the Legislature will the Election probably come off—I [*wish*] intend, to go to see friend Campbell and will defer my visit to him until [*unti*] that event occurs provided it will come off during the early part of the Session —please let me know! and say how poor Campbell is getting—I feel a deep interest in him—

Our Clark vs Hoxworth et al. suit was again continued—owing to a misdescription of the land—you did not describe the land as it was in the Mortgage—I asked leave to amend the Bill—would I not better require them to answer under Oath? They deny everything—

I have commenced about fourteen suits against the Great Northern Rail Road Company (on appeal from the Report of the Commissioners) for damages, in the next circuit court—You will be here if you are well, will you not?—There is great excitement here all the time in regard to the bailing of George High—The horse company come to Danville every day or two supposing that I am going to have him bailed out—and they are going to take him up again immediately and take him to Indiana—I will not give them any satisfaction about it—But Levin G Parmer is going his bail & old Isaac High is going to place the money ($1500.00) in his hands to secure him—I would not be at all surprised [*that*] if they should kill him (judging from the excitement at this time)—Great excitement here about the Banks no news in Danville at this time—

Please write to me immediately on the reception of this—In great haste

Yours Respy
Ward H Lamon

P. S. In taking an appeal from the report of the Commissioners of the G. W. R. R. C. on whom must the process be served will it answer to serve it on their attorney?—A very pretty little woman spoke to me yesterday to obtain a divorce from her *"Infidel Cali-*

fornia husband"—*judging from her conversation she would like to have a Special Session for that purpose as she has a flattering chance to marry again*

Yours—

[No initials at end of postscript]

Washington Decr. 22nd 1854

Hon A Lincoln
    My dear Sir

I spent but a day in Chicago and that day it was cold and snowing—and very unpleasant to get about—I only saw one member of the Legislature and that on Saturday night and he was so much engaged in some of his business affairs that I did not get a chance to mention the matter of the Senate to him.

There is the greatest anxiety here as to the election of a Senator from our State—The peculiar connection of Douglas with the State & the Nebraska question causes that election to be looked to with more interest than that of any other State—I saw Richardson to day—He says Shields will be elected by 6 majority but he knows nothing about it—Col Caruthers told me to day that the Delegate from Kansas (Whitfield) says that Kansas beyond all doubt will be a Slave State—If that be so, what will Douglas, Harris, State Regr. et cet. do by way of apology to all those to whom they asserted so positively and pertinaciously that Kansas would *inevitably* and certainly be free?

I should like to hear from you during the first of the Session—

Very truly
Your friend
Richd. Yates

Bloomington Ill.
Tuesday morn

Mr Lincoln
   Dear Sir

Judge Davis has talked with me about going north to see some members, and since then has shown me your your letter I told him in the first instance that I thought I could go to-day but I find now that I cannot leave before the last of the week & may be not until the first of the next—

The reason for my delay is that about a week since my wife's sister came to visit us at the Pike House and the next day was attacked with a Typhoid fever She has not been dangerously sick but as there was no other man to rely upon I could not think it right to leave She is now recovering and as soon as she can be moved to my own house where she will have a plenty of attention I will go

I wish you to call upon me freely for any assistance you think I render you or *use me in any way you may think you can make me available*

I shall come to Springfield when the session commences

Yours truly
L Swett

Friday night. Jany. 12. 1855

My Dear Sir:

I have yours of the 6th this evening, it being the second letter only I have received from Springfield since the ball opened. I have not written since the Legislature came together as I supposed an election of Senator would be made the first week. We have had all kinds of rumors and reports here from Springfield, but your letter is the only reliable information I have seen. I received your dispatches for which I felt very much obliged to you as they gave us the first news. It took the Locofocos aback very much, as they had been bragging very loud that the special session in Sangamo had given them the House. I immediately told G. that L. had not received his letter, and he immediately telegraphed L. to know if it had been received, but he has heard nothing in reply. He wrote several days before the Legislature met, and I think it must have been received.

Things look mixed, but I have great faith and more hope that they will come out right in the end. I wish I could be at S. two hours. John H. Addams ought certainly to be your friend—I understood him to be for you the last time I saw him. You are certainly the first choice of nearly every man who voted for him in Joe Daviess County, and I am certain he would like to carry out their wishes in giving his vote for Senator. He is a conscientious, excellent man and will do what he believes to be right. But it is now no use to write as the "hash" will be settled before this reaches you.

You would feel flattered at the great interest that is felt for you here by all who know you, either by reputation, or personally. As to Sweet, what a devil of an idea that he should offer for U. S. S. But that is *entre nous*. Yates wants to come in terribly, and he has requested me to write to one or two friends and say *after you,* he wants a chance.

If by possibility the election should not have taken place before you get this, shew to Addams what I say about him.

They have come out right in Iowa at last, and I hope it may be the same in Illinois,

Yours Truly
E. B. Washburne

H. of R. Jany. 17

My Dear Sir

We have news of the postponement of the election for Senator to the 31st inst. That gives the Locos here great hopes of electing Shields or not having any election. They say they have 48 votes for Shields certain. The postponement will give me time to write some of my friends there.—Wait Talcott is in the biggest kind of a lawsuit for an alledged infringement of a patent, and I advised his agent here to employ you by all means, and he has written out to Wait to engage you. I shall write him to do so if he have not already. I think that will be a good pull on him. I have a letter from Ray tonight, *Entre nous*—He wants a position in our House next Congress and I am going to write him if you are elected, we will all take hold and help. I think he can do something with some of the Anti-Nebraska Democrats. He also wants the Legislature to do something for him in connection with the census. All these matters can be worked in. As soon as Giddings returns from N. Y. I shall try and get him to write again to Lovejoy. I will write John H. Adams among others. Let me hear from you, and please advise me by telegraph of the result of caucus & election.

Yours Truly
E. B. Washburne

When the Illinois Legislature, on Thursday February 8, 1855, turned to the business of electing a United States senator, Abraham Lincoln received 44 votes on the first ballot, James Shields 41, and Lyman Trumbull 5, but it soon became apparent that Governor Joel A. Matteson, rather than Shields, was the actual choice of the Nebraska men, and when Mr. Lincoln became convinced of the fact that he could not himself be elected, he instructed his Whig supporters to turn to Trumbull, with the result that Trumbull was elected on the tenth ballot.

Later, Joel Aldrich Matteson, whose "double game," in connection with the senatorial contest of 1855, Mr. Lincoln had so bitterly resented, became involved in the Illinois canal script scandal. The following document, in Mr. Lincoln's holograph, is found among the papers. It was probably written in 1859 or 1860.

It is now less than three weeks to the election—For months we have been trying to get an unequivocal declaration from democratic newspapers and democratic [*members of*] candidates for the Legislature, whether it is, or is not their purpose, at the next session, to release Gov Matteson from the payment of the money obtained by him through the Canal Script-fraud—But we have tried in vain—

There is nothing left for us, but an appeal to the tax-payers—We say to them "it is your business"—By your votes you can hold him to it, or you can release him"—"Every year a part of the price of all you sell, from beef-cattle down to butter and eggs, is wrung from you in gold, to replenish a State Treasury" "To a certain extent, this is indispensable; but it is for you to say whether it shall be thus wrung from you to be litterally stolen, and applied to establishing banks, and building palaces for nabobs." "Will you attend to it?"

Several years ago, the Auditor sold certain State lands, receiving therefor, as the law required, certain internal improvement script—This script was deposited with the then Governor, not being cancelled, or destroyed—Recently it has been discovered that a portion of this script has found its way out of the Governor's custody to New-York, where it has been funded and State bonds issued for it payable to *Peter O Strang*—Thus this Script was once paid for with State lands, and then again with State bonds—But this is not the end—The bonds are brought to the Treasury here, and bought in with the gold of the tax-payers—One Lowe brings them and gets the gold for them—It turns out that the bonds are filled up in this Lowe's handwriting, and then transferred from *Peter O Strang* to Lowe, also in Lowe's handwriting—Who is *Peter O Strang*, and how he got the script out of the Governor's custody, to treat it as his own, get State bonds for it, nobody seems to know—But this much is known—Matteson was Governor when the script *may* have gone from the executive custody, and Lowe was his agent at New-York, to fill up State bonds in rightful cases—Only a few days ago Lowe was in Springfield, and a suit was commenced against him for the money obtained from the State on the bonds—For a time the Sheriff could not find him; but at last he was found concealed in Matteson's house—And this too, after the Sheriff had been once turned away from the house, by Matteson himself—

[In Lincoln's holograph]

EXPLANATION.

In April 1849 I loaned Nathaniel Hay two hundred dollars for which I took his note at six per cent for first six months and ten per cent afterwards—At the time, he owed me some trifle for fees— Afterwards from time to time I had bricks of him, and once he paid me ten dollars in money—In January or February 1855 we made a turn by which he paid the First Presbyterian Church twelve or fourteen dollars for me—On the 2nd of March 1855. we had a settlement including all these things, and as the old note was already nearly covered with former settlements and credits, he took it up, and gave me the note and due bill herewith filed, the note being for the original principal loaned and the due bill for a balance of interest due— After this, in June 1855, he furnished me bricks for the foundation of a fence, amounting to fifteen or sixteen dollars, which I have always considered as having substantially paid the due bill. In August 1855. he furnished me bricks for the pit of a privy, for which he or his estate is entitled to a credit on the note—The exact amount of this last lot of bricks I never knew but I suppose the Administrator can find it on Mr. Hay's books.

June 9. 1856   *A. Lincoln*

[This document has been copied in a clerkly hand]

New Orleans La
June 4th 1857

Honl. A Lincoln
Springfield Illinois
     Dear Sir
     Your letter of the 27th ult, enclosing draft for $69.30 on the Metropolitan Bank of New York—in full for advances and fee—in the matter of the colored boy John Shelby, has just been received—permit me Dr Sir, to return my most sincere acknowledgments for your kind services in this matter—

     I should never have ventured to trouble you, had not the boy mentioned your name, as that of one, who would take an interest in his behalf—and had I not recognized in you an old friend of my father—

I owe an apology to the lady for misinterpreting the cause of her silence—but I was of course disappointed, at receiving an answer to neither of my letters—and besides I thought my correspondent was a gentleman, as the boy spoke of Mr. Grimsley—

I am glad that he has returned safe—should he come south again —be sure and let him have his papers with him—and he must also be careful not to be away from the boat at night—without a pass, which it is the duty of the Captain to procure for him—

What right Col. A. P. Field had to charge a fee of $25, I am at a loss to imagine as he had nothing to do with the matter—and so far as I know, rendered no service whatever—

Again sir permit me to thank you—and to assure you that any service I can render you in this part of the world will give me pleasure—

With much respect
Truly yours
B. F. Jonas

Washington, Jany. 3—1858

Hon. A. Lincoln,
    My Dear Sir,
    . . . I have written you freely & just as I feel, & presume it is unnecessary for me to assure you that I shall continue to labor for the success of the Republican cause in Ills. & the advancement at the next election to the place now occupied by Douglas of that *Friend,* who was so instrumental in promoting my own—

Yours very truly
Lyman Trumbull

My wife who is sitting by me says you are too modest to understand whom I mean by *"that friend,"* but he who magnamimously requested his friends just at the right moment to cast their votes for me, & without which I could not have been elected will, I think understand it.

When the campaign of 1858 opened, Mr. Lincoln received invitations from all parts of the state of Illinois to visit them and deliver political addresses. Typical of many others are the following:

> *Courier Printing and Bookbinding Establishment,*
> *Alton, Illinois, May 14 1858*

Hon A Lincoln

    Dr Sir You must come down and speak at our County Meeting at Edwardsville on Tuesday (18th) Much depends on it, and there will be great disappointment if you don't Come

> Answer
> *Geo F Brown*

P. S. I wish you would see C. W. Matheney about some notes I owe him. I fear he will sue me, and it is not possible for me to pay him yet. Please see him and let me know what you can do—

> *B.*

> *Galesburg May 25th '58*

Hon Abram Lincoln—

    Dear Sir: I have been requested by Hon. S. W. Brown—Mayor of this city and other gentlemen connected with Lombard University to invite you to come up here on the 10th of June and deliver an *after-dinner* speech—on the occasion of the annual commencement. The reasons they give for wishing you to come particularly, are 1st a speech from you will make the commencement-dinner digest well —2dly You have many warm friends in this city who wish to see you and have you help them stir up the Republicans in the county. The college speech should not be strictly political but made up of anything you please; but we intend to have the county called together sometime during your visit—and then you can fire as loud a political gun as you please. Your coming to this city will do a great deal of good and I hope you will not decline unless you are needed more elsewhere. I am now, as you may already know, editing the only Republican paper in this city & shall be glad to do what I can in the coming elections.

Ver Respectfully
Yours—*E. H. E. Jameson*

P. S. If you should come—be here on the 9th—if you cannot please inform either myself or Mr. Brown and oblige.

J.

Ridge Farm Ill. 5th Mo. 31. 1858

Abram Lincoln

There is a report in circulation in this section of Country that thou and some others are conspiring to defeat the election or rather the nomination of Lovejoy—This may seem a small matter to thee and one that is none of my business—for surely thou hast a perfect right to electioneer for whom thou please but there are some things involved in this matter that I feel quite an interest in, in which I suppose we are mutualy interested—first I am anxious that Lovejoy should be reelected to Congress and next I am very anxious that Lincoln should succeed Douglas in the senate I am more anxious for the election of Lincoln than for Lovejoy—tho I dont like Lincoln personally—have much reason to dislike thee—and did once lend my influence to defeat thee and perhaps added the feather that turned the scale but that was between thee & Trumbul but when the election is between thee and Douglas I am for Lincoln decidedly

The mischief that I want to advise thee of is that an attempt is making to excite a Jealousy between the old free soilers & the old whigs and Americans of this senatorial district—and thereby elect a democrat to the state senate—and a democrat representative from Edgar County—and one or two votes may turn the scale between thee & Douglas

If the democrats can manage to create a jealousy between the Abolitionists and old Whigs they may succeed in electing a democrat senator in this district and a democrat representative from Edgar County I greatly desire that thy name may not become implicated in such a family quarrel—I am certainly partial to the free soil element of the republican party—and expect recruits from the whig & democrat parties to be partial their own immediate families—but we look for honorable dealing—I fear nothing dishonorable from thee—but I fear thy name may become involved with some who we know are not acting honorable

We the Abolitionists—supported Norton twice before the Republican party was formed and to my knowledge no leading free soiler has since bolted a republican nomination—because the candidate was from the whig or democrat party—therefore I deem it meanness in some whig [&] lawyers to pursue the vindictive course they have and we feel indignant at their [u] meanness—And I am anxious that thy name be kept clear of so mean—company—for I am anxious that thou should succeed Dug not as I said before that I love thee much —but because I think thee trust worthy—& that thy principles are correct whilst we know Douglas is rotten to the core—[&] but we must all act not only honorably but wisely if we beat him.

Thy friend *Abraham Smith*

Daily Evening Journal Office
Chicago, May 31st 1858

Hon A Lincoln
    Dear Sir
Enclosed I send you a slip cut from this mornings *Democrat* by which you will see that the idea is carried that the friends of Mr. Seward are opposed to your election.

This idea cannot be too soon set at reast. If it is understood in any quarter that your election is to be regarded as a triumph over Mr Sewards friends, they may be rendered lukewarm while now they know no other candidate for Senator than A. Lincoln and are united and earnest in that behalf in this section of the State, in many counties of which they are the majority

Mr Seward has taken no part *and expressed no opinion* upon affairs within our State and attacks upon him or his friends are as unjust as they are ungenerous. Especially do they feel sensitive in being assailed for being faithless to you, for I do not risk anything in saying [*though*] from my personal knowledge I do not think there is one among them who would not consider himself outside the Republican organization if Douglas was to be brought forward as our candidate.

Of course you are not held responsible for what Wentworth says and yet the impression has obtained that you are to further his claims for Governor, in consideration of his support arising perhaps from the fact that he never does anything except for a consideration.

The truth is Wentworth is not reconciled to his fate and still has some yearnings for the Senatorship and if under loud mouth professions for you he can succeed in dividing us he thinks with Micawber "something may turn up" to his advantage

Our friends in this section of the State are earnest and active and will be strongly represented at the convention on the 16th at which time I hope to meet you.

In great haste
Very truly
Charles S. Wilson

Hon A. Lincoln
Springfield
Ills.

Chicago June 1st 1858

Hon. A. Lincoln

Dear Sir—Your favor was duly received—I delayed answering it for a day or two in order to enquire—We have certainly received some injury from the N. Y. Tribune, but not enough to alarm us—There is no trouble immediately at home, but rumors from the rural districts show that some of the brethern have thought that the puffing of Douglas meant something—These things are not serious enough to alarm us but will bear watching—If D. should come home

—denounce Dred Scottism and the South and modify Squatter Sovereignty some he might effect us some, but still I believe he cannot hurt us seriously—If that is done the Bushman organization will have additional strength—If the two wings of the democracy coalesce we shall loose none of our friends—and seperate we can beat them any how

I see no cause for alarm—our Springfield convention will set all right both here and at the East

Unless we do something very rash we have got them I think certainly but my opinion is always given subject to your better information as to the Center and the South

Say to Mr. Johnson that the matter he wrote about will be attended to at the Convention

Yr friend
N. B. Judd

———•———

The following letter indicates that religious bigotry was used as a political device even in Mr. Lincoln's time.

21st June. 1858

A. Lincoln Esq:
    Dr Sir:

I wish to make a suggestion. There are in our county over 100 Catholic Irish votes. as yet they are not set. But we cannot get them. The strong hold of Catholicism is in the Slave States. Despotism suits the spirit of Catholicism better than Freedom. Taney is a Catholic, and the Southern "State Equality" doctrine, as elucidated by the "Dred Scott" dictum, they will be ready to endorse. They like also to be on the side of the Powers that be. Again the rank and file vote according to the crook of the Priest's finger. There is a large Catholic vote in this State and it will go as a unit. Now the priest of Springfield officiates at Jacksonville & Winchester. Cannot a spring be touched somewhere that will commit the priests to Buchanan in

this State & as consequence the rank & file? It should be done Early.
I know it can be done.

> Yours truly
> N. M. *Knapp*

P. S. The Fillmore men are falling in beautifully with us. My Resolutions are getting them here. I wish you would look them over.

———•—•———

The question of Mr. Lincoln's position on Mexican War appropriations, raised in Joseph Medill's letter of June 23, 1858, evolved into a campaign issue which persisted until Mr. Lincoln's election to the presidency.

CONFIDENTIAL

> *Chicago June 23. 1858*

Friend Lincoln

The *Times* of this morning makes a most savage onslough on you in regard to your votes while in Congress on the Mexican War supplies. We have not before us the Globe record and do not know how to reply Ray & I wish you would examine the article and write us a statement which we can use editorially, or as the basis of an editorial, in reply

The Times article uncontradicted or explained is calculated to do mischief. Tens of thousands of our party are old Democrats and you Know their sentiments on the Mexican War supply question. It missed Corwin. The game of the *Times* is to make a *personal issue* on Senator—and not a party fight. That's its programe

> Yours in haste
> *J Medill*

P. S.

Please reply without delay. Scripps Ray & I were confering to day as how we should meet the charge without coming to any definite conclusion, because we were not posted in the facts. I agreed to write to you.

> *J M*

Chicago June 23rd 1858

My Dear Sir

The Chicago *Times* of this morning contains a violent attack upon you, charging you with having voted against a bill for supply the American Army in Mexico with medicine and nurses—and, without saying so in as many words—striving to fasten the impression upon the public that you uniformly voted in Congress against supplies for the Army in Mexico.

I have not been able to get the Congressional Globe of that Session, and shall therefore deny the charge generally tomorrow morning, upon [*the*] my recollection of the facts in the case. Will you please furnish me with proper data for setting this matter at rest, or will you see that the *State Journal* publishes what will supply us with the requisite materials for making a defence.

Sheehan expresses his determination privately of making the contest a personal one as between yourself and Douglas. He and the pack he leads should be met promptly at every point.

Respectfully and Truly Your Friend

Jno. L. Scripps

Chicago Ill. June 23d 1858.

Honl A Lincoln

Dear Sir

The attack upon you in to days "Chicago Times" is far more dangerous than many persons might suppose:—the charge of your refusal to vote for the appropriation Bill is the most potent & dangerous weapon that can be used aginst you in the rural districts:—of course (even if true) it would have no effect with men of sense but it is true and Douglas and his yelpers Know it in all its breadth & depth that it is the very thing to *take* in the byeways & hedges:—when I was stumping with Somers & Coles 2 years since they took especial pains to try it in every speech they made until I spoke to you about it and you pronounced it false & I made them eat the statement:—I saw Messrs Scripps & Arnold about it this morning & they neither one knew anything about its falsity:—C L Wilson is not here nor is Judd:—Scripps agrees with me in the importance of an early refutation and is quite anxious to present the facts & figures in the morning but Brown is away & he can't leave the office:—I consumed the morning in finding the "Globe" & finally succeeded in finding one at the Historical Society from which if it is possible I propose to obtain some statistics this P. M.:—I suppose of course the papers will refute it unless indeed they are as Scripps & myself were impressed with the belief that it is true: but then it behooves all of us to see our Editorial friends & see to it that such refutation is full clear & distinct and that the charge of lying is retorted on them with a vengeance:—the little gentleman Johnson (I believe) would be an excellent hand to take the "Globe" & collate all the statistics relative to the appropriations bills & shew how you voted & how others (now democrats) voted on the same questions:—they think they have made a terrible onslaught we ought to return the charge equally as effective:—the devil ought to be fought with fire:—Scripps says that neither Sheahan nor Douglas wrote it:—I did not go to Wentworth for his Globe as I was advised that John is willing to see the attack & would not lend his Globe to refute it:—don't let us lose ground by inattention to these apparently trifling but really formidable matters:—the fight is as effectually between you & Douglas as if you were in the field for a popular vote:—

> In Haste Your Friend
> *Henry C Whitney*

Chicago, Monday

My Dear Sir

We want an autobiography of Abraham Lincoln, the next U. S. Senator from Illinois, to be placed at our discretion, for publication if expedient. "A plain unvarnished tale" is what we would desire. *You* are the only man who can furnish the facts. To save the imputation of having done so to us, you might give Herndon the points, and he would send them to us. We do not care for a narrative only a record of dates, place of nativity, parentage, early occupation, trials, disadvantages &c &c—all of which will make, if we are rightly informed, a telling story.

Will you oblige us if you can?

The consolidated *"Press & Tribune"* appears on Thursday morning as a nine column sheet. The report is that we are coming out for Douglas!

Yours Very Truly
Ray, Medill & Co
by Ray

[This note was written June 29, 1858, by C. H. Ray]

Daily Press and Tribune Office
No. 43 Clark Street
Chicago, July 3rd 1858

Hon A. Lincoln
     My Dear Sir

Mr Medill has just shown me a letter from you in which you express the desire that nothing shall be said by the Republican papers of the State to anticipate your charge of conspiracy against Douglas when you next meet him on the stump.

I regret exceedingly that I did not earlier know your wishes upon this subject. I had been reading upon it at odd intervals for some months and, after two or three office discussions, prepared three articles upon it, one of which appeared on Saturday morning last, the second this morning. The third article has reference to what has yet to be done to complete the object of the conspirators—viz to carry slavery into the free States.

While I do not flatter myself that my humble efforts to elucidate the subject can in the least interfere with your line of argument or render it any the less new and interesting to the public, still if I had the slightest [*wishes*] intuition of your wishes in the premises, I certainly would not have said a word on the subject in advance of your meeting with Douglas.

Will you please communicate freely with us upon any subject on which you have a preference as to the line of policy we should pursue. We shall receive any suggestions from you as a special favor.

Your speech at Springfield has given the most unbounded satisfaction to Republicans generally. Douglas must be met with positive and direct charges of recreancy, and be held up as the traitor to freedom that he is.

Very sincerely your friend

J. L. Scripps

Mr. Lincoln delivered his famous "House Divided" speech before the State Republican Convention at Springfield on Wednesday, June 16, 1858. This was one of many he had made before he challenged Senator Douglas to a series of joint debates on July 24. A copy of Mr. Lincoln's challenge, in the handwriting of Norman B. Judd who delivered it, the holograph of Senator Douglas's tentative acceptance, and a holograph copy of Mr. Lincoln's reply are in the papers, but because they are published in the *Complete Works,* they are not reproduced here.

One of the most extraordinary copies in Mr. Lincoln's holograph is the letter presumably written by Horace Greeley to Joseph Medill on July 24, 1858. It reflects a favorable opinion of the "House Divided" speech, indicates a wistful longing for the conversion of Senator Douglas, and manifests a touch of Mr. Lincoln's humor.

to you

New-York—July 24—1858

My Friend:

You have taken your own course—don't try to throw the blame on others—You have repelled Douglas, who might have been conciliated, and attached to our side, whatever he may *now* find it necessary to say, or do, and, instead of helping us in other states, you have thrown a load upon us that may probably break us down—You [*know*] knew what was almost the unanimous desire of the Republicans of other states; and you spurned and insulted them. Now go ahead and fight it through—You are in for it, and it does no good to make wry faces—

What I have said in the Tribune since the fight was resolved on, has been in good faith, intended to help you through—If Lincoln would fight up to the work also, you might get through—if he apologises, and retreats, and defines, he is lost, and all others go down with him—His first Springfield speech (at the convention) was in the right key; his Chicago speech was bad; and, I fear, the new Springfield speech is worse—If he dare not stand on broad Republican ground, he cannot stand at all—That, however, is *his* business; he is no wise responsible for what I say—I shall stand on the broad Anti-Slavery ground, which I have occupied for years—I can not change it to help you fight; and I should only damage you if I did— You have got your Elephant—You would have him—now shoulder him! He is not very heavy after all—

As I seem to displease you equally when I try to [*help*] keep you out of trouble, and when having rushed in in spite of me, I try to help you in the struggle you have unwisely provoked, I must keep neutral, so far as may be, hereafter—

Yours,

————————

————Esq
    Chicago
    (very) Ill

"What have I ever said in favor of "negro equality" with reference to your fight? I recollect nothing."

This letter has been copied entirely in Lincoln's holograph. The accompanying envelope is addressed to Lincoln by Joseph Medill, and is endorsed by Lincoln
   "J Medill
   Greely"
The first page of the letter contains a pencilled notation, possibly in the hand of John Hay, "Copy   Greeley to Medill?"
There is no explanation of the words "to you" in the upper left hand corner. Possibly they were the first words on the second leaf of a letter which Lincoln interrupted in order to make this copy and return the original to Medill.

Winchester July 24

Dear Sir:

We see Douglas' appointments; his friends here are giving out already, that you will not meet him. You must come Here when Douglas comes without fail. You are on the right track. Your Springfield speech particularly pleases us. You are justified now in unsheathing the sword & throwing the scabbard away. Run back on his track, reveal in your way his tortuosity pitch into his motives; things that look stale to you the masses never knew, or have forgotten, or fail to place in juxtaposition with his recent attitudes—

But you need no suggestions

Write
Yours—*Knapp*

———•———

Norman B. Judd's comments on the Douglas proposals for the conduct of the Debates were characteristic of that Lincoln partisan.

Chicago 27 July 1858

Hon A. Lincoln

Dear Sir—Enclosed I send you Judge Douglass reply—It is a clear dodge, but he has made the best case he could—Browning has seen it and thinks you should accept his proposition as to the places named, if he will make a fair arrangement—I would put in writing my negotiation with him. I enclose you herein a pass sent me by Capt. Turner.

I suppose you will make the proper arrangements for answering Douglass at [*his present*] the places he proposes to speak as it is to a great extent the debateable ground—I have a letter from Judge Trumbull received this morning—He says he hopes to be in Chicago on his way home this week—I cannot see that we have any thing to fear if D. is properly attended to

Yr friend
N B Judd

·

———•◆•———

From this letter, written by Dr. Charles H. Ray, of the Chicago *Press and Tribune* came word that Mr. Lincoln's reputation had penetrated the effete East.

Norwich, Chenango Co. N. Y.
July 27th 1858

My Dear Sir;—

You will not consider it an unfavorable reflection on your antecedents, when I tell you that you are like Byron, who woke up one morning to find himself famous. In my journey here from Chicago, and even here—one of the most out-of-the-way, rural districts in the State, among a slow-going and conservative people, who are further from railroads than any man can be in Illinois—I have found hundreds of anxious inquirers burning to know all about the newly raised up opponent of Douglas—his age, profession, personal appearance and qualities &c &c, I have been among my old acquaintances obliged to answer more questions relative to you, your prospects in the fight, and your chances of a victory, than about all other things beside. In fact, you have sprung at once from the position of a "capital fellow" and a "leading lawyer" *in Illinois,* to the enjoyment of a national reputation. Your speeches are read with great avidity by all political men, and, I need not say commented upon in a way that would minister abundantly to the appetite for praise, which, I presume, you possess in common with all the world and the rest of mankind.

I tell you this that you may know that interest in your fight is not confined to Illinois, and to put you on your mettle for other and higher efforts in the oratorical way. You certainly owe it to yourself and not less certainly to your party friends who have honored you with a unanimity of choice that is without parallel except in the histories of Clay, [*Mr.*] Benton and Calhoun, to leave nothing undone which may promise to give you a vote. The reputation you have already acquired by entering the lists against a "Giant," will be made permanent by success which no false delicacy must keep you from trying to win by any legitimate means in your power. You have

217

a chance which comes to but few men of each generation. It is for you to make the most of it.

You may have sent me those notes which I have teased you about so frequently. If you have not, I beg you, do not delay their preparation an hour beyond the time necessary to give them completeness and an intelligible shape. They will be forwarded to me here.

Your Bloomington speech is admirable—more popular than the convention speech at Springfield; hence, better for the hour. Homely illustration, *ad captandum* hits and striking comparisons are what the people want.

Excuse my freedom of suggestion and advice, and believe me

Yours very sincerely

C. H. Ray.

Hon A Lincoln

Chicago, Tuesday

My Dear Sir,

It was my suspicion that Abe Lincoln was not born with a silver spoon in his mouth; and that suspicion more than any thing else impelled me to make the request which I did. Matthias Mount, on Mackinaw, whom you know very well, used to tell me—I know not with how much truth—of your joint adventures in rail-splitting and the like, for wages that would now seem ridiculously small. He told me enough to make me desirous to learn more; and I take it that the public to whom you are an object of concern, have the same curiosity that I feel. In my way of thinking, you occupy a position, present and prospectively, that need not shrink from the declaration of an origin ever so humble. If you have been the architect of your own fortunes, you may claim the more merit. The best part of the Lincoln family is not, like potatoes, under the ground. Had you not better reconsider your [*request*] refusal?

About that late paragraph of which you complain: It was done in my absence. As no man is ubiquitous or can be omniscient, something things in the management of a daily paper must be trusted to subor-

218

dinates; and sometimes somethings go wrong. That paragraph was one of them. I think Medill did it. It seems to have made no stir; perhaps it escaped observation. I hope so.

Yours Very Truly

C. H. Ray

Hn. A. Lincoln

Mr. Lincoln's old friend, Henry Clay Whitney, who shared his life on the circuit, reported in the following letter the reaction of the Douglas adherents to the first of the joint debates.

Chicago August 26. 1858

Honl A Lincoln

Dear Sir

Gus Herrington who is one of Douglas' intimate friends told me that Dug had made elaborate preparations to meet you in debate at Ottawa and that he Dug was highly pleased with the result:—that Dug had now got you where he wanted you:—that you had *dodged* on the platform:—that even if you replied to the platform query at Freeport &c it would be too late:—you *had* dodged and he had got you:— this & other things indicates to me that they are much chagrined at the mode in which you disposed of the platform query:—Gus has repeated to me frequently since that you could have vanquished "Dug" by dissenting from and disapproving of all of that platform that D. read and taking bold ground against its propositions:—he thinks you should have done so & then have said to the Abolitionists that *you* was the leader & *they* must obey:—it is evident to me that D.'s object (and that it was a matter of grave deliberation in which Dickey was consulted) to drive you from a *conservative* position to one or the other extremes:—my view is that it was devised with care & caution & that they will try it every where:—I also think that they were much disappointed at not trapping you at Ottawa:—at the risk of being presumptious I will suggest that in opening at Freeport you should not allude to Douglas' catecism of the platform but if he alludes to it as he will probably shut him up on it as you did at Ottawa and by adding that at the State Convention which nominated you a platform was laid down which asserted your principles fully [& beyond that it was no one's business to inquire:—] you ought also in the opinion of your friends to ring in the Trumbull argument on to him as to striking out the submission clause:—your friends also think that you ought not to treat him tenderly:—he is going to try to intimidate you: you have got to treat him severely and the sooner you commence the better & easier:—I don't of course mean that you ought to call him a *liar* or anything of that sort but that you ought to let him know that you are "terribly in earnest"

In Haste Yr Friend
H C Whitney

Knox Ville Ills Aug 30 1858

Mr A Lincoln

Dear Sir I Send you a List of names with the names of persons & their PO. respect[*fully*]tively . . .

Mary Berry, Pecatonica P. O. This Lady is an old freind of mine & She will make you many votes—Send her a Package. She lives 12 miles east freeport . . .

Morristown P O Henry Co. . . . Sarah Stevenson (this lady will make you more votes than 1/2 the men) . . .

now I have Sent you the names of influencial men & some of them are on the other Side of the question & some of them is on the fence the most of them is on our Side & is thorough going men Those 2 Ladies will take great Pleasure in Ciculating a Package of any Dockuments you may Send them they are old friends of mine & I have written to them on the Subject & I know they will Do all they Can & If you Should have any Documents to Circulate in this Region Send them to my address & I will DO all I can for you

Yours in haste Repectfully
David E. Edgar

My old friend Henry Chew, the bearer of this, is in a straight for some furniture to commence house-keeping—If any person will furnish him, Twenty-five dollars worth, and he does not pay for it by the first of January next I will Sept. 25. 1858.

A. Lincoln

Witness *C. M. Sherby*

[This is in Lincoln's holograph and is endorsed by him:]"Paid. Check sent to S. Little."

———◆———

In the election, held on Thursday, November 2, 1858, Mr. Lincoln secured a popular majority, but because of inequitable apportionment, Senator Douglas was re-elected by the Legislature. Typical of many letters of condolence and encouragement which Mr. Lincoln received are the following:

Charleston Ills., Nov. 5th 1858.

Hon. A. Lincoln,
    Dear Sir,—
The Returns are in and we find ourselves beaten as to the *main* object of the strife, and though I doubt not you are overwhelmed with letters, I hope this may not be unwelcome to you, though cannot bear congratulation upon a *complete* success in the axtraordinary canvass you have just terminated. I know it would be impossible for me to feel worse over any political defeat whatever; for beside the general interest I took in the question at issue I had come to regard you personally with feelings such as I never had towards any man except Henry Clay and the disappointment and chagrin I feel are very bitter. Yet you have *won* a *victory* for the popular voice of Illinois has sustained Lincoln, and when we look at all the States that have voted, we see that every free state has sustained you. Douglas gets to the Senate on the bare circumstance of unequal districts in the State, in *spite* of the popular vote.
But you come out of the fight with Laurels as the Champion of

those principles for which the free states contend, with the applause of the whole Republican Host.

The way seems paved for the presidential victory of 1860. Douglas can do no more than he has done if he were a candidate for the presidency. You have shown that you can carry the vote of Illinois under the most unfavorable circumstances, and as your Defeat is only due to unfortunate circumstances by which he has had an unfair advantage, I look with anxiety to the nominations of 1860 which will give you a chance upon a wider field to meet our enemies where they cannot skulk behind gerymandered District lines to deprive you of the fruits of honest victory.

We here are Determined to stand at our guns, and will try to disabuse the public mind of the false impression that our cause is lost or endangered by this loss of the legislature of Ills.

I assure you I feel the deepest regret at the Defeat in the Legislature and I could not help writing you this, which is the only way I can vent my feelings at present. But though it is hard to bear Remember that the Republicans of this Region glory in you yet & will not rest while anything remains to do to that they can do to uphold you.

> Yours Truly
> *H. P. H. Brownell*

> *Chicago Nov 5 1858*

My dear friend:

I don't think it possible for you to feel more disappointed than I do, with this defeat, but your popular majority in the State will give *us* the privilege of naming our man on the national ticket in 1860—either President or Vice Pres't. *Then,* let me [*say*] assure you, Abe Lincoln [*will*] shall be an honored name before the American people. I am going to write an article for the Atlantic Monthly to further that object.

> Your friend in distress
> *Horace White*

I believe you have risen to a national reputation & position more rapidly than any other man who ever rose at all.

Springfield, Ills. Novr. 8. 1858

Hon: H. Greely
    Dear Sir

This will introduce our mutual friend John G. Nicolay, who resides here—He wishes an arrangement to correspond for your paper
—He is entirely trust-worthy; and, so far as I am capable of judging,
altogether competent for such a situation—I hope you will conceive
it your interest to engage him—

Yours truly
A..*Lincoln*

[In Lincoln's holograph]

Brighton, Mass. Nov. 22nd 1858.

Dear Sir.

With the greatest respect, I solicit the Autograph of so distinguished a gentleman as Hon. Abram Lincoln, of Ill. I was in hopes
to have seen you Senator from Illinois, but was very much disappointed in seeing Douglas probably elected.

In hopes that you will answer this note,

I have the honor to be, with Sentiments of the highest respect,
Your Most Obedient Servant.

Charles H. Gordon

In the following letter the governor of Illinois solicited the collaboration of Mr. Lincoln in preparing his message to the Legislature.

PRIVATE.

Belleville, Illinois,
JanY, 2, 1859.

Dear Sir:

On getting to Springfield I shall desire to consult you as to what I
shall say in my message to the Legislature about Kansas.

May I ask you to write out, hastily as you please, your views on that subject, that I may make such use of it as I deem proper in preparing my message?

I shall be at Springfield on Monday or Tuesday next.

Yours very truly
Wm H. Bissell

Hon. A. Lincoln.

Jonesb[*oro*] *Jan 10/59*

Mr Lincon
     Dear Sir

I have a Son an[d] an only Son in jail at Springfield & He Requests me not to Come to his Trial as he dont want me to see him in Prison, I have employed some 2 or three lawyers but I hear you are a Host at the Bar I would like for you to defend my Son if you will Clear him

I will give you 500 dollars do all you can and if you cannot Clear him I will pay you for your trouble if you need any help, employ it & I will pay you a Reasonable fee if you doubt my ability call of Mr. Cover Corgum or McHenry Witnesses in the case

Pleas let me hear from you
take hold of the cas immediately

J. B. Jones
P. M. C. G.

The text of the following veto message, signed by the governor of Illinois, is in the holograph of Abraham Lincoln. As one who had been the victim of apportionment inequities in his contest with Senator Douglas, it must have afforded Mr. Lincoln particular satisfaction to write these words intended to prevent further abuses. Naturally, perhaps, it has not been published in Mr. Lincoln's *Collected Works*.

Gentlemen of the House of Representatives.

I herewith return to your Honorable body, in which the same originated, the bill entitled "A bill for an act to create Senatorial and Representative Districts, and apportion the representation in the General Assembly of the State"—

I object to same bill becoming a law, because it's effect, as a law, would be to continue the control of the General Assembly in the hands of a minority of the people. This being substantially the very objection urged against the Lecompton Constitution, by the authors of this bill, in common with others, it is but fair to presume that it found its way into this bill, by mere over-sight, and that it's authors will be glad of the opportunity, now afforded, to expel it, and to give the bill such shape as to fairly represent the people.

I also object to said bill becoming a law, because, by it, the new county of Ford is placed wholly within the ninth Senatorial District, and also wholly within the eighteenth Senatorial District.

I also object to same bill becoming a law because, by it, in the matter of giving excesses, the provision of the tenth Section of the third article of the Constitution is disregarded, I insist that, by this bill, the spirit of the constitution is violated in the *unnecessary* departures from the principle of single districts. A glaring instance is the thirty-second representative district, composed of the counties of Champaign, Piatt, DeWitt, Macon, Moultrie, Shelby and Effingham, and to which three representatives are given—The map, and census tables show that these seven counties divide neatly into three separate districts, each entitled to a representative, the smallest in population being greater, and the largest much smaller, than several other single districts established by this bill.

For these reasons, I object to said bill becoming a law, and herewith return it to the House in which it originated.

Wm H Bissell

Springfield Feby 22d 1859

———— •◆• ————

Despite the fact that these local printers declined the publication of the Debates, Follett, Foster & Company, a Columbus firm, gladly undertook the work.

Springfield, Ill.
March 21, 1859

Hon. A Lincoln
    Dear Sir
We have concluded not to print the Debates you can tell the other man to go ahead we cannot do it well now.

Accept our thanks for your courtesy and good feelings in the matter.

Your Friends
Truly
Johnson & Bradford

STATE LIBRARIAN'S OFFICE,
LANSING, MICHIGAN

April 21ˢᵗ/59

Hon Abraham Lincoln:
    Dear Sir: Wishing to make additions to our State Library, will you have the kindness, to send us, your Daguerreotype, to be placed in our picture Gallery?

Yours truly
J. E. Tenney
State Librarian

———— •◆• ————

The telegram which James A. Briggs sent to Mr. Lincoln on October 12, 1859, led to the delivery of the Cooper Institute Address, certainly one of the most important, if not the *most* important speech of the pre-presidential period. Mr. Lincoln, a few months later, gave this account of the episode: "Last October I was requested by letter [*sic*] to deliver some sort of speech in Mr. Beecher's church, in Brooklyn—two hundred dollars being offered in the first letter. I wrote that I could do it in February, provided they would take a political speech if I could find time to get up no other. They agreed; and subsequently I informed them the speech would have to be a political one. When I reached New York, I for the first time learned that the place was changed to 'Cooper Institute.'"

ILLINOIS & MISSISSIPPI TELEGRAPH COMPANY

Springfield Oct 12 1859

BY TELEGRAPH

From New York Oct 12 1859

To Hon A Lincoln

Will you speak in Mr Beechers Church Broo[k]lyn on or about the twenty ninth (29) november on any subject you please pay two hundred (200) dollars

James A. Briggs

Hon. A Lincoln

Joliet Nov 28th 1859

Dear Sir

Several of our citizens your friends being assembled thought we would like to have an address upon the occasion of the death of John Brown (in the event of his execution of which we have no doubt) Can you address the mass meeting at this place (Joliet) say about Dec 7 at 7 P M. If so we will arrange a big thing for you! Please answer us immediatly as we desire to arrange a meeting at once & write us your charge—

We discussed the propriety and impropriety of your delivering an address as regards your political standing and came to the conclusion that you might use this occasion with profit to yourself If you should hold the same opinion we should be pleased to be honored with the favor we ask

Truly your friend
H C Bissell

The following letter from Joseph Medill may refer to the letter written him by Horace Greeley on July 24, 1858, which Mr. Lincoln copied, carefully omitting names.

Washington Jan 10, 1860

A Lincoln
> *My dear Sir*

Judge Kellog read me a portion of a letter from you, yesterday, in which you speak of having a letter of Greeley's to me etc Will you please enclose it to me in "Care of Hon J. F. Farnsworth." I have my mail matter all addressed to his care as we board at the same house, and by that direction my letters & papers are delivered at the hotel. I do not recollect the precise language employed by Greeley in that letter.

After I see it again I can then judge of the propriety of making, or rather of letting Judge K. make public use of the contents in his controversy with H. G. I have agreed to let him read it at all events. He joins me in requesting that you send the letter to me.

> Yours truly
> *J. Medill*

P.S. I is very doubtful whether our folks succeed in electing Sherman. I fear the "Americans" will be driven to vote with the Democrats which will beat us

> *J M*

Douglas feels elated over the result of the party conventions in Ohio & Illinois. He says he will have every delegate from any N. W. State. He is trying to rub out the remembrance of the Anti LeCompton fight and the doctrins of the Freeport speech Yesterday Iverson gave him "fits" in the Senate, Today Green speaks, against him. The Southerns swear by all the Gods that he shall not be nominated at Charleston But I observe that his friends here are willing to take any platform that the South may ask, provided he be the nominee.

Breckinridge is supposed to have bowed himself out of the ring by that Lexington speech Simeon Cameron is as busy as a d——l in a gale of wind Seward's friends begin to talk about his "claims" since his return,

J M

To the Young Men's Central Republican Union was transferred the management of the political lecture which Mr. Lincoln had agreed to deliver in Henry Ward Beecher's Plymouth Church.

69 Wall St. New York.
February 9, 1860.

Dear Sir.

The "Young Mens Central Republican Union" of this city very earnestly desire that you should deliver—what I may term—a *political lecture*—during the ensuing month. The peculiarities of the case are these—A series of lectures has been determined upon—The first was delivered by Mr Blair of St Louis a short time ago—the second will be in a few days by Mr C M. Clay, and the third we would prefer to have from you, rather than from any other person. Of the audience I should add that it is not that of an ordinary political meeting. These lectures have been *contrived* to call out our better, but busier citizens, who never attend political meetings. A large part of the audience would also consist of ladies The time we should prefer, would be about the middle of March, but if any earlier or later day will be more convenient for you we would alter our arrangements.

Allow me to hope that we shall have the pleasure of welcoming you to New York. You are, I believe an entire stranger to your Republican brethren here, but they have, for you, the highest esteem, and your celebrated contest with Judge Douglas, awoke their warmest sympathy & admiration. Those of us who are "in the ranks" would regard your presence as very material aid, and as an honor & pleasure which I cannot sufficiently express.

Respectfully &c
Charles C Nott

To
Hon. Abram Lincoln

Ohio State Agency,
25 William Street,
New York, Feby 15 1860

Hon A. Lincoln,
    Dear Sir

Your letter was duly recd. The Committee will Advertise you for the Evening of the 27th Inst. Hope you will be in good health & spirits, as you will meet here in this great Commercial Metropolis a right cordial welcome.

The noble Clay speaks here to-night. The good Cause goes on.

With kind regards

Yours truly,
James A. Briggs.

Des Moines Feb 15th 1860

Dear Sir

Was much grateful yesterday in receiving a letter from Col Curtis who in speaking of the nomination for President puts your chance in the front rank & Chase & Seward in the rear not but that they are Reliable men but that we must get a man that while he is reliable is also available. . . .

Hawkins Taylor

Hon A Lincoln
Springfield
Illinois

It is comforting to know that the promoters of the Cooper Institute address kept their promise to compensate Mr. Lincoln for his effort.

Ohio State Agency
25 William Street
New York, Feby 29 1860

Hon. A. Lincoln.

Enclosed please find "check" for $200. I would that it were $200,000 for you are worthy of it.

You "hit the nail on the head" here, & long, very long will your speech be remembered in this City. It did great good. It was so inlaid and linked with truth, that it *convinced men.*

I hope you will return this way home. Come, do not fail to come here on your way to Ill. Just write me a day or two before you come, & *dinner will be ready,* & we will have a good time. Do not fail to make about *five* speeches in Connecticut. You have a *special call* there, & a duty to perform. With kindest regards & best wishes,

Yours truly,
James A. Briggs.

My regards to your son. Should he visit this city,)
)
tell him to come & see me.   )

New York March 4th 1860

Dear Sir

I do not feel able to promise *now* to go to Ohio at the time you mention. After the Conventions, it may be possible for me to consent to do so. But I can not make any such engagement now.

My judgement is that Hon Abraham Lincoln will not only make a more effective speech than I could, but draw a larger audiance. Think of that

Yours
Horace Greeley

D. S. Pope Esq
Burton
Ohio

The success of his Eastern tour and his "availability" made Mr. Lincoln a strong contender for the Republican nomination to the presidency in 1860. At the State Convention, held in Decatur, on May 9 and 10, the Illinois Delegation was instructed for Mr. Lincoln. The following letter, written by Mr. Lincoln's Kansas friend, Mark W. Delahay, indicates the situation as it existed three days before the National Convention assembled at Chicago's Wigwam.

Tremont House
Chicago, 10 P M May 13th 1860

Hon A Lincoln
    My Dear Sir

Since your Springfield friends have been fairly located matters have been looking up, I have taken to their quarters a number of the Iowa Delegates, some of the Minnesota and all the Kansas, I have taken *"Cottonwood"* into my Room, he is sound, Ross & Proctor of Kansas I think can be managed their prefference is 'Chase, But even with the Seward Delegates you are their 2nd Choice— Greely is here as a Proxie for Origon, and is telling a crowd now around him that N Y can be carried for 'Bates, I think he is calculated rather to injure Seward,— Some of the N. J. men talk very well as I fast learned from Col Ross—and so do some of the Mass men—they say they are for a success—I have induced the Penn^a Delegates to stop talking about their man as an *'ultim attum'*, They have mooted one thing, that would Kill them off and I have admonished them to abandon it, which was to call Ills Ind, Penn^a & N.J. Delegates together to harmonize between you & Cameron, such a move would appear like a *"Slate"* and Seward is too potent here to attempt such a meeting, his friends would probably *Slate* us, if it were done— I have been up late & Early and am perfectly *Cool* & hopeful—

Delahay

Dear Lincoln

We are here in great confusion things this evening look as favorable as we had any right to expect. Indiana is very willing to go for you, although a portion are for Bates, Genl Steele is taking them in charge. Eight of the Ohio men are urging you on with great vigor Gov Corwin is for McLean, we hope to in the end get them all. Pennsylvania says Cameron or no body, but that starch must be taken out of them. Horace Greeley is working for Bates. Judge Davis is furious, never saw him work so hard and so quiet in all my life. I have had several talks with Ashmun of Mass, he talks very kindly is not for Seward. Wentworth is for you today in good faith can not tell what he may do tomorrow. Iowa feels like going with you on 1st ballot we will do our best and if we fail we must submit.

Vy Truly
Jesse K Dubois

13th May 1860

Chicago May 14th 1860

Hon A Lincoln

Your chances are brightening Illinois Indiana Iowa Main & Newhapshie will present a Solid front for you as they Stand this morning, Ohio & Pennsylvania devided Ohio inclineing for you we want all our deligates on hand it was a grate oversight in their not coming early

we have precured a Parler at the Tremont House making the best fight we can, we are in good spirits will keep you advised

Yours Truly
W. Butler

Tremont House
8 oclock PM Chicago, May 14 1860

Dear Lincoln

Things are working admirably well now, The Stock is gradually *"rising,"* Indiana is all right, Ohio is prepared to do a good part after *Chase* has had his compliments paid him, New Hamshire and a part of N Jersey are talking out for you—also Mass—*"Cottonwood"* made a splendid hit in a German Meeting to day—*they* all conceed that you can be easily nominated for *Vice President,* but we are not *biting* at the *Bate* we are not pressing too hard your claims, we are making friends every where—Penn<u>a</u> & N York are quarrillin, Penn<u>a</u> says we cant give our vote for Seward N York in return says N York will not go Cameron, and they *whisper,* that a man with Democratic anticeedents *cant* be *nominated* for Pres—this all to my mind looks as well as we could wish, *Dubois,* says he wishes me to say they all feel encouraged, I wish *Herndon* was here, send up all your *spear friends* who can prudently aid in the outside Pressure— some of the Penn<u>a</u> Delegates have said to me that they will be quite as well satisfied with you as with Cameron—they are not a unit & a consideration—in case you are nominated you must come up upon a request and address the Delegations at the *"WigWam;* you need have no fears about our offending any one, In Haste, with high hopes

Truly Yours
Delahay

Tremont House
Chicago, Monday May 14 1860

Dear Sir:

Things are working; Keep a good nerve—be not surprised at any result—but I tell you that your chances are not the worst. We have got Seward in the attitude of the representative Republican of the East—*you* of the West. We are laboring to make you the second choice of all the Delegations we can where we cannot make you first choice. We are dealing tenderly with delegates, taking them in detail, and making no fuss. Be not too Expectant but rely upon our discretion. Again I say brace your nerves for any result.

truly your friend
N M Knapp

MAY 1860

CATON LINES

ILLINOIS AND MISSISSIPPI TELEGRAPH COMPANY

Springfield 15 1860

BY TELEGRAPH FROM CHICAGO MAY 15 1860

To A Lincoln

We are quiet but moving heaven & Earth nothing will beat us but old fogy politicians the heart of the delegates are with us

Davis & Dubois

PAID

CATON LINES

ILLINOIS AND MISSISSIPPI TELEGRAPH COMPANY

May 16 1860

BY TELEGRAPH FROM CHICAGO 16 1860

To A Lincoln

Prospects fair friends at work night & day tell my wife I am well

Jesse K Dubois

1475 PD

CATON LINES

ILLINOIS AND MISSISSIPPI TELEGRAPH COMPANY

May 16 1860

BY TELEGRAPH FROM CHICAGO 16 1860

To A Lincoln

Dont be frightend keep cool things is working

Judd

SCOL 55

Chicago May 17th 2 Oclock. PM

Hon A Lincoln

There are two propositions now before the Convention which will terminate the Struggle One is that the nominee Shall receive 103 Electoral Votes before he Shall be declared the nominee of the Convention this is brought up by your friends as a test question between you and Mr Seward. The hole contest as now Spoken of is between you and Seward. Though your Vote may start off Small by watching the Vote on this question you Can give Some Idea of your Strenth

The Pennsylvania delegation puts forward as another test question a motion to Exclude the pretended deligation for Texas Kansas Nebrasky Kentucky & Virginia The two latter I think will be Sustained by the convention the balance excluded. All are for Seward as assertained

The Newyork men will fight hard on these two points a defeat on either whips them

we have done all that can be done If whiped, we expect to meet defeat Knowing we have done all in our power

Yours Truly

Butler

CATON LINES

ILLINOIS AND MISSISSIPPI TELEGRAPH COMPANY

May 17 1860

BY TELEGRAPH FROM CHICAGO 17 1860

To Hon A Lincoln

Am very hopeful dont be Excited nearly dead with fatigue telegraph or write here very little

David Davis

16 COL 85

MAY 1860

ILLINOIS AND MISSISSIPPI TELEGRAPH COMPANY
BY TELEGRAPH FROM CHICAGO 18

1860

To Hon A Lincoln

Vote just announced whole no 466 necessary to Choice 234 Lincoln 354 votes not stated cn motion of Mr Evart's of NY the nomination was made unanimous amid intense enthusiasm

J J A Wilson

CATON LINES

ILLINOIS AND MISSISSIPPI TELEGRAPH COMPANY

May 18th 1860

BY TELEGRAPH FROM CHICAGO 18 1860

To A Lincoln

God bless you we are happy & may you ever be. Your success is as sure in November as it has been today

W. H. Lamon
W. W. Orme

26 135 PD

CATON LINES

ILLINOIS AND MISSISSIPPI TELEGRAPH COMPANY
BY TELEGRAPH FROM CHICAGO 18

To Abe Lincoln

We did it glory to God

Knapp

655 PD

May 18

ILLINOIS AND MISSISSIPPI TELEGRAPH COMPANY

BY TELEGRAPH FROM CHICAGO 18

To Hon A Lincoln

> You were nominated on 3rd Ballot
>
> *J J Richards*

655 PD

CATON LINES

ILLINOIS AND MISSISSIPPI TELEGRAPH COMPANY

BY TELEGRAPH FROM CHICAGO 18

1860

To A Lincoln

City wild with Excitement from my inmost heart I contratule you

> *Jesse W Fell*

1160 PD

May 18

CATON LINES

ILLINOIS AND MISSISSIPPI TELEGRAPH COMPANY

BY TELEGRAPH FROM CINCINNATI 18 1860

To Hon Abe Lincoln

My humble congratulations great Enthusiasm our guns thundering all Abe

> *Wm Dickson*

111 55 PD

May 18

MAY 1860

CATON LINES

ILLINOIS AND MISSISSIPPI TELEGRAPH COMPANY

May 18 1860

BY TELEGRAPH FROM CHICAGO 1860
To Hon A Lincoln
    I congratulate you. Shall you be up tomorrow morning answer
C H Ray

1055 PD

ILLINOIS AND MISSISSIPPI TELEGRAPH COMPANY

1860

BY TELEGRAPH FROM CHICAGO MAY 18 1860
To Abraham Lincoln
    The republicans of the United States assembled at the Wigwam
want you here tonight will you come
J J Richards

1790 PD

ILLINOIS AND MISSISSIPPI TELEGRAPH COMPANY

May 18 1860

BY TELEGRAPH FROM CHICAGO 1860
To Hon A Lincoln
    Dont let any one persuade you to come here
Leonard Swett

958 PD

CATON LINES

ILLINOIS AND MISSISSIPPI TELEGRAPH COMPANY

May 18 1860

BY TELEGRAPH FROM CHICAGO 1860

To A Lincoln

On consultation the Penna folks say do not come here till after New York has gone home

C H Ray
J S Scripps
J Medill

231 COPD

CATON LINES

ILLINOIS AND MISSISSIPPI TELEGRAPH COMPANY

May 18 1860

BY TELEGRAPH FROM CHICAGO 1860

To A Lincoln

Do not come without we telegraph you

Dubois & Butler

655 PM

CATON LINES

ILLINOIS AND MISSISSIPPI TELEGRAPH COMPANY

BY TELEGRAPH FROM CHICAGO MAY 18 1860

To Abraham Lincoln

Do not come to Chicago

N B Judd

555 PD

CATON LINES

ILLINOIS AND MISSISSIPPI TELEGRAPH COMPANY

May 18 1860

BY TELEGRAPH FROM CHICAGO 18 1860

To A Lincoln

Dont come here

G Koener

355 PD

[*—In pencil:] Koerner

CATON LINES

ILLINOIS AND MISSISSIPPI TELEGRAPH COMPANY

BY TELEGRAPH FROM CHICAGO 18 1860

To Hon A Lincoln

In connection with your debates with Douglas we have announced your biography Please designate your pleasure if any as to who the writer shall be

Follett Foster & Co
Tremont House

25 1311 PD

May 18

ILLINOIS AND MISSISSIPPI TELEGRAPH COMPANY

BY TELEGRAPH FROM CHICAGO 18 1860

To A Lincoln

The feeling appears to be for Clay By the whole But second ballot is counting strong for Hamlin think he will be nominated on 2nd ballot

Wilson

241

Chicago 18th May 1860

Dear Lincoln

It is not my wish to further talk of matters here as the Telegraph has preceeded my information, I want very much to return by your City—But at present I cant say that I will be able to do so, I have a dispatch saying that I was mobed in 1855 by my enemies & that on my return I will be *mobed* by the friends of Lincoln—I am excited & exhausted by speaking &c "Excuse me," it is the happiest day of my Checkquered life.

Truly yours
Delahay

ILLINOIS AND MISSISSIPPI TELEGRAPH COMPANY

BY TELEGRAPH FROM CHICAGO 18 1860

To A Lincoln

Senator Hamlin is Vice Prest no man could be better for you
Jno Wentworth

1265 PD

ILLINOIS AND MISSISSIPPI TELEGRAPH COMPANY

May 18, 1860

BY TELEGRAPH FROM CHICAGO 18 1860

To Abraham Lincoln

I shall probably be appointed your Biographer in behalf of Follet Foster & Co Columbus the matter is under consultation among your friends if so I shall go immmediately to Springfield
Horace White

3116 ORD

Chicago May 18th 1860

To the
Honorable Abraham Lincoln
of Illinois
    Sir,

The representatives of the Republican Party of the United States assembled in Convention at Chicago, have this day, by an unanimous vote, selected you as the Republican Candidate for the Office of President of the United States to be supported at the next election; and the undersigned were appointed a Committee of the Convention to apprize you of this Nomination and respectfully to request that you will accept it A declaration of principles and Sentiments adopted by the Convention accompanies this Communication.

In the performance of this agreeable duty we tak leave to add our confident assurances that the nomination of the Chicago Convention will be ratified by the Suffrages of the people.

We have the honor to be
with great respect & regard
Your friends and
fellow citizens

Geo: Ashmun
of Massachusetts
President of the Convention

Wm. M. Evarts of New York
Joel Burlingame——Oregon
Ephreium Marsh of New Jersey
Gideon Welles of Connecticut
D K Coulter of Ohio
Carl Schurz of Wisconsin
James F Simmons of Rhode Island
John. W. North of Minnesota
[Wm D Kelley] of Pennsylvania
Geo. D. Blakey of Kentucky
Peter T. Washburn of Vermont
A. C. Wilder of Kansas
Edward H. Rollins of New Hampshire
Francis S. Corkran Maryland

THE LINCOLN PAPERS

Norman B. Judd Illinois
N. B. Smithers, Delaware⁰
Wm H. McCrillis, Maine
Alfred Caldwell, Va.
Caleb B. Smith, Ind.
Austin Blair, Michigan
Wm P. Clarke, Iowa
B. Gratz Brown, Missouri
F. P. Tracy, California

. . . .

and four more

CATON LINES

ILLINOIS AND MISSISSIPPI TELEGRAPH COMPANY

1860

BY TELEGRAPH FROM CHICAGO 18 (*) 1860

To Hon A Lincoln

Dear Sir! A committee of the convention will wait upon you by special train Saturday Eve to inform you officially of your nomination for Prest of the United States

George Ashmun
President

28WCH 145 PD

[*—In pencil:] May

St Louis May 19th/60

Hon Abram Lincoln,
Dear Sir

Having heard with grate satisfaction of the honor conferred upon you by the Chicago Convention and feeling that there are thousands of your friends and well wishers who would be happy to possess a

244

bust of you which shall be a truthfull representation and a work of Art I would like to model one provide you are willing—to grant me the privilege—If you are I will come to Springfield any time when it may best suit you to sit for the modilling—I am an Italien Artist and any references you may require in regard to my capability will be furnished by prominent parties in St Louis who are your friends. Hoping to receive an early answer I remain

Yours truly
Pietro G Peran

State of Connecticut
Norwich, May 21 1860

Hon Abram Lincoln
Springfield, Illinois
    Dear Sir

Allow me to rejoice in common with the multitude and to express my cordial congratulations upon the nominations of the Republican Convention at Chicago.

Your name excites the most lively enthusiasm in this State and cheers the friends of freedom with the hope and expectation that in 1861 the General Government will be honestly and faithfully administered and that it will then be seen that fidelity to the constitution will secure the greatest liberty without infringing upon the natural or legal rights of any section of our common country.

That God may direct events so that you shall be the Chief Executive of this Nation and give you wisdom to discharge such high duties in his fear and to his acceptance is the main desire of

Your friend & obedient
servant
Wm A Buckingham

NB. I am happy to say that I am much better than when you were here and have fully recovered my voice

(P.S. The mistake of putting no Southern man on the ticket will weaken our efforts in the Cause here immensely—but we must remedy the evil as far as possible by increased energy! *C*)

May 21. 1860

My dear Sir,

Well, you have "cleared us all out"! The gods favor you, and we must with a good grace submit. After your nomination for the first post, my chances were of course ruined of becoming heir to your old clothes! It became a necessity to choose a vice P. from the North East, and of democratic antecedents. But after old Kentucky had come so liberally to your rescue, I think you might have complimented me with more than 2 *votes!* Still we won't quarrel with you on that account: Nature does not aggregate her gifts: and as some of us are better looking men than yourself; we must cheerfully award you the post of honor! Allow me then to congratulate you and believe me truly devoted to your success; and command my poor services if needed.

Yours truly,
C. M. Clay

Hon. A. Lincoln
Springfield
Ills.

———•••———

Among the hundreds who congratulated Mr. Lincoln was David Wilmot, of *proviso* fame.

Tremont House
Chicago, May 21, 1860

Hon Abm. Lincon
    Dr Sir—
I hoped to have made my respects to you, and to have tendered my congratulations, before returning East; but will defer it to some

other time, when less fatigued myself, and when you are less thronged by visitors. I intend to visit the West again during the Canvass, probily in Sept.

I have great confidence of a successful in Penn^a I go direct to Phil^a, where I shall remain for a few days. If I learn anything worthy of note I will drop you a line from that City

Very respectfully
Your Obt. Sevt.
D. Wilmot

Urbana Ohio
May 21st 1860

My Dear Sir

You are in that happy position that every man feels that he has a right to speak to you by the "word of pen"—

Having just returned from Chicago and feeling somewhat patriotic—I desire through you to congratulate the Great and growing Republican party—that their representatives at Chicago—selected for a standard bearer in the coming Presidential contest the "Greatest and Best man"—If this is not true (and I don't believe you know whether it is or not) *I am,* not the *liar*—it is the rest of "mankind" that *lie*—for every body *here,* and between here and Chicago except Frank Wright says it is true—He claims that position for S. P. Chase of Ohio—But comes down gracefully—takes courage—and thanks God for giving the people *wisdom* and *virtue enough* to select the second best man—Now Mark this, "Abe Lincoln" has a "Pole" long enough to Knock *"National Democracy"* in Ohio to the tune of *Ten Thousand Majority.* The sanguine boys say *twenty—In no* contingency can Ohio be classed as *doubtful*

Now my Dear Abe, if you have any old Shoes, Boots, Pants indeed any article of clothing suitable for a *growing* family—will be acceptable—especially shirts or under clothing of any Kind, for I desire to get as near your *hide* as I can—I feel *"Irrepressible"* love springing up in my heart—It is entirely *disinterested* It has been *growing* on me for the last *three days*—so I can now say of a truth that I love you—& Mrs Lincoln and all the little & big Lincolns—yea, the generations of Lincolns yet *unborn* You can send the articles asked for any time between this and the 4th March 1865—Send by express care of

F. M. *Wright*

Quincy May 22 1860

Hon A. Lincoln,
  Dr Sir,
  As I do not expect to occupy the Executive Office, in the State House at present I invite you to take and use the same at your pleasure, until it may be wanted for executive purposes.

Respectfully & Truly
Yours &C
John Wood

May 29th. 1860

Respected sir
  in view of the intimacy that at one time subsisted between yourself and me, I deem it to be my duty as well as privilege, now, that the intensity of the excitement of recent transactions, is a little passed from you and from me, after the crowd of congratulations already received from many friends, also to offer my own *heartfelt gratulation* on your very exalted position in our great republican party.
  No doubt but that you will become tired of the flattery of cringing selfish adulators—But I think you will know that what *I say, I feel*—For the attachment commenced in the Black hawk campaign, while [*we*] messed together, with Johnson, Fauchen, & Wyatt,—when we ground our coffee in the same tin cup with the hatchet handle,—baked our bread on our ramrods around the same fire,—ate our fried

meat off the same piece of elm bark,—slept in the same tent every night,—traveled together by day and by night in search of the savage foe,—and together scoured the tall grass on the battle ground of the skirmish near Gratiot's Grove in search of the slain,—with very many incidents too tedious to name,—and *consummated* on our afoot and canoe journey home, must render us incapable of deception—

Since the time mentioned, our pursuits have called us to operate a little apart; yours, as you formerly hinted, to a course of political & legal struggle: mine, to agriculture & Medicine—The success that we have both enjoyed, I am happy to know, although we must act in vastly different spheres, that we are enlisted for the promotion of the same good cause: the cause which, next to that of revealed religion (which is humility & love) is most dear: the cause of Liberty, as set forth by true *republicanism* not rank *abolitionism*—

Then let us go on in the discharge of duty, trusting, for aid, to the Great Universal Ruler.

Yours truly   *Geo. M. Harrison.*

WAVERLY TIOGA CO N.Y.

May 28, 1860

Hon
Abraham Lincoln
    Dr Sir

I take the liberty to address you, hoping in this way, to obtain an item of information to *gratify my own private curiosity,* and I will be gratified to recieve over your own signature such information as you may possess, if any, on the subject.

In the Convention of 1789, to form a constitution for the State of Penna, The name of Abraham Lincoln appears as a delegate for the City of Philda. You will pardon my curiosity when I inform you that I was a delegate in the Reform Convention to amend the Constitution of Pa. in 1838—and as the proceedings of the Con. of 1789 were furnish to each member The name of Abraham Lincoln sounds to me *quite familiar*—& I am curious to know the Relationship between him & the great Western Giant—

Very Respectfully your Obt. Servt.
Hiram Payne

LOAN AGENCY, COLLECTION AND
INSURANCE OFFICE

Chicago, Illinois, May 29th 1860

Hon. A. Lincoln.
Springfield Ill.

Dear Sir—We enclose herewith blanks for an application and medical examination hoping that we may be honored with the privilege of insuring your life— We also enclose Statement of our company for 1859— If you should conclude to insure please file up and sign enclosed blank application, and get any regular physician to make the examination. If you will give us your application for $2,000. we will take the *cash* payment *when you are elected President* and will charge you no interest from now to *November.*

Yours respectfully,
L.D. Olmsted & Co.
pr W.H. Bridgman

Washn. City May 30. 1860

My dear Sir,

It is too bad to write you three letters in a week; but having received your note this morning, & having had a long interview with R. W. Thompson this morning, thought it best to write you the result. I did not of course mention any thing of your having written to him; but told him that he held the fate of Inda. in his hands & possibly with it the Presl. Election & I was anxious to know what he had

250

decided on. He replied, (I give you the purport of the whole conversation,) that he did not desire to commit himself positively till after the Baltimore Convention, but that his opinion was as follows. The Chicago platform contained some things with which he did not agree; but knowing you, & having confidence in you, both from personal knowledge & from having read your discussions with Douglas, he had the highest possible confidence in you, and the most assured conviction that you would do right. That Indiana must not be carried by the Democracy; and that he *expected* to oppose the formation of any Bell Electoral ticket in that State, so that it might be carried for you, as, in that event, it would certainly be. He also added that he had recently been at his birth place in Culpepper, Va, speaking there; & that at Hon. Mr. Pendleton's, in company with a dozen Southern Whigs, he propounded to them the question what he should do, if it was clearly ascertained that the Bell men had the balance of power, & that running a ticket in Indiana could give the State to the Democracy; & they all agreed that the [*State*] Democracy should be beaten, & the State given to you. He added that this was not for public repetition.

I cannot give you all the conversation; but there is *no doubt* that after the Balt. Convention, Mr. Thompson intends to come out publicly for you, as the only candidate who can carry Inda. against the Democracy, & probably suggesting that the Opposition should run Lincoln tickets in the North & Bell tickets in the South, carrying in this way every possible State against the Democracy.

The Philadelphia demonstration was a magnificent one, & our friends say the most significant of all was the Fillmore Rangers & German Reps. marching *together* in the procession. Still Pa & N.J. are to be our hardest States to carry.

In haste

Yrs truly
Schuyler Colfax

Have written this while debate is
going on; but trust it is coherent

Washington, May 31— 1860

My Dear Sir,

Mr. Wade to whom I presented your respects replied— "Tell Lincoln that he is not far from the Kingdom of Heaven—that I am only waiting for the adjournment to take the rostrum for him" A true man is that same Ben Wade, as we call him— He is full of confidence & has not a doubt of your election—

Gov. Seward has returned & looks & talks right— He is doubtless greatly disappointed but seems more like himself than while the canvass was pending. He made a capital speech in Executive session today— It was reported here a few days ago that Mr. Weed had been to see you, & some of our best friends here seemed to fear that his object might be to get some assurance from you in case of our success— He is known to be a very shrewd fascinating man, but I remarked to the Gentleman who spoke to me on the subject that you was too prudent & cautious a man to get complicated by promises to any body— I mention this that you may know how easily suspicions are aroused, & that you may appreciate the importance of keeping entirely free from committals of any sort— There is certainly no occasion for anything of the kind in your case, & I doubt if they do not generally weaken more than they benefit any man— You will pardon me for making these suggestions—being from Ill. I perhaps hear more of these matters than most others— One New York Gentleman remarked to me that they wanted to know in New York whether they were to be treated as outsiders, as if any body supposed that Republicans in New York would be treated differently from those in other States— The very fact that a prominent Republican should make such a suggestion or harbor such a thought, shows a wrong feeling— So far as I can judge the nominations have taken well & our friends are in the best of spirits— Thus far everything is right— sure—

I enclose you a line from Judge Reed, which is very encouraging, coming as it does from a quarter where we had most to fear—

Mrs T. unites with me in kind regards—

Truly Yours
Lyman Trumbull

Decatur June 1st 1860

Hon Abraham Lincoln
    Dear Sir

I am gitting mad(e) a few Walking-canes out of the rales you & John Hanks made in this County in 1830 having a silver band on them and your picture in them. Will you be so kind as to send me a small Lock of your hair to place in with the Pictures

Wishing you Great & Tryumphant Success. I remain your friend
                         John M Murry
                              Decatur Ills

To the Hon Abraham Lincoln
Springfield Ills

THE BANK OF THE STATE OF INDIANA

G. W. Rathbone, President
Samuel Bayard, Cashier

                         Branch at Evansville
                         Evansville, June 1. 1860

Hon. Abraham Lincoln,
    Dear Sir,

At the request of our mutual friend Wm. Jones of Gentryville, I sent to you herewith, a cane, the first work on which was done by yourself thirty five years ago.

I enclose a copy, in part, of Mr. J's letter to me.

It affords me pleasure to forward the cane, and to join in Mr. Jones' good wishes in your behalf

                    Very truly yours
                    G. W. Rathbone

OFFICE PRESS & TRIBUNE

51 Clark Street,
Chicago, June 2nd 1860

My Dear Sir,
Permit me to introduce to your acquantance Judge D. V. Bell, of this city, who has been commissioned by a gentleman in Michigan to present to you the *Chair* occupied by the President of the late National Republican Convention during its sessions in this city. Judge B. is at the head of our principal Commercial College, was formerly a citizen of Michigan, in which State he held the office of Auditor and filled other important trusts. He is an intelligent gentleman and ardent Republican, and I know you will be gratified to make his acquaintance.

Very Truly Yrs
J. L. Scripps

Hon. A. Lincoln
Springfield
Ill

ILLINOIS AND MISSISSIPPI TELEGRAPH COMPANY
Young America Ill   June 4th 1860

to Hon A. Lincoln
    Dr Sir
Accompanying this is a true copy of the Message received by me *for you* on the morning of Friday May 18th and is the first intelligence you received announcing your nomination for President at the Chicago Convention. You will recollect me as the telegraph Operator in Springfield during said Convention. You would confer a great favor upon me by certifying on the accompanying sheet under the name of "Wilson" that this was the first intelligence you received announcing your nomination   That said intelligence was recd by me &c &c—By doing so you would confer a great honor & favor upon

Your humble servt
J. B. Pierce

Chicago   June 4th 1860

Hon Abraham Lincoln
Springfield. Ill
    Dear Sir.

By the U.S. Express of today, I forward to your address a "rustic chair" which at the request and with the compliments of the maker and donor, Mr. Meese of Jonesville Michigan, I have the honor to present for your acceptance.

This chair was expressly made for the person who should be nominated as a candidate for the Presidency by the National Republican Convention, and during the Sessions of that body it held conspicuous place among the Seats of honor in the great "Wigwam", where it was deposited by the Michigan delegation.

It is, as will be seen on examination, composed of thirty four different kinds of wood, appropriately labelled, and symbolizing the *union* of the Several States including Kansas, which are respectively represented; the whole ingeniously combined in a Structure, which though rude in form, may be considered an Emblem of the "*Chair of State,*" which, through the united suffrages of your fellow citizens, it is believed you are destined soon to occupy.

On behalf of the donor, I respectfully ask your acceptance of this token of his patriotism, and with profound admiration of your personal character, and an ardent love for the great principles of freedom, of which you are the acknowledged representative, I have the honor to be, dear Sir,

Most respectfully Your Obdt. Servt.

D. V. Bell

Albany, June 20, 1860

Dear Sir,

The Sketches which I enclose will give you an idea of the style of the Writer of whom I spoke in connection with a Life of yourself.

I enclose, also, an article from the same Pen, on "Douglass." If D. should *not* be nominated we shall have many of his Friends with us.

I saw a leading Democrat from Pennsylvania last Week, who says that they are without hope in that State.

Though greatly disappointed, in this State, I find no Republican, and no Friend of Gov—Seward, not entirely satisfied with your nomination, and we shall carry the State in any contingency, with ease if the Democracy remain demoralized, and by an earnest canvass if they unite.

Truly Yours,
Thurlow Weed

Hon. A—Lincoln

Jackson, Miss,
June 15. 1860

Hon. Abraham Lincoln,
    Sir,

You having received the **Black Republican** Nomination for President of the *United* States I deem it not imprudent to propound to you several important interrogations, to which I demand immediately a reply covering the whole of them without dodging or shifting one way or the other, either to the right or to the left— Viz—

1st—Suppose you should be elected President of the United States and the South would not submit to your *inauguration;* What would you do?—

2nd Are you opposed to slavery as it now exists in the slave States, and if so, do you believe that Congress has more power to remove it from these States than to protect it in the Territories?

3rd Were you in favor of Jno Brown the Traitor, or do you now occasionally drop a silent tear or two in honor to his Memory?

4th What do you think of the Wilmot proviso in another form?—

5th—As I do not presume you will vote for your self for President, do you intend to vote for Douglas the Traitor if nominated, or for Bell & Everett the Union Savers?

I am a voter and I want to know exactly every inch of ground you stand upon—I want to know for I want to vote for the right kind of a man—If you suit me I'll go for you—If not away with you ! !

I am for what is right, and nothing wrong, nor will I submit to any thing that smacks of Jno. Brownism, Japaneseism nor any other kind of modern *isms*. Give me the good old times of Washington of Jefferson & Madison—I want nothing else—I want nothing more. If you should be the lucky man to restore these good times to the troubled people—then I say Abraham Lincoln "thou art the man". Lord send it—Amen!

Address me immediately

> Yr friend
> *Tho. T. Swann*

> *New York   June 16, 1860*

My dear sir.

I was about to begin this letter by saying that I congratulate you on your nomination, but when I consider the importunities which will beset you as a candidate and the cares, responsibilities and vexations which your success will throw upon you, I do not congratulate you. It is the country that is to be congratulated. I was not without apprehensions that the nomination might fall upon some person encumbered with bad associates, and it was with a sense of relief and infinite satisfaction that I with thousands of others in this quarter heard that it was conferred upon you.

It is fortunate that you have never gathered about you a knot of political confederates who have their own interests to look after. You will excuse the frankness of an old campaigner who has been engaged in political controversies for more than a third of a century, if I say that I hope you will allow none to be formed around you while you are before the country as a candidate for the Presidency. I have observed that those candidates who are most cautious of making pledges, stating opinions or entering into arrangements of any sort for the future save themselves and their friends a great deal of trouble and have the best chance of success. The people have nominated you without any pledges or engagements of any sort; they are satisfied with you as you are, and they want you to do nothing at present but allow yourself to be elected. I am sure that I but express the wish of the vast majority of your friends when I say that they want you to make no speeches write no letters as a candidate, enter into no pledges, make no promises, nor even give any of those kind words which men are apt to interpret into promises. Several of our Presidents have had a great deal of trouble from this cause, and I suspect that Fremont if he had been elected would have had quite as much as any of them.

I hope that what I have said is no impertinence. I feel the strongest interest in your success, but it is only the interest of a citizen of our common country. What you do and say, concerns not yourself alone, but the people of the United States. I think you will be elected and I am anxious that you should go into the Executive Chair with every advantage for making the most judicious and worthy appointments and lending your aid to the wisest and most beneficial measures.

                                   I am, dear Sir,
                                   faithfully yours
                                   Wm C. Bryant

Hon. Abraham Lincoln

                                   Boston, June 18th 1860

Respected and Dear Sir,
    Excuse me for troubling you with a single line. In South Reading, of this State, ten miles from Boston, where most of our business men transact their daily business, we have just formed a "Lincoln Club." Our "Club" held a *ratification* meeting on Thursday evening last, as please be informed by accompanying papers. My purpose in troubling you, is to ask, can you not cause to be sent us a *piece* of a rail, or a *rail entire,* with the splitting of which you had some connexion. We wish it to exhibit in our *Clubroom.* If you can do us this favor,

I assure you will put us under renewed obligations to you. In your home in Illinois you can perhaps hardly appreciate how much pleasure and interest would be awakened by the possession of a memento such as we ask, especially in a town where the Club came very near "Christening" itself "Rail Splitters of So. Reading."

Will you, Sir, if it is practicable for you to send us a *rail* or *part of a rail*, cause such a relic to be sent, addressed to me, *South Reading, Mass*, and the expense will be cheerfully paid at this end of the route.

With assurances of High Regard, and sentiments of Respect, and Confidence in the triumphant election of the Republican Candidate,

I remain,

Yours Truly

Geo. W. Copeland,

Pres. of "Lincoln Club," South Reading.

Hon. Abraham Lincoln,
Springfield, Ill.

OFFICE PRESS & TRIBUNE

51 Clark Street
Chicago, June 18 1860

My Dear Sir,

I am hard at work at the biography, and now need the remaining notes, which I trust Mr Nicolay will be able to send me without much delay.

Since I returned from Springfield it has been thought best, provided satisfactory arrangements can be made, to bring the work out in New York. Parties have been written to on the subject, and Medill will go down to New York and complete arrangements should the answer seem to render it advisable. In that event I will complete the MS. here, and take Springfield in my route to N. Y.

Very Truly Yours

J. L. Scripps

Hon. A. Lincoln
Springfield Ill.

Orange N J, June 19th 1860

Mr Lincoln;
   Dear sir,
   As will be seen by the enclosed article taken from the journal of this place, I was seriously injured by a premature explosion while in the act of firing a salute in honor of yourself, and Mr. Hamlin.

My object in writing you this note, is to solicit from you, or Mr. H. some renumeration for my sickness, produced by the above cause. I am a *poor man* and have nothing but what I labor for, from day to day; and now that my means of gaining a support are cut off for some time to come, I will be very thankfull to you for any favor however small to enable me to get through my present state.

To assure you that I am not imposeing upon you, I have clipt the article above refered to, and if it is necessary, I could give you a score of newspapers, of different places in this vicinity, containing an account of the accident. But I thought it was useless to do so.

If upon due reflection you see fit to transmit "a little of the needfull" the faver will be thankfully received, and never forgotton.

I remain your most humble and obedient servant.
                                        Wm E. Matthews

P S.
My address is
Orange.
Essex County,
New Jersey

THE ORANGE JOURNAL
EDWARD GARDNER, EDITOR
                              Saturday Morning, June 9, 1860

SERIOUS ACCIDENT.
   On Thursday evening, while firing a salute in honor of the Republican candidates, Mr. Wm. E. Matthews, of Scotland St., was seriously injured by the premature discharge of the gun. He was engaged

in loading the piece at the time of the explosion. He was dashed several feet from the gun, and when taken up it was found that his arm was shattered and burned badly. He was also badly burned about the face, but we understand his injuries are not likely to prove of a fatal character. Mr. Amzi Wright, who was also engaged in loading, received some slight injuries to his hand.

OFFICE PRESS & TRIBUNE

51 Clark Street,
Chicago, June 19 1860

A. Lincoln
    My Dr Sir
I Start to N Y to night on a little business that may or may not result in benefit to our cause. A fortnight ago we cautiously opened correspondence with a reliable discreet, influential Republican in New York City suggesting to him to Sound Bennett of the Herald, and if he found him open to conviction to ascertain his terms. He has seen B. and finds him not unwilling to "dicker", terms moderate, and, "no cure no pay" Our friend advises that Ray or I, go down to N Y, bringing Judd with us. I Start to night, Judd towards the last of the week. I'll have a preliminary interview with his "Satanic Majesty", before Judd arrives, and ascertain his State of mind &c, &c. We deem it highly important to spike that gun; his affirmative help is not of great consequence, but he is powerful for mischief. He can do us much harm if hostile. If neutralized a *point* is gained. We think his terms will not be immoderate. He is too rich to want money. Social position we suspect is what he wants. He wants to be in a position to be invited with his wife and son to dinner or tea at the White house, occasionaly, and to be "made of", by the big men of the party. I think we can afford to agree to that much. It is not only the damage he can do us in the canvas in the close Eastern States, but the blows he can inflict on a Republican Administration during all its term. He has a vast corps of writers and correspondents at home and abroad and a universal circulation North, South, East,

West, Europe Asia Africa and the Isles of the Sea. During the Chicago Convention I had a long and confidential talk with one of his favorite editors, who by the way is a Republican in Sentiment. He assured me that at heart Bennett was a free soiler, and if he was satisfied that a Rep. Adm. was coming into power, he would jump aboard our train v c. I had private information to the same effect last winter at Washington

When our confidential friend at N.Y. conversed with him about you, he (B) spoke quite handsomely "of you. said you were the strongest man Reps could have nominated, were honest, capable, not dangerously ultra, thought you would make a good president, and stated that if your campaign was properly fought you could be elected &c. dide'nt know what he would do &c"

I deemed it my duty to keep you posted on what we were doing I'll write you the result on my return home. From all the letters and & news we get our faith is strengthened that triumph awaits our common efforts.

Yours Truly
J. Medill

P S They are having a lovely time at Baltimore
　　Oh! the irrepressible conflict.

OFFICE OF THE PRESS & TRIBUNE

Chicago
Wednesday June 27th [1860]

My Dear Sir,

It is early yet; but it will do you no harm to begin to consider what shall be the quality and cut of your inaugural suit. It does not seem to me that you have anything else to do in the campaign, which Breck and Lane have taken off your hands. We here are overflowing with joy and thankfulness at the turn which affairs have taken; and I cannot, though worked about half to death, refrain from stopping to congratulate you upon the near prospect of your election and the consequent rescue of the country from the hands of the spoilers. You will go into power under the most favorable auspices. The Southern men to get a Northern vote will be forced to assume union ground from which they cannot secede; and your inauguration will be followed by a calm which nothing but the infernal folly of the radicals can disturb.

—But I did not set down to write a letter, only to say what you must already know—that the sky is bright and that Providence only can defeat your hopes and mar the wishes of your friends.

Yours Very Sincerely

C. H. Ray

Please make my respects to Mrs. Lincoln and Little Chin-chopper.

ILLINOIS REPUBLICAN STATE CENTRAL COMMITTEE

154 Randolph St., Chicago, June 27   1860

Friend Lincoln:

You will doubtless see the N. Y. *Tribune* & the Chicago *Press & Tribune* campaign biography for yourself in the course of a week or two. You will perhaps learn that that portion of it relating to the campaign of 1858 was prepared, at Mr. Scripps' request, by myself. Therefore I wish to put in a plea in abatement; to-wit that its imperfections are at least partially due to the fact that under a sudden emergency & an entire change of programme the whole had to be written between Monday noon & Tuesday evening, and under the cast-iron pressure of 32 pages for the *entire work*. I think you will agree that this is the best plan, for the publishers & book agents in New York say that one million copies of a biography of this size and price can be sold before November, whereas a larger & more expensive work would not reach the *masses* at all. The price will be only $2.50 per hundred or $20.00 per thousand.

We have forwarded to the various counties about 1,500 letters concerning prompt & effective township organization & have received very encouraging replies to many of them.

Breckinridge's acceptance has killed all the Douglas men in the city. They perceive now what they never could understand before

—that of the two roads open to the Democracy at Baltimore, "one led to hell & the other to damnation."

Very Truly Yours
Horace White
Secretary

Providence June 29 1860

Mr Lincoln
    Dear Father I might say"

As the Excitement has abated I thought I would take the liberty of writing I was in Chicago during the Convention and when I heard that Abraham Lincoln had the nomination I was so regoiced that I shed Tears like a child The thought struck me. what must Mrs Lincoln & Bob feel. when they heard it I almost imagined I could hear old Buck snicking in the stable Oh it was glorious and it does make Me feel good all over. and I hope now you will show them the way things stand in November.. I am and have been agent Christy's Minstrels for the past year and I am amongst these Printers almost all of my time and I am asked Every day about you and I believe I tell them the truth as near as I know=Our company are all Lincoln Men and our funny Men are giving you good hits from the stage—all the time which of course before an audience of 1000 People in a strange place—Evy Every night does no harm " Mr Lincoln as Every One is using your name in whatever manner they choose We took the liberty to place it on our Bills Hoping that you will take no Offence at my writing these few lines but I felt so well over your success and you having known myself & Sister & the family from our youths I could not help so doing= Mr Lincoln Please write me a few lines to Boston you will confer a great favor let me know how Bob & the Famly are getting along hoping you are well I remain

Your Boy
Louis A Zwisler
Formerly of Springfield

Now dont fail to write
me to Boston

Galesburg July 10th 1860.

Hon Abraham Lincoln,
    Dear Sir,

It affords me very great pleasure to announce to you, that the Board of Trustees of Knox College at their recent meeting July 3d inst. voted unanimously to confer upon you the Honorary Title & Degree of L. L. D. in consideration of the high legal attainments & comprehensive statesmanship evinced by you during the past few years. Wishing you prosperity & long life,

                    I am most respectfully yours,
                            Harvey Curtis,
                            Prest. Knox College

Hon. Abraham Lincoln
Springfield Ill.

                    Washington D.C. July 17th 1860.
        Dear Sir;

I have had the pleasure for the second time that my family got an increase of young republicans, just in that month at wich years ago the declaration of independenze insured liberty to this country. On the fourth of July 1856 a son of ours was born, whom I called "Julius Independence" and this day I have in my arms a vigorous boy, whom with your kind permission I wish to call by your honored name.

This boy is the son of a true Republican, who would be proud, if you, the selected one to the highest office in the gift of the people, would become godfather.

Surrounded by tools of the present administration in the federal capital and bothered by adversary influence all round, I venture, to macke this request and I hope that you will give some encouragement by accepting it.

I am, Sir, with highest regards very sincerly

                    Your most Obedt
                        Joseph Gerhard
Delegat at the convention in Chicago and membre of the Republican National Comittee for the district of Columbia.

OFFICE PRESS & TRIBUNE,

51 Clark Street,
Chicago, July 17th 1860

My Dear Sir,

I send you by this day's mail a copy of the campaign biography.

You understand some of the difficulties under which it has been prepared. First, I labored two weeks after my return from Springfield upon the plan of making a pamphlet of 96 pages. Then Medill made the arrangement in New York for a pamphlet of 32 pages— and the Tribune people would consent to no delay. My only resource then was to condense here and omit there, instead of writing it over as I wished upon the plan of making a pamphlet of 32 pages. After I got to New York I had the printers estimate how much of my manuscript, with the accompanying extracts, it would require to make the 32 pages. I furnished the precise amount As fast as two pages were set up [*it was*] they were stereotyped. When the whole was in type, it was found we had 35 pages, and Greeley & Co, insisted upon having the 32nd page rescued for their advertisement. I then had to [*take out*] cut down four pages, and there were only about eight pages remaining to be stereotyped. I did the best I could, but you will see that both the account of your debates with Douglas as well as the conclusion, are sadly botched. There was no help for it. I have also reason to feel a little hard at some of my Springfield friends. Before I left there, I had the promise from some them of certain material which they could likely have furnished. I was to have it without delay. After waiting a week, I wrote. My letters have not yet been answered. However, I will not complain.

I believe the biography contains nothing that I was not fully authorized to put into it. In speaking of the books you read in early life, I took the liberty of adding Plutarch's Lives. I take it for granted that you have read that book. If you have not, then you must read it at once to make my statement good.

I cannot expect that you will be greatly pleased with this performance. It fails very much of pleasing me, and of course I cannot hope any one will have a higher opinion of my own offspring than myself. But while I do not [*ask*] expect it to excite any positive gratification on your part, I shall be much pleased to know that there is nothing in it that is positively painful to you. More than this I cannot expect.

Very Truly Yours

J. L. Scripps

———•◦•———

The letter from that free soul, John Talbott Hanks, is of especial interest since the writer belonged to the environment from which his kinsman, Abraham Lincoln, emerged.

July . . 22 . . 18 . 60

Canyonvill Douglas Co. Origon

Dear unkel

while seting a lone in mi Cabing all a lone no bodey to disturbe me thinking of the past as well as the future a thought came to mi mind Conserning you—and I coud note availe mi selfe of a beter opertunity than this to write a few lines to lete you no thate I was in the lande of the living I dont no whether mi lines will be exceptable or note but howsomever I will take the responsiblity to do so in the first plais I will say that I am well and harty and I hop when this comes to hand will find you in the very beste state of health—

it has ben a bout Ten years sense I saw you laste. well do I remember the day that I bide you mi last a dew Sence then I hav allways rememberd you fur the good advice you gave me and will and will till Time is no more sence then I have sene a grate meney Changes in life and experanced a grate deal as fur luck and prosperitey I have ben up an down in the world bute no I stand purtey fair for rasing in the worlde I hav a good prospect fur making money I received a lettor from fother the other day he desires fur me to cum home he says that he dont expect to live long in the world and wontes me to cum home doe yu think ite wod be aviseble fur me unkel to returne home when now I hav be gun to prosper I love mi olde fother as well as son coud love his fother you no unkel that I was raised a poor boy I had no Chance to make mi self while growing up to man hood as I wod liked to done I was deprived ove the chance as others had I have had to work hard for mi living ever sence I was a boy Eight years old and I think now I had beter look out fur mi self when I was out to california and returned home I gave all that I had to mi fother wich was something near a thousand dolers I bout him I thought wod doe him and returned back to california to make somthing fur mi self it is trew that I have ben hear a suficent time to make a raise I will admut that but fortune is note to be maide by ever body all though I have laberd harde a nuf to make one I got tyerd of california and went from thair to origon I found this countery much beter than california fur helth and ever thing else that I have seteld down to make this mi home I wod like to see mi old friendes very well but thay dont make me a living and I have to look out fur mi self—I have just returned from the Election it was the hotes one that I ever saw in origon David Logen and his a ponent went over the State and stompte it Logen is a good speaker and a smart man this State went a ganst logen a bout one hunderd majority democratice—Sence then I have herd that you was nominated fur president I was glad to hear that fur I bleave that you can cary this State if your friends pursuse the rite corse I live not fur from old Joe Laines he is not very popler in this conty he is the gratis a ponent you will have in the State but he is loosing ground faste he was seaking fur the nomination but did not get it his son in Law bet that old Joe wod be nominated we havent herd who is nominated on the democratice side if Douglas is nominated he will be very hard to beate in origon if he is not I will bet that you will cary the State I have herd strong democrates say that thay was a going to suporte you I travild all over this countey and lecneard hard a ganste Logen I was the cose that he was beat I had a grate deal bet on the Election and I wonted to wine it be fore I close this we have got the news from the States and no all the candidates you will get this State and you may dipend on it am going to suport you and do all that I can I live her in the midest of Joe Laines friendes herd him speak meny a time I no him well he is a purfect gut and he is lowsing grond faste I going to travil fur you I well a quainted with ever Body most—I can do you some good hear more than eney Body that is hear and the hardest man to beat a lectnaring that you ever saw I wont you to answer this as sone as you can and post me all you can direct your lettors to canyonvill Douglas Co origon you muste Excus this fur I am oute ove practis a writin to old Abe

Yours in haste

John T. Hanks

Hampden July 23 1860

My Dear Sir,

Your note of the 18th inst. was received last evening, and I was gratified to hear from you. I had been on the point of addressing you several times, and the press of correspondence and other engagements really prevented.

I am not certain whether we ever had a formal introduction or not—My impression is that we have; My recollection of yourself is · more distinct undoubtedly, than yours of me I had just left the House the Session before you entered it, and members were more familiar to me than Senators to you— I remember well of hearing you speak one day— We may I think reasonably hope to become intimately acquainted in the coming four years—

We feel a confidence in Maine that she will do her whole duty There is not as much excitement as in '56, but our meetings are larger than in that year, and there is a force and determination not then seen. It shows the strength and power of a consolidated and harmonious party which was then in its infancy— *All is* well in New England, and we are looking earnestly to the great North West, and we are looking too in a full faith that she will be true in the vindication of correct principles. I cannot see but the old democratic ship has foundered and must go down.

By the way, a gentleman who has named a vessel for you enquired of me a few days since where he could obtain a Bust of you, by which his carver could execute a figure head for his ship— Can you inform me? Are they in Boston or New York, and if so where?

I will be glad to learn how the canvass progresses in your State and Ind. for my *own* gratification I think I have enough prudence not to injure the cause or any one, by what may be communicated to me

Yours Truly
H Hamlin

Hon A Lincoln
Springfield Ill

Cookstown 24 July 1860

Hon Abraham Lincoln
    Dear Sir
I left Niagara Falls on the last Friday the 20th inst. where I had a conversation with the Hon W H Seward he expressed himself entirely pleased with our ticket, and his determination to use all his influence for its success. There is a Power high above poor helpless Man that presides over the destinies of our Glorious Union, that seems to be mooveing in the present Contest, and will decide it for his own Glory and our good So mite it be

Very Respectfully
W. E. Frazer

Hon. Abraham Lincoln
Springfield Ills
    Hon,
I have the honour to write to you to know your opinion concerning the foreigners; Please have the kindness to let me know 1º If you accept et ready to support the article 14th of our platform of Chicago 2º If you are against the people who profess the Roman Catholic Church. We have a large number of Irish men here; many of them are [*disposed*] dissatisfied of the democratic pretention and

they will be willing to vote for the Republican Candidate for the presidency if they did positively know the true opinion of Hon Abraham Lincoln

Excuse my liberty in writing to you but my best wishes being for the prosperity of my glorious adoptive country, I cannot resist to serve it with my little ability

I am, Hon Abraham Lincoln,
With a profound admiration
Your very humble Servant
F. E. Leseure.

French Teacher at the Academy, Paris, Ills
Paris Illinois July 26th 1860 ./.

New York
Augt. 14, 1860

Dear Lincoln.

This day is very rainy and it is hard work to find anybody—

There is very little use Staying here, but I thought I would see Greeley anyhow, and would see Mr Weed at Albany—They told me at the Tribune Office, that Greeley does not show himself until from 2 to 5 oclk—

Henry Winter Davis was at West Point, & I met him by appointment at the Astor House last night

He Says that everywhere through this region, & where he has been, that the Election is considered a foregone conclusion—that no one doubts that you will be elected— There is no excitement because the election is considered certain—

This feature dont please me, & yet, it is very difficult to make a vigorous fight, when the ranks of the enemy are broken & distracted—

The magnificent meeting at Springfield has a fine moral effect every where—

Henry has a strong desire that your administration should be a success—thinks if it starts out right that it will be—that the body of the opposition in the (house) Southern States will stand by it—and that it can perpetuate its power for several successive Presidential Elections— He made suggestions that I think were very valuable & which I will tell of you in person— Maryland will go for Bell—but if the Democracy were united she w^d not— He thinks that Douglass has a considerable body of supporters in all the Slave states— enough, if they ultimately vote for Douglass to give several states for Bell—

Henry dislikes the union movement generally, & the Union with either branch of the democracy is condemned by him emphatically—

I may stop in Indianapolis & Terre Haute on my way home—not certain however,

> In haste
> Yr friend
> *David Davis*

PS—
Our friends in Pa think there is a fair prospect for Delaware

REPUBLICAN NATIONAL COMMITTEE

Astor House 39
New York, August 18 1860.

Hon. Abr. Lincoln—
My dear Sir—

Yours of the 14th reached here during my absence, yesterday, at Albany. To your question—*"How does it Look now,"* I have the satisfaction of replying *Well!* Our advices from every quarter are such that we do not see how there *can* be any reasonable doubt that the contingency whereupon Gov. Wise was to march upon and take possession of the Federal Capitol will certainly occur. Just now, our Republican friends in Maine are having a brisk fight—your friend Douglas being among his "friends", aiding them by his presence and counsel. I do not think these doubtful, although the "Squatter Soverigns" boast largely of what they will do. I have recently spent a few days in that State, and found the Republicans thoroughly awake and confident of victory. If the victory is decisive, there is no longer a chance for even a *fight* in the other New England States.

Our advices from New Jersey and Pennsylvania are of a character to leave no doubt that the Republicans *must* carry *both* of them—and by very large pluralities. The same of this State of New York. There *can* be no combination made which will endanger our success. In truth, I feel sure that we will lose nothing east of *Indiana.* Of the prospects in that State, as well as *Illinois,* of course, you are as well, and better posted than we can be *here.*

Our Committee have made pretty liberal outlays for Indiana, and hope the election of Gen. *Lane* in October, together with a Republican triumph in Pennsylvania, will really *settle* the election of President, and leave us nothing to do but to "receive, count, and assort the votes", and proclaim Abraham Lincoln and Hannibal Hamlin, President and Vice President elect, of the United States.

As you ask my opinion whether your acceptance of the invitation to Springfield, Mass. would "*help* or *hurt,*" I answer very frankly that I do not think it would "help". The travels of Douglas in search of his "father's grave", and his "anxious mother's" *pantry* are freely commented on by the Republican papers, who hold up *your* quiet and dignified retirement in contrast. You could not go to Springfield, without your journey being in some measure a *political ovation.* As such, it would relieve Douglas of the charge of being the *only* stump candidate for the Presidency. It would also be construed by the Democratic papers into evidence of Republican alarm. In this view, it might "*hurt*". Everything east, I believe is well. The election is ours now. The triumph is ours.

Of course, you will not misunderstand my frankness. Our Republican masses would turn out to give you such a greeting as no man ever received. We would all rejoice to take you by the hand. But we can wait until some of your Cabinet find it convenient to come along with you!

Trusting you will pardon this long and hastily written letter, and let me hear from you again, I subscribe myself

Your friend and Obedient Servant

Geo. G. Fogg

Elizabeth Town Ky
August 19 . . 1860

Hon Abraham Lincoln
  My dear Sir

Your letter of the 16. . Inst was received by this days mail, and I hasten to reply, not only to acquit you but to clear myself of any knowledge of the statement of some correspondent in The N. Y. Herald saying *"that you had been invited to visit Ky, but that you suspected it was a trap to inveigle you into Ky in order to do violence to you"*

I will tax your patience by adverting to our correspondence. It was generally understood that you were born in this Town (Elizabeth Town) and as there was some difference of opinion about the place & also about your parentage, that I took the liberty of writing to you on the subject, to which you frankly & promptly responded.

That letter called out another from me, in which I did not invite you to visit Kentucky, but in speaking of the place of your birth & of your recollections of the old Homestead, I made a passing suggestion that it might be pleasant for you now in the turn of life to visit the scenes of your Nativity. To which in your letter marked *Private* dated June 4th you use this playful language "you suggest that a visit to the place of my nativity would be pleasant to me—Indeed it would—But would it be safe? Would not the people Lynch me? The place on Knob Creek marked by Mr Read I remember very well, but I was not born there. *As my parents have told me, I was born on Nolin very much nearer Hodgens-Mill than the Knob Creek place is—My earliest recollection however is of the Knob Creek place"*

The remark about the Lynching, no man of any sense would have understood it in any other way than a little playfulness & pleasantry on your part—I at least so understood it, and was about to reply to it in the same humor, that a visit here would subject you to a good many attacks—But they would be for office under you, as it was regarded as a foregone conclusion that you would be the next Prest—unless the split in the Democratic party let in Bell The mark *Private* on your letter I supposed simply means that it was not for publication, had it been marked Confidential, no body would have seen it. But as it was I showed it to Mr. W. B. Read who was attending our

Court & one or two other acquaintances & spoke of it to others who like myself had a curiosity about your birthplace.

The reason why I did not reply, was through a little delicacy, least my object might be misconstrued.

I suppose you have noticed the vote of Ky for Clerk of the Court of Appeals in which the Bell Candidate beat the Breckenridge man upwards of 25,000 votes. That Breckenridge is in a minority in Ky I have no kind of doubt, but I do not deem the late election a fair test as a great many Douglas men voted for Coombs. But I have no doubt that if the parties stand as they are now in November that Bell & Everett will carry the State of Ky by a considerable plurality of votes—

An old neighbor & friend of mine Saml. Young told me to say to you if I wrote to you again that he would vote for you, his sister married a Hanks—& he married a sister of my old Friend Charles Sawyar who lives near Mattoon & who tho nearly 80 years of age headed a Lincoln torch light procession at that place not long since & carried a fence rail on his shoulder—as did every other man in the procession—Not long since a relative of mine from New York visited this place & aided by some old Citizens hunted up the remains of the old Cabin in which your father resided, he had 8 feet of a log sawed out & took it to New York The old house has been removed several times, was once a human residence, Twice a slaughter house & now a stable—excuse me for going into these little particulars. I thought you would not be displeased to hear of them—I have seen in the illustrated papers a likeness of yourself—I was almost on the point of saying that if you had a correct Photograph of yourself that I would like to see it.

I do not suppose that you intend to visit Ky But if you do I would like to see you personally and would be surety that you would be pleasantly received—I wish it understood that this letter is private & not for publication, but if you desire a reply from me to the N Y Herald I will with pleasure prepare a statement

Truly yours
Saml. Haycraft

Philadelphia September 3. 1860
1119 Chestnut Street

Dear Sir

Mr Brown arrived on Saturday, and sent round to me, the minia-
ture with the letters of yourself, Mrs Lincoln & Mr Nicolay. It is a
magnificent work of art, and must be a faithful likeness. It corre-
sponds with your bust, of which I have a copy.

To day, Mr Sartain, and Mr Brown have been with me, and I
may say the engraving is commenced, and is promised to be finished
in two Weeks. Mr Sartain will have the constant benefit of Mr
Brown's advice, and no pains will be spared, to make the engraving,
worthy of the picture.

Mr Brown was greatly pleased with his visit to Springfield, and
particularly with his reception by you and Mrs Lincoln

Please to present my best respects to Mrs Lincoln

and believe me
very truly yrs
John. M. Read

Hon. A Lincoln   Springfield
Illinois

Springfield Ill Sept 24th 1860

R. L. Miller Esq

Dear Sir—Your letter of the 16th addressed to Hon. A. Lincoln,
came duly to hand. He thanks you for the favor, and is pleased to
hear that political affairs look so cheering in your county, and State.
He remembers Robert Rutledge very well indeed and sends him his
regards.

Yours Truly
Jno. G. Nicolay

Pittsburg Penna   Sept 28 1860

Abraham Lincoln Esqr
    Dear Sir

Enclosed please find a "Lincoln nail" the nail is invaluable the circumstances with which it was connected making it so. it was manufactured yesterday in a moving procession of 50 000 Republican Freemen. a belt run from the wheel of a wagon connected with a nail machine situated on the wagon while moving in the procession was in full operation manufacturing "Lincoln nails" and as they were manufactured they were distributed to the people, Sir this is a genuine article observe the "L" on the head of the nail show it to your little wife, I think it will please her curiosity. I have a little wife myself She is one of the most enthusiastic Lincoln wemen in Pennsylvania in all my Family can put in 3 votes for Lincoln Hamlin & Freedom I hope God that the American people may hit the nail on the head this time in your election please accept this little token enclosed a tribute of respect to yourself & the greate cause of Truth & Justice which you represent

                    very
                        Respectfully
                            Yours
                                Samuel Greer

9th ward   Pittsburg   Pennsylvania

BANK OF NORTH AMERICA
                    New York Sept 29. 1860.

ENCLOSURES RETURNED
OCT 19TH 1860   *

Hon. Abraham Lincoln.
    Dear Sir,

I enclose two letters from Capt. Abner Doubleday, of the 1st Regt. U.S. Artillery, whose contents will explain themselves. They are the last of a large number, all, until recently, pointing to the purpose of the Charlestonians to seize the forts in their harbor. The arrival, some two weeks since, of an Engineer officer to strengthen the defences of Ft. Moultrie, led him to suppose that the open boasts of Mr. Buchanan's sympathy and complicity with the treasonable intentions of the secessionists, were to be disproved by energetic action on his part. Capt. D. is from this state, and being an avowed Republican is looked on with much suspicion by the people around Ft. Moultrie; so much so, that we have strong suspicions some of his letters are occasinally opened. I send you these letters, not because it is more your business than mine to try and save the country from the disgrace, apparently so sure; but because the almost certainty of your election may give you means of information and an influence, which may avail to prevent it. Your success is simply a convenient pretext, for the desire to secede, my brother writes, has always been rampant in Charleston. I enclose you a map of his making, showing that if the forts once pass into the hands of the traitors, no revenue cutter could lie off, and blockade the harbor, for the first foul wind would drive her ashore. If the forts were properly manned, the attempt at secession, if made, (which is doubtful), would not succeed, for the duties would be collected at Ft. Moultrie, and postal and judicial advantages would be cut off, so that they would bear their present burdens and receive none of their present accommodations. Please return me as soon as convenient the letters and map. Mr. Chas. Ridgely, banker, of your city knows me; in case you should have any suspicion of a hoax, please inquire of him. Considering your election as the surest means of disabusing the Southern mind of its baseless fears, I am working for your election, though I shall never have any favors to ask of you, as President

Resp'y Yours
W. *Doubleday*

No 310 New Street Philadelphia, September   th 1860

Hon Abraham Lincoln
    Dear Sir

You will excuse the liberty I have taken, of addressing you without a personal acquaintance, or a formal introduction! As you are the candidate of the party, of which I have the pleasure of being a member, (you thereby becoming public property,) I do not feel as though I was committing a breach of etiquette, by addressing you on a subject that I think is of vital importance to yourself, and one that I hope you will give due consideration and act accordingly!

If the Political signs of the times are not deceptive, you will be duly and constitutionaly, Elected President of the United States; at our coming Election by a majority of your fellow citizens; If Such shall be the case, it becomes necessary that you shall be duly inagurated into office, and that your life and health shall *be preserved*, to carry out the doctrines, and principles on which you will be elected!

Now Sir in my humble opinion it will require on your part, if *elected* the greatest vigilance, and precaution to preserve, your life and health, and it is to that end, that I write, to give you due warning of what I fear will be your end unless you are most watchful and vigilent on that subject!

I have given the subject of the very sudden, and I may say, mysterious deaths of some of our free State Presidents, and the sudden Political somersets of the Vice Presidents who by law succeeded them to the Presidency much thought, and a very thorough private investigation, and I think a stronger case can be made out, in favor of the theory I am about to advance to you, by circumstantial evidences, and remarkable coincidences, than has suspended many a poor creature between Heaven and Earth by our Courts of justice!

In 1840 a National Convention of the Old Whig Party met at Harrisburg Pennsylvania to nominate candidates for President and Vice President, and at that time the feelings of a large portion of the whigs were for the nomination of Henry Clay, but the convention in its wisdom, and for expediency concluded to give that great man Henry Clay, the go by, and nominated Gen Harrison, And

I believe that if you will refer to the vote of that Convention, you will find that Gen Harrisons vote was exclusively from the free States, and that the votes of every Southern delegate in that convention was cast against Harrison (*unanimously*) And when the convention came to the nomination of a candidate for Vice President John Tyler, a hypocritical virginia Slave owner, who Shed crocodile tears because Henry Clay was not nominated for President, was selected, not from any worth or merit, but to satisfy the slave interest of the convention;—The ticket was made and sent to the people for their rejection or approval, and and as you well remember Tippicanoe and Tyler too, were put through by the people with a rush, and as every honest whig supposed to the entire satisfaction to a large portion of the people of the United States, what was the result, Gen Harrison was installed into office on the 4th of March 1841 and lived just one month when he *died* suddenly, (and I may say mysteriously) which caused this country and I may say the nation to mourn for the loss of that good old man;—

It was well known that Gen Harrison was a free State man, with strong feelings against the extension of *our nation's curse negro slavery*, and in favour of freedom, and free Teritory, which was the cause of the Southern vote of the convention which nominated him, being cast solid against him;—

After Harrisons death his remains was placed in a sarcophagus to be conveyed to North Bend, its final resting place, and a committee of Congress was appointed to accompany the funeral cortage to North Bend. The Chairman of that Committee was the Hon Thos. Ewing Senator from Ohio, and when they arrived at the place of distination the Sarcophagus was opened and to the surprise of all, the head and chest of the corpse was very much swollen, and the face and breast was as black as though the blood had been drawn to the skin by bruises;—The matter was talked over by the Committee and I am informed it was declared by a Doctor who was present, that nothing but Poison would produce that result, and suggested an investigation, when Mr Ewing replied, close up the Sarcophagus and deposit it in its final resting place, for said he, if on investigation it should be found that Poison was the cause of his death, it would involve the country in a civil war.;— Thus his body was consigned to the grave without investigation, and the People left in ignorance as to the real cause of Harrisons Death, which, was by Poison beyond a possability of doubt;—

By Law, that *arch Traitor* John Tyler assumed the responsibilities of the office that the people had elected Harrison to fill, and he being a southern Pro Slavery man, and a fit and willing tool of the Slave Oligharchy, went back to his first love (viz Loco-focoism) and turned traitor to the party that had elected him, and you know well what his history was, Whilst he held the reins of government in his hands, and how well and truely he carried out all of the dictations of the Southern Slave party, and how he betrayed the Whig Party that had elected him, and how heartily he was and is dispised by the whole country north, up to the present time; *He lived out his term of office and received the reward of his masters;*—

In 1844 James K Polk of Tennessee a southern Pro-Slavery Loco-foco was elected President, and George M Dallas a northern Loco-foco with southern views, (who betrayed his own State, as Judas betrayed his Master) was elected vice President:— *They being the right kind of materials,* ready and willing to carry out all of the mandates of their Masters:— *They lived out their terms of offices* to the full and entire satisfaction of the two hundred and fifty thousand Slave owners of the South, and they received their rewards:— They were elected by a palpable fraud, viz. Polk Dallas and the tariff of 42, Polk is a better tariff man than Henry Clay, The tariff is safer in the hands of Polk and Dallas than in the hands of Clay and Free-lynhyson, all of which was a known and willful fraud on the People, and our *cold Hearted unprincipled President James Buchanan,* then traveled through Pennsylvania, making Tariff Speaches and promulgating the fraud in almost every County:—

In 1848, Gen Zachy. Taylor, that good honest Southerner, was elected President, and Millard Filmore, an anti-slavery man of New York State was elected Vice President:— Gen Taylor was duly inaugurated into office, and entered on his duties, as President of the United States, and his Administrative policy was much feared and doubted by many of the *Anti-Slavery extension men north,* and as you know his policy was uncertain for some time after his inauguration But he being a true national man, and strictly honest, and free from all sectional prejudices, soon dispelled all fears from the minds of those who had doubted him before, And as you are better acquainted with his political history than I am, I will only illustrate my position by quoting sufficient for that purpose;— He was decidedly opposed to the further extension of slavery into territory north of 36,30 and desired, and was using the whole force and power of his Administration to bring New Mexico into the Union as a free State;—He also believed that the Missouri compromise was strictly constitutional, and one of the most sacred compromises of the slave question, and I am credibly informed that five days before his sudden death, he had high and angry words with some of his prominent Southern friends, on the subject of extending Slavery into New Mexico, and that he said to thim, he was the President of the whole United States, and that he had found certain States and territories free, and he would never with his consent, agree to force or extend that damnable curse into any territory that is now free, or north of 36,30, and would use all of his power against it; consequently he did not suit the Slave Oligharchy, and on the 9th of July, one year four months and five days after his inauguration he *died suddenly*, as did Harrison, and with the same apparent disease, which caused the Nation to mourn again for the loss of that good old Chieftain President;— His death was attributed to his eating a cherry pie the day befor his death;— I have no doubt but the pie was the cause of his death, but in the pie was *poison* for I cannot believe that an old soldier who had been used to the hardships of a camp life for thirty years could be killed by eating a simple cherry Pie; if there had been no poison in it, but my opinion is that the *Borgias were about;—*

By law the New York anti-slavery man Millard Filmore succeeded Gen Taylor as President, and it was strange to see what a perfect somerset he turned, how soon he became what he chose to term a National Man, and how soon he lost all of his long cherished Anti-Slavery notions, and how soon he became a pet of the slave Power at Washington, and that his former *York State notions* did not suit in a Southern atmosphere, and he had then discovered that he suddenly becam very *National* in his views; How willing he was to advocate and sign the fugitive Slave law, as a finality on the nigger question, and then what a favorite he became with the whole South. *He lived out his term of office, and received his reward,* and after he retired from office, before going home to Buffalo, he made a tour through almost the entire South, and you remember how he was feasted, toasted, and eulogized, by the Slave owners from Maryland to Lousiana, and cheered on his road throughout the entire south, and as soon as he struck free territory, how he made a straight line for home, not stopping to receive the congratulations of his free State friends;— There is much more that might be said in relation to Mr Filmore, and the Slave propagandists, but I have said enough. The original contract between the high contracting Parties, I suppose has been strictly carried out;—

In 1852 Franklin Pearce, a week kneed, New Hampshire Locofoco, was elected President, and he being rather of a *fainting disposition,* and of a femanine tendency, and very unsteady in his nerves, and easily flattered, which made him a fit subject for the Slave power to opperate upon, and well he done their biddings, the result was the repeal of the missouri compromise (which measure was headed by that *arch Demagog, Stepen A Douglass*), The civil war in Kansas with all of the enormities connected therewith;— The sacriligious outrages of the border ruffians in spreading broadcast over the territory death and devastation;— The violation of the ballot boxes;— The passage of laws that would disgrace the heathen, are all evidences of the unholy dictations he received from his masters, and in Short he went over to them body, soul, and breeches, and *he lived out his term of office* and done his biddings nobly, and received his reward;—

In 1856 James Buchanan a cold Hearted, Pennsylvania Locofoco was elected President, and shortly after it was known that he was elected a delegation of Southern Slave Owners with Governor Wise of Virginia at their head made him a visit at *Wheatland* and after the interview between the President elect, and the slave oligharchy, it is generally reported and believed that Mr Buchanan was rather stubborn, and would not work right in the traces, as to the policy of his coming Administration and the Slave power went home some what discouraged with the coming President, and they were in great consternation for a time and the southern papers, many of them actually threatened that the southern electors should vote for some other candidate, or person for President instead of Buchanan, for he was not right on the Southern questions;— But after further consideration the electors did vote for Buck, and he was elected;—

In due time Mr Buchanan engaged rooms at the National Hotel in Washington City, and that fact being published all over the country which caused a perfect rush of office seekers and politicians, to the National When Mr Buchanan arrived and during his stay at the National there was near fifteen hundred guests;— And over five hundred of that number were poisoned, and about fifty of them *died;*— And what is most strange in the matter, there were but three (I believe) of the guests who belonged to the south who were afflicted, and they very slightly;— when it is known that a large majority of the guests were southerners;— The first theory started was that Poisoned Rats had got into the water, but that theory soon exploded, and then an other idea was concocted, viz That the cause was the Poisones Gases that came from the *Sewers* that were connected with the Sinks of the Hotel, but that too soon exploded, likewise;— And finally a committee of scientific Gentlemen were appointed to give the matter a thorough investigation and if possible determin what was the cause of the dreadful distruction of life and health, and after a thorough and careful investigation it was found to be *Pulverised Glass mixed with very fine pulverised Sugar* but on consultation it was determined not to make the real cause public because it would be dangerous on account of it being so easy for servants by that means to poison the whole community;— Now you see how cunningly the whole thing was managed, the Poisoned Rat story answered for a time, but was soon abandoned, next the *Sewer dodge* was taken up and answered for a short period, to divert the attention of the anxious public, that too had to be abandoned, also. And when the real cause was ascertained, it was thought best not to make it public on account of the servants;— Thus you will see how nicely the slave power manages to keep the public ignorant of their *black deeds;*— Mr Buchanan was warned of his danger by several letters without signatures but he gave them no notice, and at the time it occured it was really a fearful thing to think about, but since the southern policy has been fully developed, the whole thing becomes perfectly clear, and plain, and not mysterious as it at one time appeared, we hear southerners swearing vehemently almost daily, that if Lincoln is elected he shall never take his seat &c, and I do not know how they are to prevent it unless it is by making *Poisoning Presidents* a part of their Nigger doctrin;—

Mr Brackenridge, the Vice President being a true southern Pro-slavery man, would have been a very acceptable swap for Mr Buchanan, at that time, he being a man in whom they could have full confidence and would be entirely satisfactory to the slave power;— Mr Buchanan was however permited to live, but he would not be now living, if he had not sold himself to the Slave Oligharchy Body and Soul, and gone over to them more thoroughly than any of his predecessors;— The *Borgias* of Washington were after him, as they will be after every President, who does not consent to the Pro-Slavery side of the question as soon (or before) he gets into office, And I am satisfied that the lives of our Presidents depends on their views and opinions of a certain domestic institution which our beloved country unfortunately is cursed with viz Negro Slavery;—

Now I will ask you in all sincerity can these things be accidental;— Do not the *coincidences and facts combined* show strong indications of foul play and are not the coincidences very remarkable;— Pro-Slavery Presidents live out their terms of offices and those having different views are doomed to short existances in office, and their deaths are sudden and mysterious;— Sir our beloved country is under a more despotic rule than almost any other country known, and that too under the name of Democracy without a single trace or land mark of true democracy being left, for such old Federalists as ten cent Jimy to swear by;— And the *Borgias* of Washington are ready to do the biddings of their masters faithfully whenever it shall be deemed expedient to get a President or high official out of the way of the Slave Despots;—

I being stongly impressed with the belief that Free State Presidents were foully dealt with, took occasion to give that matter my particular attention and in my private investigations of the attempt to poison Mr Buchanan, I happened to get hold of the Head waiter in the Ladies dining room at the time the occurrence took place;— He having once been head waiter for me, was very friendly, and much attached to me;— I said to him John, how is it about the attempt to Poison old Buck, you was there at the time, and I would take your opinions about it sooner than I would those who held higher rank in society than you do, this some what flattered his vanity, and after a little hesitation, he said well it was not Poisoned Rats for *Devil the* poisened rat was there ever in the house as long as I was there;— nor was it the Poison arising from the *Sewers* for if it had of been that, it would have afflicted all alike;— Well said I John what do you think then was the cause of the Poison being in the House, after some little delay in answering, he said to be candid with you, my opinion is that it was in some very *fine pulverised Sugar* that the Steward of the Hotel bought a few days before Mr Buchanan arrived, for said he we had no occasion for that Sugar, we had a large quantity of all kinds of sugar in the store room when that was bought;— plenty of *crushed, sand, St Domingo,* and *brown Sugars,* plenty of all kinds necessary for a Hotel, and the Steward had no occasion whatever to buy the 4 or 5 barrels of that very fine pulverised sugar, said he I never saw such fine pulverised sugar before;— I then said to him John if the Poison was in that Sugar how did it happen that so many of the Northern people were Poisoned, and only about three of the Southerners when you know that a large majority of the guests were from the South;— Och, you an old Hotel keeper, and dont see how that could happen, why you know that for *Tea* nearly every person from the North drinks tea, and those from the South Coffee, and we all had our orders, that when any person called for tea to hand them that fine pulverised Sugar, and when they called for Coffee to hand the crushed or St Domingo Sugar, and said he that is the way that happened, and he then remarked you did not hear of any of the family, or the servents being poisened;— I then said who was the Steaward, well said he his name is —— —— and he is an Irishman;— I then asked if he was a *roman Catholic,* he said yes sir the same as I am, and I will tell you no lie about it;— I then asked him what had become of the Steward he said he could not tell where he went, he left Washington, and I cannot tell where he went to;— I then asked him, do you suppose he was paid for his services in that black deed;— well said he my opinion is that any person who is base enough to do the deed, that he would be rascal enough to not do it without being well paid for such wickedness, said he I am shure of that;—

This was before the Committee of Scientific Gentlemen were appointed to investigate and determin the real cause; and after the cause was ascertained, it proved to be in this fine pulverised Sugar, just as John had told me he believed it was, and the Poison was fine pulverised Glass mixed with fine Pulverised Sugar;— And there is no doubt but the compound of Sugar and glass was specially prepared by some one for the occasion, and placed in a position where the Steward was directed to go and get it, and if it could be traced out you would find that the whole thing was done by the directions of the Slave power, thinking to get old Buck out of the way, and to make room for Breckenridge their friend to take his place;—

Now Sir dont you think the proofs are strong, and the remarkable coincidences are unexplainable;— And it certainly behooves you to be cautious and pay heed to the warnings before you, And I will suggest (to you) that when you go to Washington City preparatory to your inauguration, that instead of going to a Hotel, that you select some kind friends house in Washington where you know you will be safe untill after you are inaugurated, and on taking possession of the White House, that you make a clean Sweep of every living creature from that establishment, and that you bring your *cooks with you* from your home, those whom you know to be honest true and faithful, and cannot be bribed or bought, for as certain as your name is Abraham Lincoln, unless you are cautious, your *Reign* will be short, and you and Mr Hamlin will both be put out of the way to make room for a creature of the Senate who will do the biddings of the Slave Oligharchy and unless you do as many of your predecessors have done, go over to the Slave Power body and soul, you will be slipped out of existance unless you ar watchful, as sure as you now live;—

You are the candidate of the great reform party, and we who are working for your election hope to see you live, and carry out those great national reforms, and we hope you will stand firm to your principles, and give us a good old Henry Clay Tariff for protection to American industry, and Manufactures, which we hope to get under your Administration, together with all other reforms laid down in the Chicago Platform, and if elected we do not want to see the head cut off of our Party as has been the case with the two last Whig Presidents but we want you to live;— Therefore your salvation is caution and vigilance;— In the selection of you servents be careful not to have any Roman Catholics or Papists about you, have none but American born, black, and white, and have nothing but Protestants about you, and then I will feel as though you will be comparatively safe;— We of Penna. desire to see you live out your term of office, and to see the Principles on which you will be elected faithfully carried out, and to see a quietus put to this vexatious and interminable *Nigger agitation,* and the Slave extension question forever Settled, and the country once more in Peace, Prosperity and quietness;— And we desire further to see you faithfully carry out all of the compromises of our (Mag-na char-ta) the Constitution, to so administer the affairs of Government that justice will be done to all, and by so doing our Southern Brethren, will learn by you that justice can be done to all, North, South, East and West, even if their President is as they in their perfidy choose to call him, a d–d Black Republican.

Very Respectfully Yours
Oliver H. P. Parker
Late Proprietor of the Franklin House of this City

[The following note attached after page I in volume, perhaps written by another hand and certainly on different stationery.]

Mr Lincoln, will please read the accompanying document, *which is not an application for office,* but is on the Subject of the preservation of his life and health, and future welfare; Although you may have had warnings of the same nature, the writer thinks perhaps there certain facts therein contained that cannot be otherwise obtained,

New Lebanon   Oct 2/60

Abraham Lincoln, Esqr
    Sir.

With a little assistance from you, I can secure a number of votes to help you in geting a Home in the White House for the next 4 years We are all *wide awake* or the most of us, in helping the Glorious Cause of makeing a home for you in that Little White House, and that Dear Little Mrs Abraham Lincoln the Mistress of the Same Little House. Now if you will send me Something, I can help you to Something also. I think if I had $50. or $100. or 200. I can use that for you on the 4 of next month.

    Yours Truly
    J. H. Weed

[The following on back of folder]

Please direct
J. H. Weed
New Lebanon
Columbia County
N Y

Oct 8/60
Mr Lincoln

Dear sir

After making a slight appology perhaps I may be excused for troubling you with a few lines in the way of asking a favor of you. And that is I know of no other name in your city to write to now would you confer a favor on me by going to the bagage master in Springfield and see if I have a box there it [*it*] was checkt in indianopolis a bout the 15 of last Dec to go to springfield ill via Lafayitte and I gave my check to Mr Rolins at camp point to get the box for me and he has left country and the check is lost the Number of the check was 52 if you will give me what information you can or get the box forward to me to Tennessee station Mcdonough Co ill

Any favor I can do you in return either by request or otherwise I shall not be backward

Truly Yours
G Savidge

When Pennsylvania and Indiana went Republican in October 1860, the success of Mr. Lincoln's candidacy seemed assured.

OFFICE OF THE CIRCUIT CLERK AND RECORDER

OF

DEWITT COUNTY, ILLINOIS

Clinton, Ills Oct 10th 1860

Hon A Lincoln
Dear Sir,

It has become my melancholly duty to inform you that Judge Davis is in a d—l of a fix; he was seized with a *griping* about noon today, which has greatly endangered the roots of the hair of all the members of this Bar; his unfortunate condition was produced by Telegraphic Despatches received from Penn. & Ind; When he first received the election news he was trying an important criminal case, which terminated in his Kicking over the Clerk's desk, turned a double somersault and adjourned court until after the presidential election—and in his delirium he actually talks of Lincoln's Election as being a fixed fact—and says he knows that Douglas is sorry he didn't die when he was little— For several weeks the Judge has been very much engrossed and would often mention, in his reveries the names of Weed, Cameron, Connor, Judd, H Winter Davis, and occasionally with much spirit would mention the name of one Damn Duncan of Louisville (a Bell man from what I could judge) hoping he had lost his $10,000.00 on Indiana—he looks care worn, and forcibly reminds us of "Old hundred" and at times looks like an Old Umbrella stuck in the mud— He talks of going to Decatur to hear Tom Corwin on Saturday next and from there to Springfield after that to spend the Sabath—should he come to your place you will confer a favor on his numerous friends by looking after him a little—

I write in haste— Hoping you & family are very well—and that you may be the next President

> I am
> Your friend
> *Ward H Lamon*

———•—•———

Credit for Mr. Lincoln's beard has previously been given to a little girl, Grace Bedell, who, on October 15, 1860, urged that it would improve his appearance, but from the following letter it becomes apparent that the "True Republicans" of New York had already made the suggestion.

Oct 12: 1860

To the
Hon. Abm. Lincoln
  Dear Sir
Allow a number of very earnest Republicans to intimate to you, that after oft-repeated views of the daguerreotypes; which we wear as tokens of our devotedness to you; we have come to the candid determination that these medals would be much improved in appearance, provided you would cultivate whiskers and wear standing collars.

Believe us nothing but an earnest desire that "our candidate" should be the best looking as well as the best of the rival candidates, would induce us to trespass upon your valued time.

> Your most
> sincere & earnest
> well wishers
> *True Republicans*

P.S. We really fear votes will be lost to "the cause" unless our "gentle hints" are attended to.

T. R.

Address in reply, box 1444 New York City

C. D. L.

October the 13d 1860

Mr *Lincoln Sir* i rite to you to tell you to be on your gard du not eeat every Thing you have orded to be brought   be Carful not to be Posined by those rufings Mr Lincoln Sir i hope that the Lord Will Spair Your Life to mak the the Country in A beter Condison sir i like the Republican Movent and i hope sir we shall put everthing Rite may the lord keep you from the Snars That lies befor you der sir the day this not Fair disent sir Whe hope that your life Will Be Long and plesent the four years and We Will put you theor a gain so no more At Present From Your Frind

Joseph Lee   Salem Mass

Philadelphia, Oct 15, 1860

Dear Sir—

The contest is altogether over in Penna—utterly abandoned by the Democracy. They have kicked out the Bell men, and mean to die decently. The Douglas straight ticket has now no force, and will not be pushed with any energy. Many of that Camp will not vote at all —others will vote for you, and some will vote for the Douglas electors on the Reading ticket and scratch the balance. Our own men will, notwithstanding, vote, and poll more than they did for Curtin.

You need not be surprised at a full 100,000 majority here over the Reading ticket. I trust Trumbull will be saved.

Yours tr
A K McClure

Hon A Lincoln

Quincy Ill. Oct 17. 1860

Hon A. Lincoln
   Sir

   Please accept the accompanying fish—a Mississippi River Salmon —the finest one caught at this place this season—with the sincere compliments of the undersigned. He confidently believes that the fish which he caught this morning will grace the table of the next President of the United States

Respectfully
Samuel Artus

Oct 17 1860
Lawrence Kansas

Mr Lincoln

   As I have every reason to Expect that you will be our next President—I want to warn you of one thing—that you be Exceeding Careful What you Eat or Drink as you May be Poisoned by your Enemys as was President Harrison and President Taylor. Now I Voted for both those Presidents—And Would like to Vote for you— But cannot—But am anxiously Waiting for the 4th of Nov. When it Shall be Declared that your are the President Elect—
   Yours With Great Respect

R S Bassett

Chester Del. Co. Pa. Oct 17th 1860

Mr President

I now endever to do all I can to put you on your gard. When you cross Masons & Dix. line keep you eye's OPEN and look out for your enimeys or they will poison you or do something to take your life. Same as they tried to serve Old Buc. Look, Sharp

Truly Yours

F. R. Shoemaker

To Mr Abraham Lincoln

Washington D. C. Oct. 18th 1860

Dear Sir.

On your arrival in this city to make arrangements for carrying out the will of the people—which is to be expressed during the ensuing month—you will find our Hotels excessively crowded and every way disagreeable places of sojourn for yourself and family. Allow me therefore to suggest the propriety of your coming directly to my house on your arrival in Washington, and making it your home until the White House shall be made ready for your reception. I can assure you that yourself and the members of your family who may accompany you, will receive a most cordial welcome from Mrs Robbins and myself, and that everything will be done on our part to make your sojourn with us pleasant and agreeable.

We occupy a house on C street a few doors east of the mansion of the late Col. Benton—the house that was occupied either by Mr Dix, or Mr Winthrop, when you were in Congress.

I am one of the oldest republicans of this city,—was one of the late Dr Bailey's earliest friends here,—have never asked for nor held a government office,—have never prosecuted a claim before Congress, and have rarely visited the Capitol. But, I *have* diligently prosecuted the business of my profession, and with some success,—as you will percieve by the accompanying argument and decision.

Neither Mrs Robbins nor myself are votaries of fashion, and had we been so, our politics would have been a bar to our entry into the circle of our Self-styled West End aristocracy. We live comfortably and we trust sensibly, in view of our responsibilities here and hereafter. We have never played the courtier to persons in power, and we are not surrounded by needy expectants of office.

In addition to chamber accommodations, we can give you the exclusive use of a large room for your conferences with gentlemen friends, whilst our parlors will be at the service of Mrs Lincoln for the reception of her friends; and Mrs Robbins' treatment of Mrs L. will I am certain convince her that Washington is not the utterly heartless place that it is generally supposed to be.

I sincerely hope that the above invitation will be accepted without hessitation by yourself and Mrs Lincoln—whatever may be result of the election—

That a kind Providence may guard you both against sickness and casualties and in good time safely locate you in the People's Palace, is the sincere wish of Your friend

Z. C. Robbins

Hon. Abraham Lincoln
Springfield Illinois

———•·•———

Even before his election Mr. Lincoln received military intelligence. Both Major David Hunter and Captain George W. Hazzard were members of the suite of the President-elect on his journey to Washington. Hunter became an important Union general; Hazzard died of battle-sustained wounds.

PRIVATE AND   *Fort Leavenworth, Kansas*
CONFIDENTIAL   *Oct. 20th 1860*

Dear Sir:

Your success and safety being identified with the great Republican cause, the cause of peace, union and conservatism; must be my apology for addressing you.

On a recent visit to the east, I met a lady of high character, who had been spending part of the summer among her friends and relatives in Virginia. She informed me that a number of young men in Virginia had bound themselves, by oaths the most solemn, to cause your assassination, should you be elected. Now Sir, you may laugh at this story, and really it does appear too absurd to repeat, but I beg you to recollect, that on "the *institution*" these good people are most certainly demented; and being crazy, they should be taken care of, to prevent their doing harm to themselves or others. Judicious, prompt and energetic action on the part of your Secretary of War, will no doubt secure your own safety, and the peace of the country,

>   I have the honor to be
>   Very Sincerely,
>   Your mo. ob.
>   *David Hunter*,
>   U. S. Army.

Hon. A. Lincoln
Springfield, Ill.

P.S. I had the pleasure of meeting you in early days at Chicago, and again at the great Whig Convention at Springfield in 1840.

>   *Cincinnati Sunday 21st October 1860*

Dear Sir

The Honl W. L. Yancey made a very egotistical and insulting speech in the Opera house last night to a large audience. I enclose a sketch of it taken from the Press, a Breckenridge paper, which considering the source is a very fair article. Mr Y. referred in bitter terms to the *black* republicans and made frequent contemptuous allusions to Senator Seward's late speeches in the N.W. but he did not once mention your name or that of any other presidential candidate. After trying to impress upon the buckeyes the pecuniary advantages of humoring the south, he proclaimed in a tragic air, that he would resist by force "the aggressions of the north" if they were longer continued. The questions submitted to and answered by Mr. Douglass at Norfolk were handed to the chairman (the city postmaster) but that official retained them in his possession and Mr. Y. did not indicate whether your election would be another "aggression". When he announced that if quiet withdrawal from the union constituted treason he was a traitor he was overpowered by a shower of hisses which could not be stifled by the long continued cheers of the post office, custom house and federal courts officials who were ranged in the front of the parquette.

The late letter of Amos Kendall to the Constitution seems to have silenced *its* guns and may cause Mr. Buchanan to indicate his views as to "peaceful secession" I have watched the War Department very closely for the last six months and I have little doubt that Secretary Floyd is playing into the hands of the secessionists. Not only have the southern and Pacific states been all supplied with their full quota of the new rifled (Minié) muskets but the southern arsenals have been piled up with them, drawn from the armory at Springfield Mass. as fast as they could be fabricated.

Two southern arsenals, Augusta Georgia and Baton Rouge La. have each a guard of fifty men while at *each* point the arms ammunition and ordnance stores are sufficient to equip twelve thousand men. The arsenals at Fayetteville N.C. Mount Vernon (near Mobile) Ala. and Little Rock Ark. with the Depository at Alexandria La. (all full) are totally unprotected and can each be captured by a party of twelve men. The armory at Harpers Ferry was guarded from the time of John Brown's invasion till a short period after his death, but it is now totally unprotected.

The garrison of the forts at Charleston S.C. consists of two companies (108) men commanded by an officer incorruptible to be sure, but who is incapable of any physical exertion. The important fortifications at Smithville N.C. have no guard, while at Pensacola (the finest harbor on the Gulf) three immense forts have an aggregate guard of 54 men. The fortifications at Savannah, Mobile, New Orleans and Baltimore have no garrisons. At Fort Monroe (Old Point Comfort) Virginia there are eight companies (450 men) with an energetic and patriotic commander but I hear he is to be super-seded by a favorite of Jefferson Davis.

So long has southern influence and southern patronage controlled our army that I know only one officer of any rank in it who is not an avowed admirer of the peculiar institution.

The exception is Col. Sumner, a cousin of the Senator. Even the juniors who do not boldly stand up for slavery affect to deprecate any reference to the subject. The command of the army and of the military geographical departments of Texas Utah and New Mexico is conferred on Virginians. Every Military Bureau is presided over by a Virginian or the husband of a Virginia wife. The Colonels of four of our five mounted regiments are southerners; The Adjutant General is brother in law of Senator Mason of Virginia; the Act'g Com. Genl. the Surgeon General, the Judge Advocate General and his assistant, and the Qr. Mr. General all Virginians. The grossest favoritism has been practised to secure this result. Gen. Totten of the Engineers has been relieved from duty in his bureau to make a place for his junior Col. De Russy whose wife is a native of Nor-folk. The Governor, Lieut Governor and Treasurer of the Military Asylum (Soldiers Home) are all Virginians; so are the Commander of the Recruiting Station at Jefferson Barracks Mo.—the Discipli-narian of recruits at Governors Island N.Y. and the Commander at Carlisle Barracks Pa. This last officer earned his reward by escorting John Candlebox Calhoun from Weston Mo to Lecompton & back in January 58 when the returns of the election for state officers under the Lecompton Constitution were to be announced. Gen. Harney who served the administration so faithfully in Kansas has just been recalled from Oregon and is waiting in Washing to join the south-ern movement, *I believe*. Gen Johnston the pet & protege of Jeff. Davis is also on leave—so is Lt. Col. Hardie of the 1st Cavalry (a pet of Toombs); the gallant Col. Magruder of Va who wanted the Prince of Wales to go to shoot buffalo; and Maj. Beauregarde of Louisiana who will be the Vauban of the southern army. All these officers are in intimate relations with secession senators and they are all at Washington.

I would respectfully commend to your notice that paragraph re-ferring to the army and navy in the late disunion article of the

Charleston Mercury. An effort will be made to induce our five cavalry regiments to declare for southern institutions; but if Col. Dimick remains at Old Point Gov Wise will not surprise and capture that fortification.

The officers named at the bottom of the previous and the top of this page will go all lengths so I believe would our Qr. Mr. Genl. J. E. Johnston.

This letter is written without consultation with any living soul. I send it to you because I think you ought to possess the knowledge I have attempted to convey

Very Respectfully
Geo. W. Hazzard
Captain U. S. Army

Abraham Lincoln
Springfield Illinois

Bath Oct 22 1860

Abraham Lincol Esq

 Dear Sir I take the oppertunity to Drop you a few lines About A litte annicdote that hapened in our town A young man in our town By the mame of J T Van Camp A Stage driver There was A Democrattic meeting heald In this place on friday evening Oc 19 Just About the time that The Speaker was taking his Stand that had bin Erected for Him Befor the hotel doore the Stage Driver roled A Dri good Box across the Street and took His lamp and Set it on the Box and got up on it and Began Speaking in your Behalf At the Sane tin of the Denocratick Speake Began I Should Judge there was three hundred peple there An in less than twenty Minnets the Stage Drive had 250 of them at his Stand and a beter Speach we never heard Cheers went up For him on al Sides and When he was Don he was caried In the hotel and order was *presented* to him for A new hat we thoughtt this was worth reminding you of And if you would Just Send Him Some little thin as a reward It woul Do the party a great De of good and leave quite a joke on the Demo party he ownes a little Stage rout here and he has Bet It against $100 that you will Be the next presadent

Yours Res   *Charles G Seagraves*

Just Direct to J T Van Camp
Bath Northhamton Co
Pa

Irvington Oct 30th 1860

Dear brother Lincoln.

I suppose you will be very much surprised to hear that you have two sisters, who live many miles away from you in New Jersey, and though we are unknown to you, still your name is very familiar to us, and is often mentioned in our conversation with each other. We have read the life of your childhood with interest, and have followed you in imagination from your earliest days up to the time when in crowded halls you boldly declared your sentiments in regard to the slave system, and your opinions coinsided so well with our own, that we determined to adopt you as our brother, and call ourselves by your name.

My friend and I live two miles apart, still we meet very often, and then what a time we have calling each other by our new name, and advocating our brother's cause.

We are very anxious for your success, and we feel that there is no one so capable of standing at the head of our Union as yourself. We are confident of one day seeing you President of the United States, and when you are established in the White House, I think Minnie and I shall have to beg our fathers to take us to Washington, to be introduced to the President, for in this country we young folks are all princes and princesses, and have a right to be presented at court.

If you can find a little time to spare from your political pursuits, nothing would delight us more, than to receive a few lines from you.

Please direct to Libbie S. Bailey, Irvington, Essex Co., N.J.

Your sister
Libbie Lincoln

Peoria Ills
Nov 2d, /60

Hon. Abraham Lincoln
    Dr Sir
    I have this day sent you by express a barrel of flour manufactured
in the procession at the dedication of the Wigwam in this city on
the 31st Augt. last. Mr W. Peterfish made and presents the barrel
& Messrs George Field & Co the flour which you will please accept
as a small token of respect for your able support of the Tariff
                              Yours respectfully
                                  John Comstock
                                      Pres. Rep. Club

Mr. Lincoln was invited to receive the election returns in the Springfield telegraph office.

ILLINOIS & MISSISSIPPI TELEGRAPH COMPANY
                    Telegraph Office Springfield Nov 5 1860
To Hon A Lincoln
    Dr Sir
    If convenient for you, we would be happy to have you and any
friends you may wish to bring, spend tomorrow night with us, where
you can receive the good news without delay. Not wishing to have
a noisy crowd inside, the doors will be closed at 9 oclock p m
                              Respfly
                                  C. F. McIntire
                                      Manager
                                      Springfield Office

CONFIDENTIAL

Montpelier Vt Nov 5, 1860

Hon Abraham Lincoln
    Dear Sir will you allow me a humble citizen to say a word of
caution I believe Harrison was poisened and when you go to the

White House do clear out all those servants & have good Northern Servants who will be true & cant be bribed I ask no favors but this that you *will* take care of yourself and not let them poison you

Yours truly
Zenas Wood

Nov 10 Now your Election is sure & I renew the caution & wish & pray that your life may be prolonged

Z W

My dear Sir

Among the thousands of congratulations that will pour in upon you from all parts of our country, you will, I hope, set some value on that of a literary man and not a party-politician; but your firm, fast and constant friend during the contest, which has now so happily terminated.

Most faithfully Yours
Park Benjamin
24 West 17th St
New York. Nov. 7, 1860.

Columbus, November 7, 1860.

My dear Sir,

You are President elect. I congratulate you and thank God.

The great object of my wishes & labors for nineteen years is accomplished in the overthrow of the Slave Power. The space is now clear for the establishment of the policy of Freedom on safe & firm ground. The lead is yours. The responsibility is vast.

May God strengthen you for your great duties.

Very truly,
S. P. Chase

Hon. A. Lincoln.

302

New York. Nov. 6. 12. P.M.

Honorable Abraham Lincoln,
God has honored you this day, in the sight of all the people.
Will you honor Him at the White House,
One of those who are glad today.

Indiana Asbury University
Greencastle, Ind., Nov the 7 1860

Hon. Abraham
Lincoln
    Dear Sir
As this is the first time that we have had the honor of addressing
you, that as we are school boys, but had the honor of voting for you
and, are happy to congratlate you in your happy success, now for
a little advice we want you to split the Democratic platform into
Shivers all

please answer
Abes boys

ILLINOIS & MISSISSIPPI TELEGRAPH COMPANY

Nov 7th 1860

FROM ALBANY 7TH 1860
To Hon A Lincoln
  All safe in this state

T. Weed

555 & 140 COL

THE LINCOLN PAPERS

Nov 8th [1860]
From Pensacola Fla

To Abraham Lincoln
You were last night hung in effigy in this city

A Citizen

1055 PD

Springfield, Ills. Nov. 9. 1860

For Lieut. Gen. Scott, with the respects of
A. Lincoln—
Mr Lincoln tenders his sincere thanks to Gen. Scott, for the copy of his "views &c", which is received; and especially for this renewed manifestation of his patriotic purposes as a citizen, connected, as it is, with his high official position, and most distinguished character, as a Military Captain—

A.L.

New York
Nov 9 1860

Honl Abraham Lincoln
Springfield
Ill
  Dear Sir
As a lover of our common Country I venture to suggest to you that it becomes your duty in the present grave Crisis of the Nations History to repair at once in person to Charleston S C and other southern cities and by direct intercourse with the people through the medium of public addresses make known to them your determi-

304

nation to administer the Government, not only according to the letter, but in the spirit of the Constitution.

It is folly to blind our Eyes to facts in connection with the present agitation & excitement of the public mind, consequent on your election to the Presidential Chair—

No reasonable man can fail to perceive in this condition of things the imminent peril which threatens our existence as an United Nation of Soverign States— To my mind a visit, at once to be made, by yourself through the Southern Section of our Country, would accord not less with the promptings of fearless patriotism, than an honourable self respect—

It is proper for me to say that I have been no advocate of your election to the high office to which you have been called— I earnestly & honestly laboured for your defeat—this however is past— I trust that it is not out of place now to appeal to your patriotism, and invoke you to rise superior to all party considerations, and throw the influence of your present position in favour of the Nations highest interest.

I am Dear Sir
Very Respy
Yr Obt Svt
Wm. H. Price

77 Front Street
New York City

Bryan Hall Chicago Ills.
Nov 10/1860—

Hon. Abraham Lincoln,
  Dr. Sir

This will be handed to you by Geo. P. A. Healy Esq. the eminent Artist, whom Congress has commissioned to paint a series of Presidential portraits to grace the White House, which, although I am a Virginian, I am *heartily* glad you are so soon to occupy.—

305

From the accompanying circular you will observe that I have purchased Mr Healy's private gallery, embracing the portraits of all the Presidents, & of many other eminent American Statesmen.— As Mr Healy is now en route to the South, I have commissioned him to stop at Springfield, & solicit of you the kindness to give him two or three sittings, that he may add to my National Gallery, the portrait of the President Elect.—

Commending Mr Healy to your kind consideration I am, Dr. Sir,

Yours with great respect

Thos. B. Bryan

Will Mr. Lincoln please attend to this letter personally

Haverhill—Mass—Nov 10th.—1860.

Hon. A Lincoln—

Sir—I have been much impressed to write you a few lines which concern your personal safety. I have seen three score years & have noticed something of the world. I suppose I shall not be the only one who will remind you of your danger. You have been chosen President of these United States—so was Harrison—so was Taylor— but where are they? No doubt they were put out of the way—sacrifices to Slavery—And what became of Rantoul a native of my own native town—Beverly—Mass—who bade fair to become president of these U.S.—taken away so suddenly that his wife even could not be with him.

How was it with the wholesale poisining of the Anti-Slavery men at the National Hotel at Washington—where not one of the proprietors or servants were affected—Be continually on your guard. "A word to the wise is sufficient—

Respectfully Yrs—

A. W. H.

Hillsboro, Ill. Nov, 10th, 1860.

Mr Lincoln,
    Dear Sir,

I am so overjoyed to hear you are elected for the Presidency, that I can not express my delight any other way, than by writing to you. I have been looking forward impatiently ever since your nomination, to the sixth of November, in hopes you would be elected. Though I am a little girl, I can realize the curse of slavery, and want slaves to be kept from the territories, and I believe you are the only candidate that will do it. When I read about those noble men that formed the constitution, I want it carried out, and we all know, they were opposed to slavery. I hope too, the South will soon learn, that they can trust a northern man to be President, and that the states and people will be happy under your government.

I hope you will excuse the liberty a little girls has taken to express her joy.

                    Most respectfully,
                            Yours,
                        Helen T. Haskell.

Columbus Inda.
Nov 12—1860.

Hon A. Lincoln

Dr Sir—Allow me to suggest to you that you are and will be until the end of your Presidential term in personal danger from *Border Ruffians* at all times— I have heard some of them say that you should be killed— You owe it to your friends but more particularly to your Country to use great caution at all times and under all circumstances—We must not—we cannot lose you— The anxiety of your friends here and our Country's good is my excuse for troubling you

                    Very truly yours
                        Joseph I. Irwin

Presumably the following letter was written by the son of the governor of Virginia, and presumably also it was addressed to a person named Quicksall. There were a number of Quicksalls in Philadelphia in 1860, among them a teamster, two calico printers, a "dealer," a hotel proprietor, a restaurant keeper, an umbrella and parasol stick maker, a conductor, and a trader.

Richmond Nov. 12th 1860.

My dear friend,

This is my first opportunity, & this is but a poor one, for redeeming my promise to give you the result of my inquiries and observations among southern men as to the purposes of their section in the present crisis. You showed yourself a wiser man than the rest of us in West Philadelphia when you expressed the opinion that some difficulty would insue from Lincoln's election. The secession of the cotton states is now a fixed fact. If our Phila. papers have not already convinced you of this, you must doubt it no longer when I assure you that the unanimity and resolution of their people are unquestionable and unchangeable with regard to measures of disunion. The earnestness—the bitterness of sorrow, with which I contemplate such an event cannot blind me to the certainty of it's occurrence. But now as to the effect of such action, I express no mere individual opinion, but gather my views from those of the most judicious and the most experienced when I say that Virginia will remain in the present confederacy, and that she will remain because no effort will be made to coerce the return of her sister slave states. The secession movement will be consummated under Buchanan—recognized by him as legitimately establishing the independence of the seceding members. Thus the question cannot arise under Lincoln's administration. He cannot find any just cause of war unless in the case of a repudiation on the part of southern debtors towards their northern creditors; and this, improbable with honest men under any circumstances, will be impossible under the present. The too obvious policy of maintaining peace will compel a faithful recognition of all pecuniary obligations. Thus the matter appears to those in whom I have most confidence. The cotton states, yet none but the cotton states, and perhaps not all of those, will go out. There will be no war, and nearly as may be in such a time, there will be no great financial disaster.

The wedding came off at the appointed time. I was not unreasonably embarrassed, but have been most intolerably fatigued & engrossed by the succeeding entertainments. Remember me most affectionately to my friends. I shall write to some of them soon, and shall greet them all a little later—that is at the fixed date. Mr. Clarke & Mr. Duxet Mr. Bacon and Mr. Brown I cannot help mentioning by name, but not more especially than I do Mrs. Quicksall and your little girl.

With great eagerness to get back,

I am more truly than ever

your attached friend

Henry A. Wise Jr.

Excuse my stationery &c.
I am writing in a public
office, & with nothing at my
command but a steel pen.

H. A. W. Jr.

[On back of folder:]
Richmond, Nov. 12/60

Henry A. Wise Jr to
    of West-Philadel-
phia, stating that the secession
of Va is an accomplished
fact &c.

Marion Ala Nov 13th 1860

Hon Wm H. Seward
   My Dear Sir
   Permit me to address you from the verry center of secessionism & fire eating you will doubtless be surprised to hear that Gen. Hubbard

has turned up in the refractory State of Alabama. I came here for my health & have found great relief—But to my sorrow I find mysef in the midst of rebellion & revolution

The Cotton States are all on fire—enlisting minute men as they are called & the Blue cockade is the order of the day while secession & a southern confederacy is the almost unanimous cry—I am told by men in the highest stations & by one who has lately returned from Washington that Mr Buchanan has pledged himself that if any southern state wished to seceed He would not oppose but would aid them This is understood to be the fact by all the Cotton States hence their great hast to plunge into secession immediately—

If this turns out to be so, pray tell me my Dear Sir what will be done—I own property here & can not dispose of it nor get away—Permit me Sir to call to your mind the case in 1832 when South Carolina thretned to seceed more than 150000 men volunteered in the Northern States & tendered their services to the President—to be ready at a minutes warning & it was probably this in a great measure that cooled them down—

Now if three or four Hundred thousand men were to volunteer by whole Regiments, armed & equiped & proffer their servises to the President to be ready at His call to put down any Insurection in the Southern States, be assured it would do more to cool down these fire eaters than all the arguments in the world

This is an important town it is called the Athens of Ala it has a College & two large Female Seminarys & therefore many of the first men in the south come here, the Govr. also lives here, & I come in contact with them—They all agree in this, that the North has become so abolitionised that the South can not remain any longer in the Union with them & If Mr Breckinridge or Joe Lane had been elected President they would still be for secession it is that increaseing & controlling Northern Majority that they fear & nothing else—"This is the Truth"

They sweare that Mr Lincoln shall never be Enaugerated—as sure as He comes to Washington He will be shot, let the concequencies be what they may—

Please write me by an early mail but *do* put on a *postage stamp* for if I were to re a letter Franked by W. H Seward I should be hung before night If it was known that I had written this letter I could not stay here a day—I shall enclose this in a letter to the Hon W. M. Dunn, M. C. from Indiana—This my Dear Sir is no Land of Liberty & May God in his mercy deliver us from it

With Great Respects

I Remain Yours &c

A Hubbard

N. Y. Times Office

N. Y. Nov. 14, 1860.

Dear Sir:—

I propose to intrude for five minutes on your valuable time:

1st. To congratulate you and the country on the result of the Election.

2nd. To ask you whether possible good might not result from a note embodying the *points* of the enclosed,—to be written to some friend by you.

The main thing, you will note, is to have you say that the *South misunderstands the Republican party,* and that a *Republican Administration can alone correct the error.* I believe this is all any rational man can ask at your hands, and that it is all the emergency requires.

Whatever you may think of the suggestion I beg you to believe that it is offered with the most profound deference to your judgment, and from no other motive than a desire to smooth the way for the coming Administration.

I am,

With great respect,

Your ob't Serv't

H. J. Raymond

Hon A. Lincoln

THE LINCOLN PAPERS

Memorandum of a Private Note from
Hon. A. Lincoln.

I agree with you perfectly in thinking that any declaration of intention from me at present would be premature, uncalled for, and quite as likely to increase as to allay the existing excitement of the public mind.

The cause of that excitement is evidently an entire misapprehension, on the part of the Southern people, of the sentiments and purposes of the Republican party. That cause can only be removed by actual experience of a Republican Administration.

My views upon every prominent political issue are before the country & accessible to every one who desires to know them in my published speeches. What I said then I believe now:—and no new declaration could give it additional weight.

I have too much faith in the good sense & patriotism of the people of the South to apprehend any violent disruption on their part from the mere *fear* of future aggressions,—while I have too much faith in their honor to expect them to submit to such aggression when actually committed. I think with you that they will take counsel of their judgments, instead of their fears.

[This draft, written by Mr. H. J. Raymond, was enclosed in his letter of November 14th, 1860]

Decatur, Ills. Nov. 14, 1860.
Dear "Abe":—Nancy wishes me to inform *you* that *she* had our cottage beautifully illuminated last night, in *honor* of *your* election to the Presidency. She is a Strong Lincoln woman, and has fought *man*fully for you during the campaign. Your friends had a grand time here last night.

Yours respectfully
James Shoaff

Louisville Nov 14 1860

Dear Lincoln

I desire to tender you my sincere congratulations upon your elevation to the highest position in the world—by the sufrage of a free people—As a friend, I am rejoiced at your success—as a political opponent I am not disappointed—The result is what I expected—

That you will bring an honest purpose to bear upon all subjects upon which you are called to act, I do not doubt—Knowing you as I do and feeling for you as I have ever done—I can not but tremble for you—But all men and all questions sink into utter insignificance when compared with the good of our whole country and the preservation of our glorious Union—You are I know as proud of its past glories as any man in the nation—

Its continuance and its future will depend very much upon how you deal with the inflamable material by which you are, and will be surrounded—

The *eyes* of the *whole* nation will be upon you while unfortunately the *ears* of one *half* of it will be closed to any thing you may say— How to deal with the combustible material lying around you without setting fire to the edifice of which we are all so proud and of which you will be the Chief Custodian is a dificult task—

Upon this subject I have the views of a private citizen seeking no office for himself nor for any friend he has—

I will not even broach them in a letter—But if it would be agreeable to you I will come & see you—and I think can impart to you some information as to men & public sentiment here which may be valuable

With kind regards to Mrs L

I am as ever
Your friend
J. F. Speed

THE LINCOLN PAPERS

BANK OF NORTH AMERICA

New York Nov 18, 1860.

Dear Sir,

Since I last wrote enclosing letters from my brother, I have received many others from him, which, coupled with other information in my possession, left no doubt in my mind of the complicity of the President with the designs of the secessionists. I took my proofs, when the election was over, to the editor of the Evening Post, in which a series of articles has been commenced, exposing Mr. Buchanan's treason, with the hope that the publicity thus given to it, may force him to do at least part of his duty. These articles have been brought to Mr. B's personal notice, and both he and Secretary Floyd have denied their truth. As they are true, this looks as if they were becoming frightened, and the superseding of Col. Gardner, an avowed secessionist, by Maj. Anderson a loyal Kentuckian, seems still further to confirm this idea. My brother writes that a settled determination to have the forts, as a necessity of their positions, is evinced by the South Carolinians, who begin to ask why the President does not keep his promise to withdraw the troops. I think he is afraid, and, by directing public attention to these disclosures, hope to force him to send more troops. This would greatly simplify Mr Lincoln's position after the 4th of March. The present aspect of financial affairs here, though gloomy, is not nearly so bad as in 1857. The simple fact that our exports largely exceed our imports is a proof that in a very short time gold must flow this way from Europe in large amounts. I look to a decided and permanent improvement in less than thirty days. I do not expect any answer to this letter.

Resp'y Yours,
U. Doubleday

To Jno. G. Nicolay Esq.

Philadelphia Pa. Nov, 26th 1860.

His Excellency
(Hon.) Abraham Lincoln
President Elect. U. S.   Sir,

I used what little influence I possessed, voted for & attended the inaugurations of Presidents Harrison & Taylor with a heart big with hope. (Also for you & intend to be at your inauguration)

But alas! Too soon I followed their remains to a premature grave. General Harrison rode through the Streets of Washington in a long procession in a Snow Storm with his head uncovered & improperly clad.

I have never during my long life felt greater emotions of joy with
　　　　　2　　　　1
regard to the *future, approaching.*

I have long felt the greatest solicitude for your Hons. health, & though I am a Stranger, I have repeatedly felt desirous of writing you requesting you to avoid any & all the causes that may in the least be likely to affect so sad a calamity & deprive the Nation of its long cherished hopes, of a just & honest President. Do, I entreat, be guarded, to save the Nation from disappointment & despair.

I trust you will avoid all exposure, & take your accustomed rest & relaxation, so necessary to ones health, that you will be the better able to accomplish the Nations expectations & hope. I have repeatedly desisted from inflicting a letter on you because I know you are constantly recieving thousands that must be irksome to read. But I am so impressed that some misfortune will befal you, that I cannot remain silent.

I firmly believe there are men base & reckless enough in some of the Southern States to assassinate both you & Mr. Hamlin & that they intend to do it.

I firmly believe that some reckless culprit will attempt to assassinate both you & Mr. Hamlin either at your own home, on your way to Washington or there even at the time of the inauguration if not before.

The people of the South are so embittered, I think without any just cause, that they will not hesitate to take your lives rather than that you should be inaugurated as President of these United States, & so they would do to any other republican had he been elected.

When her public men like R. Barnwell Rhett declare in a public speech "They have elected a southern renegade spewed out of the bosom of Kentucky into Illinois, a northern whitewashed or octoroon molatto to be President & Vice President of the United States."

Our greatest fear from the South is her want of general education & information, the misrepresentations of her Statesmen, & public men, & the venality not only of hers but some of the Northern opposition presses.

The history of John Tylers, Millard Fillmores Pierces & Buchanans Administrations, show that no President can administer the Government to please them, but that they will get all the important offices & all they can from any President & the national Treasury & use it to embarrass his administration & destroy & break up his Republican & national party.

Please excuse the liberty I have taken to write this letter. I am one of the numerous family of *Uphams* not entirely unknown in the old whig, & present republican party. I am a native of the State of *Vermont.* N.Y. is now my home.

Respectfully & sincerely Yours &c.
Alfred W. Upham

I have letters from many of the most distinguished Statesmen, deceased, & still living. Pres. Harrisons, Taylors & Fillmores. If convenient please favour me with your autograph, if no more.

I believe the South are kicking up a muss for no earthly purpose than to secure a large share of the important offices, & the lions share from the National Treasury. They are no fools. They believe the North will give them liberally to keep them still &c. I hope & trust none but the ardent friends of the President Elect will secure places under his administration. Persons of intrinsic merit & worth. Any others would prove a dead weight, like a mill stone about his neck.

La Crosse Wis Novbr. 27th 1860.

Abraham Lincoln Esqr
Springfield

I hope you excuse me if I take the liberty and ask you one question.

My wife got on the Election day a little Girl, and I made the proposition that if it is a girl to give your wifes name, and if it is a boy your name Abraham. Will you have the kindness and give me a line what your wifes name is? I am very much oblige to you for any truble.

Very Respectfully Yours etc
G. C. Neumeister

Spartanburg S. C.
Nov 27, 1860

Abraham Lincoln Esqr
Springfield
Dear Sir

We understand you have a very likely & intelligent mulatto boy you would dispose of on reasonable terms being engaged in negro trading if you will let us know what you will take for the boy Hanibal known as Hanibal Hamlin and you price is reasonable we will purchase him, and are prepared to meet you with the cash at Richmond Va on the 18. Decr inst. Your early attention to the above will oblige

Yours Respectfully
J. D. Wright
W. D. Hardy
A. J. House

317

THE LINCOLN PAPERS

Chicago
Nov 28th 1860.

My Dear Sir,

After congratulating you, as I most sincerely do, not only upon your election, but on the handsome majority you received, which conclusively establishes the fact, that your highminded and honorable course, had forced to your support, many who were politically hostile to you; and no doubt, all of your opponents, who had the manliness to appreciate your merits, permit me to confer with you on a matter of vital importance to our country, the party, and especially to Mr Lincoln & his family.

Last night, as my wife and I were discussing the affairs of the nation, and the many threats that had been made against Mr Lincoln personally, two important matters suggested themselves to our minds, to wit—1st The effort to poison Buchanan and Breckinridge, *before* they entered on the duties of their offices; and 2d the fate of Harrison and Taylor, *after* they had taken their seats. From all these, in common with his many friends, we are anxious to save Mr Lincoln, and we know that you are also. To avoid the former, Mr Lincoln had better keep his movements entirely secret, for a short time before his inauguration; and I would suggest that he should not go to Washn till a very few days before that time. When there, it would be well for him to stop at the house of a true and tried friend, whose servants are also true & can be relied on.

You remember that I was born & raised in Washn & lived there all my life till 24 Decr 1855. I had much sickness, and out of a family of ten children, lost five, under the care of the best physicians there, including those who attended Harrison & Taylor. The change of climate, water, manner of living &c will probably induce sickness in Mr L. or his family; and if the arrangement could be made, it would probably be better that Mr L should take his family physician with him, which he could probably do, by putting him in charge of the Hospital there. If this arrangement is not made, I would suggest those whom he should not have, and those he should have, to attend him and his family. If the Alipathic system is practiced in his house, I would earnestly suggest that he should *not* employ Dr. Thos.

<pre>
 1   2   3   4   5   6   9
Miller Dr May Stone, Magruder,—Lindsey, Lieberman, Johnson,
   7   8
</pre>

Morgan, or Hall—These all are Democrats except Lindsey and the most bitter kind of opponents of the Republicans— The 1st 2d 4th 5th & 8th if I remember aright, attended Harrison & Taylor—the others are poor things. I would suggest that Dr Wm Jones should be called in—he is now City Post Master—was an old line Whig—turned Democrat; is not much on politics;—but is an old and excellent physician, —thoroughly experienced in the diseases of that region, and perfectly reliable. Dr Burroughs is also a good physician, and though a whig in former years, and a member of a Baptist family, is now a Democrat,—mixed up with the Catholics, & formerly drank sometimes.— He is a good physician, and very careful in giving medicine.— His Lincoln's medicines, he had better get from Mr. Stott, a good Presbyterian Druggist, on Pa Av; near 4 1/2 Street, south side. He is a first rate Druggist, and a good Republican. If Mr L. prefers the Homoepathic system, he cannot do better than get Dr. Green, who resides on C. St—just East of 4 1/2 Street. I have taken the liberty of writing you thus, hoping that you would take the trouble to see Mr & Mrs L, and put them on their guard in this matter. I have never corresponded with Mr. L. and would not do so now, under any circumstances, lest my motives should be misconstrued. Moreover, I have said things in this letter, which I wish no eye to see but your own, and no ear to hear, except those of Mr & Mrs L— When you have read this letter, and communicated the contents, and after copying the names and recommendations, please destroy it. Dr. Smoot is a good man, and I believe a good physician but personally I do not know him. He is a sincere Republican, but in this matter, I would take Jones, only, as an alipathist, or Green, as a Homeopathist— Jones has been a successful physician for more than forty years—Green has practiced both systems with great success, but prefers the Homoepathic plan.

My wife and family unite with me in cordial greetings to your wife, family & yourself.

Sincerely your friend
John Wilson

I do not believe that you would *think,* that I had any *motive* in this matter, other than that herein presented; but let me assure you, that Drs Jones & Green are merely speaking acquaintances—nothing more.

Gov: Wise of Va has a son in law practicing medicine in Washington, and residing on 9th St, between E & F. Streets. His name I do not remember, but he should be embraced with the other nine.

107 Madison Avenue
New York City
Nov 29

My dear Sir./
If you or yr Secty have no time to read this—no harm is done. If you or he has, it may afford at least an amusement.

At a political dinner party in my house last evening the guests amused themselves with "Cabinet names": & it was proposed that each should write out their ideas of expediency &c & compare notes.

Out of six, five had named John C. Fremont for Secty of War & two gave the reasons of fitness: three those of expediency as concerning the Pacific & the rail road interest.

Every one named Mr Seward for Secty of State: and Geo Ashmun for Treasury & David Wilmot for P.M Genl

Four had written the names of Badger of N. C Three of Botts of Va. Three of Etheridge of Tennessee as Southern names—Badger for Atty Genl Botts for Navy. Etheridge for Interior

I mention only the concurrences which was impromptu.

x   x   x   x   x

As a member of the Pittsburg—& Phil conventions & an alternate to Chicago (and—pardon the pleasantry—*not* an applicant for office) and particularly as a *devotee* of Gov Seward permit me to embrace

this opportunity of wishing you God speed—health—happiness & unbounded success.

Faithfully & heartily
Yr Repr friend & Ot Sert
A. Oakey Hall

Mr Lincoln
Springfield
Ill.

New York. November 30th 1860

Hon Abe. Lincoln
    Permit me to congratulate you upon your good fortune, in being
elevated to the high cockolorem chair of the nation, And although
you are away out in Illinois the home of the Great Douglass you are
not out of the reach of you forty seven million of friends wanting
office. Permit me Honest Abe to say to you that I am not particular
of having any office [*of hi*] higher than Secretary of State under
your administration. I am going to Washington on the 4th of March
next and shall have on my person a dozen howitzers to repel any
attack which shall be made upon you, you will see me [*during*]
while you are taking the oath and in order that you will [*better*] be
able better to recognise me I shall paint the 32d hair of the left eye-
brow a sky blue. Till then good bye and dont forget to make me
Secretary of State.

Yours till death
Unterrified

Shady Dale Jasper Co. Ga
Nov. 30th 1860

Hon. Abraham Lincoln
    Dear Sir
    In justice to yourself I take the liberty of forwarding to you a
circular, with which Georgia is now flooded, purporting to eminate

from Chicago Ill and calculated to add to the excitement of an already excited people— Is it possible that the within is the Northern Sentiment by which you gained your election as President of the United States?— For one I do not think this document ever saw Chicago. One word from you in contradiction will quiet the anxious conservative minds of thousands,

Respectfully
Mat. Whitfield, P M

November 1860

I raised the tallest Lincoln Pole in Ohio
I helped to elect the tallest
President in the United States,
I married a wife 5 ft 11 inches high,
I produced the largest turnips in the
State of Ohio and a pumkin
192 lbs in weight. honest *Abe*
aint I some pumkins

H Jeffords

Mr Lincoln sir.

I sing for you and I huraw for you. My father voted for you. I want you to send Me a nice presand, and I belong to the masidonean gee club I am a little girl [*a past*] Just a past my Eleventh year you will please excuse the liberty I take In writing you these few lines: every body would go long i would hurah for Lincoln.

With great respect
Mary L Raikes

pleas write me a letter if you dond send me a presand
I live near camden preble county Ohio

to—honest old uncle Abe the Rail Spliter

———•—•———

Ninian W. Edwards, to whom the following letter was addressed, was Mrs. Abraham Lincoln's brother-in-law.

Lexington Ky
Dec 1, 1860.

My Dear Sir

Will you allow me as an old Friend to take the lerty of saying to you who are so identified with Mr Lincoln by marriage and no doubt also by friendship—that it is the profound conviction of many of our best men in this region, who wish well to Mr L. administration that unless something is done within the *next Thirty* days to arrest the tide of passion in the South, he will be inaugurated on the 4th March as the Prest of a divided Empire—The Conservative men of the South have no foot hold to fight the Secessionists—If Mr L. could say publicly After he shall have been elected that the Northern states who had directly or indirectly nullified the Fugitive slave law could expect no countenance from him in such legislation And that his purpose was to bring the power of the Government to its execution he would strengthen the hands of his well-wishers beyond what he thinks

You may say—"He has already said that", Will not his utterances now go with very different force from what they have done heretofore

You may reply, Nothing will satisfy the South, but the adoption of their creed, That is trew of South C. and even that would not satisfy her for she wants to get out of the Union—but it will appease like a peace offering very many men who are now in flamed and who are led to believe—through Demagogues that they are about to pass under the yoke of an enemy

See how the South is situated—Iritated—rightfully or not to a point of secession and yet not one word is said by the North to sooth or quiet her, And thus her bad citizens who for selfish ends are anxious for disorder and confusion over ride moderate and wise counsels—

Cant Mr L. say or do some thing that will give assurance to the prudent men of the S. that he has no sympathy with the fanatics of the N. And being a Southern man by birth that he will protect their institutions by the power of the Government.

Kentucky is sound throughout with the exception of small squads of Breckinridge men scattered here and there—And yet if several Southern States go out I am afraid she will go with them—Her situation is deplorable. If she goes North, the South where is her trade, will impose burdens on it & will prohibit the importation of her slaves, If she goes South, the Slave trade will be opened in spite of her & slave property be rendered worthless—

She is therefore vastly interested in Union—So is Va N.C.—Missouri &c. I see nothing before us but endless confusion, in which civil war, more than probably connected with insurrection plays its part—Surely the moderate men who supported Mr L. will justify him in going every length short of a sacrifice of his principles to avert so dire a calamity.

I will not weary you with more, But every good man here is alarmed at the aspect of affairs—and I wish Mr L. could be made to realize fully the danger we are in, I am afraid Southern men keep away from him and that he may be induced to think, the newspapers exagerate every thing, I assure you Sir they do not, and Mr L. is the only man, that can, if he can save the country—

My Kindest regards to your wife

I am Very Truly Yr Friend
Geo B Kinkead

N W Edwards Esq
Springfield
Illinois

John Addison Gurley, then a representative from Ohio, was subsequently appointed governor of Arizona by Mr. Lincoln.

Willard's Hotel
Washington Dec. 3. 1860

(CONFIDENTIAL)
Hon. Abraham Lincoln—

Dear Sir: At the risk of being considered obtrusive I send you this letter to say, that there is a pretty general belief here that the Cotton States will go out of the union. I have had several conversations with Mr. Sherman since I came here, one an hour ago— our rooms are near to each other—& he gives it as his opinion that we had better make up our minds to that result & act accordingly. I am more hopeful, but have not as much confidence in the continued union of the states as when I saw you at Chicago. If six months could pass before any action is taken by the southern states, all would be well I think, but South Carolina will secede this month. The feeling here seems to be that you should have a Cabinet that pleases the President elect without regard to the personal claims of *any* man or the demands of any state. A common danger is doing a good deal to diminish office seeking, & our members generally desire the promotion of strong men, such as you judge will be of service to you, rather than personal or state favorites; & this feeling will grow stronger as the danger increases.

Mr. Ethridge of Tenn. is here—he will stand by you & the Union at all hazards. He seeks no office, & I think desires none. You may count on him as a fast friend. He has given me a full account of his late political campaign—& my conclusion is, that he did about as much for Bell as Forney did for Douglas!

One South Carolina member is sorry for the condition of things in his state—is at heart opposed to disunion, but I will not mention his name lest it should by some means get into the newspapers. Orr was forced into the secession movement against his will—this I have from good authority—& yet the statement may be a mistake. It is hard to get at the exact truth. Hoping that this letter may find you in the enjoyment of good health, & a hopeful spirit, I subscribe myself

Your friend
John A. Gurley

Washington, Dec. 4–1860

Hon. A. Lincoln,
  My Dear Sir,

The message has just been read & is satisfactory to no—body—It opposes secession unless a state wants to go out, & then denies any power in the Union to keep it in &c—but you will have seen it before this reaches you—

A good feeling prevails among Republican Senators—The impression with all, unless there be one exception is, that Republicans have no concessions to make or compromises to offer, & that it is impolitic even to discus making them—The articles of Weed, Webb & Greeley, so far as they discuss new compromises, or propositions [*for paying*] that the North pay the South for runaway slaves, find no sympathy with our body. Gov. Seward distinctly repudiates them —I was a little surprised that the House voted to raise a committee on the State of the Union. It seems to me that for Republicans to take steps towards getting up committees or proposing new compromises, is an admission that to conduct the government on the principles on which we carried the election would be wrong. Inactivity & a kind spirit is it seems to me all that is left for us to do, till the 4th of March, except that the President should in the mean time need some additional legislation to enable him to execute the laws; but he is so irresolute & undecided that I know not if he would use the power to preserve the Union, if it was all placed in his hands—I hear it said as coming from Southern men, that no opposition will be made to the confirmation of your Cabinet, except some of them should be taken from the South of such as they call traitors to Southern interests, when they will be rejected. Of course there is talk & speculation among friends here as to who will or ought to be your advisers, but I do not know that you would care to know all that is said—I think it would be well however if you could have free conversations with some of our leading friends—

Yours truly
Lyman Trumbull

Linden Wis. Dec. 5th 1860

Hon. and dear Sir

The ministers of the West Wisconsin Conference, of the Methodist Episcopal Church, made you a life member of their missionary society, on the fifteenth of September last, and as the Sec. of said society I am authorized to send you a certificate of the same. I therefore herewith send you the said certificate, and "rejoice with joy unspeakable" in having the privilege.

We expressed our interest in your election, as you will see by the date of the certificate, long before its grand and glorious consummation. We are indeed the true children of *Abraham,* and as such you shall ever have our prayers, for your present and eternal welfare.

Your humble, and obedient,
and faithful Servant,
Peter S. Mather

Hon. A. Lincoln.

Rev. P. S. Mather
Linden
Iowa Co.
Wis.

Washington
Dec 6, 1860

Hon A Lincoln
My Dear Sir

You are doubtless advised of the Action of the House in raising a committee of one from each State to consider that part of the Presidents' Message in relation to the Secession of the Cotton States, And being a Member of that Committee I feel anxious to do nothing that would be inconsistant with the general policy that you propose to addopt on that subject, but on the Contrary to act in accordance with it Therefore should you feel at liberty to make any suggestions (not of course to be repeated or in fact to consider you responsible for them hereafter) in relation to the remedy for the present [*trouble*] difficulties, I should be highly pleased to recieve them

It is doubtless true that South Carolina is fully determined to seceede from the Union and that she will formaly do so within the present month and it [*is*] apparent from the express language of the Message that the President will not attempt to prevent it—and it is equally certain that some three or four other States Sympathise Strongly with her. I think I am not an alarmist but I can not ignore the fact that a crisis in our governmental affairs is approaching that will require firm and patriotic men to guide the Old Ship of State safely through this storm that now seems to be growing in the southern portion of the Confederacy. These dangers should be looked squarely in the face, and a true Statesman will not underrate the dangers and difficulties that surround us—

We are right and ultimately must prevail and secure peace quiet and renewed prosperity to the Union of these States if wise and patriotic counsel prevail and that they may and I doubt not they will, is the fervent hope of your friend & Obt Sevt—

I hope to hear from you

I Remain Truly Yours
W Kellogg

Hon A Lincoln
Springfield Ills
    Dear Sir,

Some of our friends here think it might be more expedt. for you & Mrs Lincoln to stay at a friends house than at a hotel when you come on—If so, we have a spare room at our city house & Mrs Blair bids me say that she would be most happy if you would honor us by occupying it. The house is a very plain old fashioned affair & the room not a fine one, but is the one Genl Jackson intended to occupy after leaving the White house over the way & we Blairs would be delighted for you to begin where he left off.

With kind regards to to Mrs Lincoln

I am very truly yours
M Blair

Washington Decr. 8./60

Indianapolis, Inda.
Decr 8, 1860.

Hon. A Lincoln;—
Respected Sir:

The bearer, Mr Mendenhall, will present this request:—I shall be under lasting obligations if you will favor me with an autograph recommendation of my Lightning rod. It may seem a piece of small impertinence to approach you thus, but I have already the approval of the most eminent scholars in the Country, and your *name* can do me incalculable good. It is my enterprise and all I look to for a living, & I am making the most of it. I claim more conducting surface, in a better form and better connection at the joints of the sections than any other rod. Your Opinion will be thankfully & gratefully received, & cherished as a *priceless Souvenir.* Begging pardon for this intrusion, believe me,

I am, ever, Your most fervent friend.
Wm. Hall.

[Endorsed:] needs no answer

Dec 9 1860
Union Depot
Sullivan County Este Tennessee

Mr A Lincoln
    Sir I am one of your Beste Frendes I had note the chanct to vote For you & the reasen of it you had know ticket in Tennessee I am a pore man & ned all the helpe I can gite Eff it is agreble with you I wood Lik to have a offic under you you have it in your pour to Give me a offic Eff you will you Can tak my Cas & doe as you think Beste Eff you Can Give me a offic you Will Confer a Grate Favor one me I Refer you to Tho.A. R. Nelson of Tennessee I Will Remain your Frend Eff I donte Gite a offic I wante you to anser me as sune as you Recive my Letter Eff you pleas I wante you to mak Tho. A. R. Nelson one of your Cabnett I donte think ther is a Beter man in the united states I Beleve Eff you had had a ticket in Tennessee you wod had Got one half of the vote I wante you to Remember me I hope you Will anser me promptley
                                        I am your Frend Truley
                                                James M Crockett

---

John Adams Gilmer was a Member of Congress from North Carolina.

House of Reps. U.S.
December 10th 1860

Mr Lincoln.
    The present perilous condition of the Country—threatening the destruction of the Union—must be my excuse for the unusual liberty I take in writing this letter.
    Solicitous that the States may remain united, if by any fair means

330

possible, and the honor and constitutional rights of all maintained and secured; and desirous to do all I can to preserve the public peace, I venture to express the hope that you may feel at liberty, in advance of your installation, to give the people of the United States the views and opinions you now entertain on certain political questions which now so seriously distract the country.

For one politically opposed to you, and representing a Southern constituency, who, together with myself, did all we could (I trust honorably) to defeat your election, I feel that I presume a great deal, perhaps too much in troubling you with any inquiries. But the dangers of the crisis, and my desire to have allayed, if possible, the apprehensions of real danger and harm to them and their peculiar institution which have seized the people of my section, I respectfully ask whether as, President you will favor the abolition of Slavery in the District of Columbia:

2d Whether you would approve of any law of Congress prohibiting the employment of Slaves in the Arsenals and Dock-Yards where their location is in the Slave States;—or the transfer of slaves from one slave-holding State or Territory to another of like character:—

3d Whether, in your opinion, Congress has the power, directly or indirectly to interfere with slavery in the States; and whether by any policy, or any system of appointment to office, Slavery agitation, or by other ways or means, you would in any way, directly or indirectly, attempt to lessen the value and usefulness of slaves—disturb the peace and quiet of their owners, or impair the institution of slavery:—

4th Whether, on the application of any new State for admission into the Union, you would veto an act of Congress admitting the same because slavery was tolerated in her Constitution—the same being the choice and fairly expressed will of the citizens making the application:—also indicate the policy, if any, which you would favor or recommend to settle and quiet the disturbing question of slavery in the Territories:—

5th Whether you will enforce the fugitive slave law—whether you would favor its repeal. If not, whether you would suggest amendments impairing its efficiency or usefulness:—

6th   Whether you will use the influence of your position to secure the repeal of all laws passed by any State, in conflict with the fugitive slave law and intended to defeat its peaceful and proper execution.

I address you from pure motives.— The times are alarming, and fully justify your speaking on the questions mentioned now. You have in some degree my opinion of the excitement in my section, when I assure you that you hazard less to yourself, politically, in granting a request which I earnestly press solely for the sake of good, than I do in making it. But I am not without hope that a clear and definite exposition of your views on the questions mentioned may go far to quiet, if not satisfy all reasonable minds, that on most of them it will become plain that there is more misunderstanding than difference, and that the balance are so much more abstract than useful or practical; that as to them a generous and patriotic yielding on the part of your section, now so largely in the majority, would, on the one hand, be a mere sacrifice of opinion, and, on the other, the preservation of the best Government that has ever fallen to the lot of any people.

Respectfully,
Your Ob't Servt.
John A. Gilmer